GOING
Till You're Gone

All Scripture quotations are taken from the
KING JAMES VERSION.

ISBN: 978-1-936208-85-2

Cover design: Kristi Yoder
Layout design: Felicia Kern
Front cover photos: istockphoto.com
Illustrations by Nathan Wright

Second printing: April 2014

For more information about Christian Aid Ministries, see page 277.

Published by:
TGS International
P.O. Box 355
Berlin, Ohio 44610 USA
Phone: 330·893·4828
Fax: 330·893·2305
www.tgsinternational.com

TGS000816

GOING
Till You're Gone

Rethinking Retirement:
A Kingdom-focused
vision in midlife and beyond

Gary Miller

Table of Contents

Part One: A Time of Great Change

Part Two: A Time to Reflect

Part Three: A Time to Refocus

Preface

When I first began writing *Kingdom-Focused Finances for the Family* in 2009, my primary burden was for young families. Our culture has thrown an amazing array of options at them, and trying to sort through the multitude of choices while keeping the Kingdom of God in view is a daunting task. They need our prayer and support. But one of the unforeseen results of that book was that many requests poured in for more teaching on practical ways to live out Biblical stewardship. Ministers from various denominations, concerned parents, and even young people called to ask if additional help was available. There was an obvious realization that we are not always succeeding in our struggle with materialism and accumulation, and an acknowledgement that it is difficult to maintain our focus on the Kingdom of God. As a result of these cries for help, the Kingdom-Focused Living series was born.

In 2010 I began to write the second book in this series, *Charting a Course in Your Youth*. This was an attempt to encourage youth to choose to serve the Lord Jesus, not just in some superficial way, but by totally surrendering every detail of their lives to Him—including their finances.

But even as I addressed areas of concern for young families and youth, something bothered me. Somewhere, the younger generation learned how to live. Somewhere, they were taught what is really important. Their lifestyle choices have undeniably been shaped by listening to the discussions of their elders and observing their priorities. This is not to point fingers or assign blame for failures. Instead, it is a reminder that we are all responsible. We can all share in the blame for disregarding some of Jesus' basic teachings and using society as a reference point.

This book is not written to chastise those who are in their retirement years. We want to learn from them, not reprimand or rebuke them. Neither is it my goal to provide ammunition for those in their twenties or thirties who tend to be scornful of those who are, from their perspective, living out their retirement years without a clear vision. There is a great need in our churches, as well as in our society, for respect toward our elders and those in positions of authority.

Although there may be lessons in this book for those in their seventies and eighties, and even for those in their twenties and thirties, it is primarily directed toward those between those ages—those in their forties, fifties, and sixties. There are three reasons I have focused on this age group.

1. This is an age group in which radical change can still occur. With the rapid change in life expectancy, many individuals are still active and in good health in their eighties and even nineties. This means that those in their forties, fifties, and sixties potentially have many years ahead of them. If this age group catches a vision of using their resources for the Kingdom in their final years, a great deal can be accomplished for the Lord,

2. This age group is in a position of influence. Younger believers are observing how a Christian actually lives like a steward when he has more time and money than he needs. If they can see older Christians practicing self-denial during these years, it will bless them as they, in turn, grow older.

3. Many living in this middle-aged bracket are in an unprecedented position. They will have more discretionary income and more available free time than any previous generation. In a recent study conducted by Boston College's Center for Retirement Research,[1] it was estimated that those between the ages of 46 and 64 living in the year 2010 are expected to receive a total of about 11.6 trillion dollars of inheritance

money. While researchers say there are many variables, one thing is sure. This huge transfer of wealth is going to have a great impact on the lives of those receiving it. But my primary concern isn't the effect on society. What effect will this have on the church? Will this transferred wealth be a blessing? It will result in more available free time and discretionary money. But will this bless the Kingdom?

We don't know what the future holds. This country's economic situation is anything but stable, and things could change rapidly. But the purpose of this book, and my prayer for those of us in midlife, is that we determine to use all we have been given for the Kingdom of God. May the Lord bless you as you read and as you live out Jesus' teachings in everyday life.

—Gary Miller

Introduction

In the end he stood alone. His admirers, loyal associates, and ardent followers were gone. People who had eagerly listened, begging for advice and hanging on to his every word, were no longer interested. Even his closest friends and family had deserted him. In his final hour, when support and encouragement were desperately needed, they had fled. There had been a time, not very long ago, when some of the wealthiest and most famous names in society had wanted to be seen with him. He had been admired and sought after. But not now. Now he stood by himself, and as the judge pronounced his awful sentence, the angry onlookers cheered.[2]

This man was Madoff. He was 71 years old, and his sentence was 150 years in prison for operating the largest Ponzi scheme[a] in the history of humanity. For years Bernard had paid higher dividends on investments than any of his competitors could match. His company, Bernard L. Madoff Investment Securities LLC, with its unmatched dividends, was the talk of the rich and famous. But unknown to them, Bernard was simply using new deposits to pay high dividends on the old. And when the entire scheme came crashing down, he had bilked investors out of billions of dollars.

From wealthy billionaires to poor widows who were counting on deposited money to take them through their retirement, angry people

---

[a]A fraudulent investment program that pays returns to its investors from their own deposits rather than from actual profit earned. A Ponzi scheme usually attracts new investors by offering higher returns than competing investments. When new investments in the scheme slow or stop, the entire scheme folds and the investors lose most or all of their investment.

came forward, demanding justice and retribution. Bernard's scam caused untold misery, not only in the lives of depositors, but in his own life as well. His children and his wife of fifty years disowned him in disgust. And as time passed, emotional repercussions from Bernard's crime continued to haunt him. Exactly two years after the day Bernard was arrested, his son Mark, a husband and father, unable to bear the reproach brought on the family name, committed suicide in his New York apartment.

Today "Bernie," identified as prisoner No. 61727-054, has transitioned from his $8 million penthouse on East 64th Street in New York to an eight-by-ten-foot cell in the federal correctional complex in Butner, North Carolina.[3] Rather than dining on caviar with rich celebrities, you will find him eating cold sandwiches with drug dealers. The man who once recruited investors at exclusive country clubs is now only allowed to venture out of his concrete cell to get fresh air every other day, exercising in a cage on the roof.[4] It is a pathetic ending to a sad story.

Bernard Madoff's story is an example of self-centeredness and greed. With an eye only on profit and personal gain, Madoff destroyed his marriage, his relationship with his sons, and the trust his many clients placed in him. But Bernard Madoff is not the only man who has pursued a self-centered path. Self is the theme of our day. Our society constantly shouts that life is about *me*. It tells *me* that I should do what *I* want to do and go where *I* want to go. Marketers constantly proclaim that it's all about *me*, and public schools offer classes to boost self-esteem. Just pick up one of our daily newspapers and read the advice column. If your parents, spouse, or job are no longer fulfilling your desires, move on. *Me* should obviously be the primary focus in decision making.

But somehow when a Bernard Madoff comes along and puts all that self-centered teaching into practice, everyone is disgusted. No one really admires the result of a self-focused life. At some basic level we understand that we wouldn't want to live in a culture where everyone was completely living for self. And yet self continues to be promoted. We are taught that life's aim is self-fulfillment. I am to pursue things that satisfy *me*, that feel good to *me*, and that make *me* happy.

We could wish that this focus on *me* was limited to the secular world. But sadly, this self-centered emphasis has infiltrated churches and gradually reshaped their views on finances and possessions—as well as on retirement. If you listen to many prominent "Christian" teachers, you will find the same focus. Retirement is promoted as a time to enjoy life and benefit from the things you have accumulated.

We are familiar with advertisements for exotic vacations, timeshare offers, and the ever-changing myriad of recreational products offered today. In our self-centered society one would expect these. However, wouldn't marketers understand the foolishness of using self-focused advertising to attract a self-denying people? Unfortunately, even "Christian" articles and advertisements today assume that believers are best motivated by appeals to self-gratification.

Volunteering during retirement is encouraged. Why? Because of how much better it will make you feel about yourself. Retirement accounts and various financial investments are promoted. For what reason? Because they will make it easier to enjoy your retirement and do the things you have always longed to do. The theme recurs: It is all about *me*. Recently, in a brochure promoting volunteering at a Christian rest home, I noticed these words: "We want your volunteer experience to be fun and fulfilling." Is there a problem with spending our older years in enjoyable activities? Is it wrong to find fulfillment in volunteering?

There is nothing wrong with enjoying our final years. I think God Himself is pleased when we enjoy life. But there is a problem when fun and fulfillment become our primary focus. When we drift from serving the Lord to serving ourselves, we depart from a Biblical Kingdom focus.

What has caused this shift in Christianity? During the years of the early church and the early Christian martyrs, Christianity was known as a radical religion. Men and women who chose to follow Jesus willingly walked away from their former self-centered lives. Today, an observing unbeliever can often see little difference between his own value system and the materialistic focus of people who proclaim to be following Jesus. Is Christianity no longer a life-changing religion?

Several years ago I talked to a middle-aged believer who was trying to get a vision for the last half of his life. He started quietly interviewing older men in his church fellowship to understand their vision and find out how they were occupying themselves during their final years. When I talked to him after he had spoken with several of his fellow worshipers, he was discouraged.

He had asked one older brother how he was using his time and energy, and this older man replied that he was a paper hanger. The younger man told me that at first he was excited. This older man was still active and had a vision. But then the older man went on to explain. "My wife gives me a roll of toilet paper every once in a while, and I hang it up."

In a joking way he was admitting that he was accomplishing very little. But what really bothered the younger man was the fact that the older man seemed pleased with his lack of accomplishment. He seemed almost proud of it! He had worked hard in his life, and even though he was still in good health and capable of working, he had no vision for achieving anything more. The younger man found this disturbing. "Where is the older generation's vision?" he asked. "There is so much they could be doing in their older years."

I am thankful there are many other older ones among us who do have a vision for the Kingdom. There are still believers who are willing to spend and be spent for the Kingdom until the end. Yet it is easy to grow weary of the battle at times, and I think every older believer has a longing for heaven. We look at this sin-cursed, polluted, immoral world, and there are times we would like to just step off the planet. We watch with concern as the ungodly society we grew up with gives birth to a generation that seems even more intent on forgetting God. We can't help but wonder what is on the horizon. How many more Bernie Madoffs will our society churn out? How much worse can things get?

Perhaps the Apostle Paul had similar thoughts. He wrote of his desire to depart and be with Christ, which would be far better.[b] I think Paul experienced times of battle fatigue—times of wishing he could just forget the struggle and go on home to glory. But Paul didn't camp there, and neither should we. He went on to say that he knew it was needful for him to stay and bless the church of that day. In other words, Paul was determined to give all his energy to the Kingdom of Jesus Christ until he was called home by God Himself.

That is my prayer for each of you as you remember the past, consider the present, and anticipate the future. May your heart burn with a desire to be useful to the end! Regardless of mistakes or poor choices you have made, may you resolve to devote the rest of your time to God. Someday the Lord will call you home. But as you look forward to the final years of your life, I pray that you will have a growing desire to live for the Lord Jesus. I pray that as long as you live, you will maintain a godly vision, exhort and encourage your fellow believers, and keep on going till you're gone!

---

[b]Philippians 1:23

PART ONE
A Time of Great Change

One

Poverty to Prosperity

It was 1939, just ten years after the roaring economy in the United States had ground to a halt. While a few were concerned about a German chancellor named Adolf Hitler, most people in the United States felt disconnected from this European concern. They were emerging from ten years of struggle to survive and were just thankful for new jobs and an increase in orders at the factories. Unemployment was still high in 1939, but the worst was over and the economy was slowly improving.

During this time Max and Verda Foster, living in the Central Valley of California, began to discuss an idea. Max was a reporter for the local newspaper, but he had always retained an interest in farming. Times had been tough, and Max and Verda discussed ways they could increase their meager income. The grandchildren later said it was Verda who first suggested raising turkeys. And that is exactly what they did. The back porch of their small home was pressed into service, with Verda setting the timer to alert her day or night to gently rotate the eggs. This little project soon helped supplement Max's income, and eventually a small hatchery was built just off the bedroom. The back porch became Max's office.

Seeing opportunity for continued expansion, Max and Verda borrowed $1,000 against a life insurance policy and made a down payment on an eighty-acre farm, enabling them to continue expanding their fledgling business. In 1942, just three years after they started raising turkeys and with World War II in full swing, Max quit his job as a newspaper reporter and devoted himself full-time to the farming project. The small operation that began with poultry quickly expanded. Max soon added an all-Jersey dairy and began delivering chilled milk to the front doors of local residents. In the following years Max and Verda's business experienced phenomenal growth. In 1954, fifteen years after their humble beginning, the Fosters added a creamery, and in the sixties they opened a cultured products plant that produced cottage cheese, sour cream, yogurt, and ice cream. Just seventy years after Max and Verda first started their little back-porch project, Foster Farms claimed to be the largest and most recognized poultry producer in the Western United States,[5] with plants in other parts of the country as well.

By combining a small loan with diligence and hard work, Max and Verda propelled their fledgling enterprise into a formidable food production empire. But Foster Farms is not alone. Many family businesses have seen rapid change and expansion in the past seventy years, and many of us can think of scenarios similar to that of Foster Farms.

From extreme poverty to great prosperity, our older generation has seen astounding change. Those of us who are younger cannot fathom the economic upheaval our parents and grandparents saw in their lifetimes. They grew up accustomed to hard work and hard times. Many of them still remember outhouses and one-room schools. I remember hearing my grandparents talk of the changes they had seen in their lives. They went from running outside to see a passing Model T, to watching jets course across the sky, to seeing pictures of men actually walking on the moon. Amazing change!

But although their world changed, some intrinsic values didn't. These values were created by difficult times, and they have stayed with this generation even though their world has been transformed. Sometimes these traits of caution and frugality seem strange to those of us who are younger. We chuckle at their thriftiness and smugly smirk at their fear of debt and waste.

I grew up in California in the 1970s, just a few miles down the road from Max and Verda Foster. Foster Farms was a large corporation by then. I remember smiling as I passed Max Foster on his way to his office early one morning. He must have been in his eighties by then, and worth many millions of dollars, but in spite of his great wealth, he was driving an old beat-up pickup. I was just a teenager and would have been embarrassed to be seen in an old clunker like his. This level of frugality was hard for me to comprehend. But the old

Ford Courier still ran, and it was good enough for him, even with its whining motor, faded paint, and unfashionable appearance. He could have easily afforded any vehicle he wanted, but old habits die hard.

A Materialistic Paradox

Although Max's generation can be extremely frugal in some areas, they can be quite extravagant in others, and sometimes this confuses young people. How can the same senior citizen who shakes his head at paying three dollars for a cup of coffee at Starbucks shell out $200,000 for a motor home he uses only a couple times a year? Max and Verda Foster were an example of this paradox.

While Max drove his old truck to work each day, Verda cruised to town in style. She had the only Rolls Royce in the neighborhood. But although she enjoyed a luxurious mode of transportation, she retained certain traits of frugality as well. I attended school with her grandchildren and remember hearing them chuckle at some of their grandmother's saving habits. Verda had survived those early days by being extremely frugal. Hers was the generation that lived by the mantra, "Fix it up, wear it out, make it do, or do without." But now that wealth had arrived, a materialistic paradox had emerged. It was as though part of her was still living in the frugal past and part in the bountiful present.

One day a granddaughter came to school telling that Grandpa Max had finally put his foot down. "Verda," he had said in exasperation, "this has to stop. People who drive a Rolls Royce don't stop along the road to pick up aluminum cans!" Her world had changed, but she hadn't. Saving and scrimping were so much a part of her life that the habit continued—even while driving her Rolls Royce.

Many of us have observed similar inconsistencies. Recently I was sitting beside an older couple on an airplane, and I asked a little about their lives. They seemed glad to tell about the tough times they had experienced and to share their opinion about the wastefulness of the younger generation. Today times are better for them, and they enjoy frequent vacations. Although they couldn't understand the younger generation's money-squandering habits, taking their second Caribbean cruise of the year didn't seem wasteful to them at all.

Those of us who are younger can be confused by these seeming discrepancies. But we haven't experienced the economic transformation that shaped our parents and grandparents. We have been raised in a disposable society. Things are no longer made to last but rather to throw away. Though items may need very little repair, we toss them out simply because it costs more to fix them than to replace them. Life for us has been easy. We haven't tightened our belts during world wars or a depression. We haven't wondered where we would find food for the day. Yet sometimes, even though we have seen and experienced less, we assume we know more.

I have listened to young people discuss their observations of the older generation. Many of our youth have had the opportunity to travel the globe. They have rebuilt homes after a tsunami or cleaned up after massive earthquakes. They have seen the reality of global poverty and then returned home to America. Looking around at all of the self-centeredness in spending, it is easy for them to become critical of the previous generation. They ask questions like, "How can Grandpa feel good about traveling to Florida each year when thousands of children are starving?" They wonder why the older people in their communities are not more active in helping and why so many of their resources are spent on themselves.

Some of these observations are valid. Many older individuals are obviously using their abundance of time and money to seek pleasure and personal fulfillment. Why have so many older believers chosen to focus on frivolous travel, fun with the family, or hobbies and pastimes? We need to look at the reasons this has occurred and examine some basic Biblical truths we have ignored.

But we also want to look at some shining examples of individuals who have chosen to give their lives for the Kingdom even though they could have pursued personal pleasure. These believers, even during their final years, have chosen to make their lives monuments to God's grace and goodness. They are an encouragement, and those who are younger can be inspired by observing their choices.

Conclusion

In his best seller, *The Greatest Generation,* Tom Brokaw called the years following the Great Depression a time of "unparalleled progress on almost every front."[6] From a secular perspective this was true. While not everyone became financially wealthy, it was a time of prosperity unknown to previous generations. Advances in technology, communication, and travel impacted all of us. But not all have responded in the same way to this new affluence. Some have used these blessings to build the Kingdom, while others have chosen to bless themselves.

We want to look at examples of both as we consider how to develop a Kingdom-focused vision for our final years. We want to learn from the lives of those who have traveled before us. It is important, however, that we do this with charity and humility. I can't be sure how I would have responded had I been faced with this shift from poverty to prosperity.

Those who were living in the 1930s didn't know what was ahead of them. They had no idea that World War II was just around the corner, and they couldn't foresee the economic boom that would immediately follow. They didn't know what was ahead, and we don't either. But we do know that time is short and it will soon be our turn to live out our final days. Let's learn from those who have gone before us and resolve to develop a vision today for Kingdom living tomorrow.

Two
The Invisible Gorilla

In 1999 Harvard University conducted a basic psychological experiment. The experiment was incredibly simple, bordering on the absurd. Yet the surprising results have surfaced in publications such as *Newsweek* and *The Wall Street Journal*. The conclusions were so revealing that they have been featured in college textbooks and psychology curricula. In addition, a full-length book was written to analyze the findings.[7]

In the experiment six Harvard students were videotaped passing two basketballs between themselves while moving around within a small circle. Three students clothed in white passed one ball between themselves, and three clothed in black did the same. The video taken of these students was less than a minute long, and those viewing the clip were asked to count how many times the students dressed in white passed the ball to each other.

This isn't as easy as it sounds. It is difficult to count passes of students dressed in white when you have students dressed in black moving around and passing a ball as well. But it can be done, and the number of times the students dressed in white actually passed the ball is fifteen times. But while you are carefully following the movements of the one ball, something else occurs.

About halfway through the video, a student dressed in a black gorilla costume walks slowly into the middle of this milling group of students. The gorilla stops, turns, faces the camera, and then beats its hairy chest before slowly ambling off the stage. The gorilla's actions are very deliberate, and it makes no attempt to be secretive. Yet amazingly, fully half of the people watching this video clip for the first time do not see the gorilla.

How can this be? How can a big, hairy gorilla come lumbering across a screen, stop in the middle, turn and face the viewer, beat its chest, and walk off the screen, yet be totally invisible to someone intently watching the video? How indeed?

The answer is that these viewers aren't looking for gorillas. They are concentrating so intently on counting the number of times the players dressed in white are passing the ball that they miss the gorilla. They are totally unaware of the obvious.

Since that first experiment in 1999, similar tests have substantiated its findings. Recently an almost identical experiment was conducted. In this video a gorilla also walks across the stage while the players pass the ball. The gorilla stops in the midst of the players and beats its chest, and the viewers again are supposed to count the number of times the white-clad players pass the ball. Of course, this time everyone sees the gorilla. They have heard of the past experiment and are on the lookout for gorillas. But something else happens. During this experiment, the bright red backdrop behind the players slowly turns yellow, and one of the players dressed in black walks off the stage in the middle of the event. Surprisingly, as they watch for gorillas, only 17 percent notice these two obvious changes.

We See What We Look For

Results of these experiments are conclusive. We tend to observe only what we are looking for. We focus on the expected and miss the unexpected—even if it is obvious. Of course, we all like to think we are the exception. Over 90 percent of individuals polled said that if they'd had an opportunity to participate, they would have seen the gorilla. We all like to think we are more observant than average.

One of the men behind the experiments, Professor Dan Simons of the University of Illinois, said, "What's interesting is that most people firmly believe that as long as they are looking at the world, they will notice anything important that happens."[8] The vast majority of us are confident we are good observers. Yet the overwhelming evidence suggests we are observant primarily of what we are expecting to see and generally oblivious to what we are not.

This truth sobers me as I examine my own life. I tend to analyze, categorize, and compartmentalize the people who surround me. Subconsciously I scrutinize the individuals with whom I live, work, and worship. I see their traits, habits, and weaknesses and make conclusions about what kinds of people they are. And once I have them categorized, all I observe in their lives is what I am expecting. If I conclude, for example, that their theological view is a little more grace-oriented than my own, I notice and can become critical of their statements that focus on God's forgiveness and acceptance of the sinner. It seems that is all they talk about, and I conclude they are going a little too far.

Conversely, I also am aware of the brother who, in my opinion, tends to overemphasize obedience. His preoccupation with the importance of works in a believer's life annoys me. It seems like his comments are always circling around the same theme. But again, those are the comments I was expecting, and that is what I hear.

Sometimes in the midst of categorizing and analyzing the faults I was expecting, I miss the obvious. I fail to see the tremendous blessing that the brother in question is bringing to the body of Christ. I miss the gorilla.

But this propensity doesn't just occur on a personal level. Masses of people have participated in group-think and also missed gorillas. How else do you explain the nothing-can-go-wrong attitude in America during the Roaring Twenties or Germany's infatuation with Hitler in the 1930s? In each situation the masses were sure they were seeing the entire picture, but in reality they were missing huge gorillas. We must conclude that adding more observers doesn't always solve the problem. Entire nations have failed to see the obvious.

Christian Gorillas?

We could wish this human tendency had no impact on Christianity, but church history is rife with hidden gorillas. Our eyes become trained to scan the horizon for the concern we have been trained to watch for, and we miss a threat we hadn't considered.

Consider the Christians in Constantine's time. Can you really blame them for missing the potential threat created by an emperor who loved Christianity? For hundreds of years—in fact, for as long as anyone could remember—the church had been facing persecution. Just ten years before, Emperor Diocletian had issued a series of harsh edicts rescinding the rights of all Christians and demanding they comply with the heathen rituals and sacrifices of the day.

Many Christians had lost family members. Some had watched as relatives were cruelly tormented and killed. It was obvious how Satan was working, and it was clear to them that physical persecution was the primary enemy.

Then suddenly, amazing news arrived in town. The new Emperor Constantine had issued the Edict of Milan, proclaiming religious tolerance in the Roman Empire. Can you imagine the relief? After praying for reprieve for years, the Christians must have been overwhelmed with gratitude. And as the next few years passed, the news got even better! The same government that had been slaughtering church members and attempting to annihilate the church had switched to building cathedrals and offering salaries to church leaders. How could this be anything less than the blessing of God? Nothing like this had ever happened before throughout church history. Surely God must be working in a marvelous way!

From our vantage point things look different. We marvel that the church members couldn't see what was happening. They were so focused on how Satan had used persecution to attack in the past that they couldn't comprehend the great threat of a government that embraced the church. They saw Constantine as a blessing sent by God, but in their relief and jubilation, they missed the obvious. While they were rejoicing in their new freedoms, a gorilla was lumbering onto the stage.

How could they forget so quickly what Jesus had said about His

Kingdom being totally different?[a] How could they have stood idly by and let Constantine begin to use the sword to defend truth when Jesus had expressly forbidden it?[b] I can be judgmental as I look at the church of that period. Yet as I look back at all the times I thought I had a good understanding of enemy tactics and didn't, I have to humbly admit I probably wouldn't have seen that gorilla either.

What causes us to notice change? What is it that really rings the alarm in our lives and warns us to take notice? In analyzing my own life, I have come to a sad realization. Too often the changes I notice first are the ones that clash with my selfish desires. And the changes that go unnoticed are the ones that please my flesh. Too often I quickly categorize change that brings relief to my flesh as a blessing from God, and consequently, I miss the gorilla.

Poverty to Prosperity

Let's go back to the great economic change that occurred in the 1900s. My grandfather was born into a rural Indiana farming community in 1895. As a boy, I remember listening to him tell stories of farming with horses and pumping water by hand. I tried to imagine life when cars, trucks, and jet travel were inconceivable. He was married in 1918 and raised a large family in those difficult times. Neighbors lost their farms. People shared with each other the little they had. Life was hard, and any extra food they raised was taken to town on Saturdays to be sold from the back of the horse-drawn wagon. The focus was on survival, and many went without sufficient food and clothing during those difficult years.

Too often I quickly categorize change that brings relief to my flesh as a blessing from God, and consequently, I miss the gorilla.

Grandpa told of the world wars and of the tension within communities as some young men were sent away to fight while others

[a] Matthew 20:25-28
[b] John 18:36

asked for conscientious objector status and stayed home. As I listened to these stories, it was as though Grandpa had lived on a different planet. My own life was so different that I had difficulty relating. It seemed that until the end of World War II everything they tried to do was difficult. Life was hard and survival a task.

But as the years continued, change began to occur—rapid change. A post World War II economic boom began in 1945 and lasted through the early 1970s. Coupled with the rapid progression in technology, this period of strong economic growth transformed almost every area of life. Many of the modern conveniences we've become accustomed to first became available during this time. My father was a young boy during those years, and he told of their first exposure to electricity in their home. They nearly wore out those bedroom light switches that first night.

In the 1940s Grandpa and Grandma hosted a minister from California. They sat around the table and listened in breathless wonder to details of that far-off place in the West. The children heard about teeming orange groves and huge grape vineyards and tried to imagine what it would be like to live in a place without snow. California seemed like a distant, exotic country. After the minister traveled on, one of the children asked Grandpa, "Daddy, do you think you'll ever get to California?"

Grandpa told his children this could never happen. Travel to a far-off place like California seemed impossible—something reserved for the rich and adventuresome, but certainly not for an Indiana farmer.

But Grandpa did go to California. He traveled there many times to visit the very son who had asked the question. And within thirty years he would be the first in his area to tour the Holy Land. Grandpa had no idea of the changes that were just around the corner.

Those were exciting years. Crops produced well, factories ran at full capacity, and wealth accumulated. For people coming out of the Great Depression, it would have been difficult to see this change as anything but good. As farms and businesses grew in size and profitability, it seemed clear that they were experiencing the blessing of the Lord.

But did they miss the gorilla? Did they miss the effect this prosperity was having on their spiritual lives and churches?

The Poverty of Wealth

We have a difficult time being alarmed about change that agrees with our flesh. We can become concerned with natural poverty, but even though Jesus tried to warn us, we tend to forget the great inherent poverty of wealth.

> *. . . we tend to forget the great inherent poverty of wealth.*

I remember working for a wealthy man named Jim.[c] Jim had come through the Great Depression and had vivid memories of doing without necessities. He had worked hard and eventually prospered. In fact, Jim had become a wealthy man. He owned several businesses, commercial property, and several large tracts of income-producing land. Yet in spite of his wealth, Jim was miserable. He was convinced another Great Depression was just around the corner, and consequently he refused to part with anything. He built large warehouses to store all these items he might use someday. As he continually updated his properties, he stored the old cabinets, used plumbing fixtures, and miscellaneous appliances in his warehouses. Then, fearing theft, Jim hired men to patrol these warehouses. Jim constantly worried that he might lose something he had accumulated. Consequently, as his possessions increased, so did his anxiety. Jim was an older man now, and his daily life was consumed in a vicious cycle of worry over theft, stock market fears, real estate concerns, and anxiety about the future. He well understood the burden of poverty, but he had failed to account for the inherent poverty of wealth.

Conclusion

Pick up almost any magazine dealing with retirement, and money is the theme. Articles seem to redundantly circle around the same question: "Are you saving enough?" Reading these publications would give the impression that successful retirement depends primarily on the size of your portfolio. Advertisements show pictures of laughing, gray-haired senior citizens touring Europe or leisurely strolling the

---

[c]Here, as in many short stories throughout the book, names and details have been changed to protect identity.

decks of a cruise ship off a sun-washed island. The message is clear. After a lifetime of hard work, you owe it to yourself to relax and enjoy life. "Those Golden Years," they say, "are a time to enjoy the fruits of your labors. Finally you will be able to live off that large mutual fund and do the things you have always wanted to do."

But as we continue to look at living out the last half of our lives, we want to examine this prevalent message of our culture. Is it correct? Is it Biblical? Does God intend that we use these years to serve ourselves? Is this a time to sit back and focus on our nice possessions, wonderful families, and ability to travel? Could it be that God has more in mind than restaurants, recreation, and relaxation? In the midst of all these wonderful pleasures that tickle our flesh, are we missing something vital? Could we be missing the gorilla?

Three
Life in the Thorn Patch

It was on a construction site in the late 1980s when I first met Andrei. He had emigrated from Romania, and as we worked, he shared the struggles of his past. His story was similar to those of many other believers who escaped from communist countries during the 1970s. Andrei had been a part of the underground church in Romania. He knew what it meant to choose Christ though opposed by culture, public opinion, and threatening government officials. He had grown up listening to horror stories from church leaders just returning from torture chambers, and he understood the reality of persecution. Attending worship services with one ear tuned to the sermon and the other listening for the secret police had been a constant reality. To Andrei, this was Christianity. It was all he had known.

Finally, after years of meeting in secret, smuggling Bibles, and hiding from police, Andrei had an opportunity to escape. With the help of believers, he was concealed in a vehicle and taken across the border to a neighboring country. The situation was so dangerous that his friends had packed Andrei into a tiny metal compartment and welded it shut to avoid detection by the police. Finally, after hours of hiding in a cramped position, struggling to get enough air through the tiny holes drilled in the side of the box, Andrei arrived safely across the border. After a while his family was able to join him there, and together they escaped to America.

I met Andrei several years later, but recalling his escape and that first taste of freedom was still thrilling for him. With bright eyes and an animated voice, he loved to tell, in broken English, of those first worship services. The joy of singing without fear and the abundance of Bibles were blessings almost too good to be true. America was a wonderful place to live. No one looked over his shoulder, services were never interrupted, and they had more food than his family could eat. This was obviously the blessing of God!

But several years passed, and at the time I worked with Andrei, he was beginning to have some doubts. Though he was still thankful for the liberty in this country, he had made some observations that alarmed him. Andrei had watched the lives of many believers who had come from Romania and was concerned about the changes they were making. He knew these people. He had observed their faith in the midst of intense persecution. He had seen them stand against a fierce and determined assault by the government authorities and watched them shine like cities on a hill.

"We sent our children to schools where the teachers taught them day after day that there was no God," Andrei said. "And I don't remember even one of them succumbing to that teaching! We knew what the atheistic teachers were pounding into our children, so as soon as they arrived home, we'd spend time teaching them again from the Word of God."

It had been a time of great spiritual warfare. The fight was intense and the battle lines clear. The conflict was black and white, with everyone aware of Satan's tactics. Parents recognized their own weaknesses and the need for constant prayer and vigilance in the fight. But then everything changed. After moving to America, the Romanian believers enjoyed peace and prosperity. The dramatic change was unbelievable. No longer did someone watch by the door during services, nor did they need to hide their Bibles in the attic.

But Andrei noticed that in this great land of freedom these same people who had so faithfully stood under oppression were having trouble dealing with liberty. Their young people were being heavily influenced by the fashions and fads of the day. Older members of the church were losing their original passion for the Gospel, and it was becoming more difficult to interest people in regular church attendance. Prayer didn't seem quite as essential, and fasting was almost a thing of the past. Daily devotions with the family didn't seem as important, and some of the marriages were struggling.

The Romanian believers had come to America with a strong work ethic, and many became prosperous. Now, with all the business concerns and newfound wealth to enjoy, their zeal for the Lord had diminished.

One day, after sharing some of his concerns for these persecuted but now prosperous Romanians, Andrei made this startling statement. "I have considered," he said soberly, "moving my family back to Romania."

Back to Romania?

This was before the fall of Nicolae Ceausescu and the communist regime. Persecution and torture were still regular occurrences in Romania. Was it possible that Andrei was considering leaving a country of ease and affluence and moving back into a setting like that?

I remember going home after these discussions and pondering, *Is prosperity so dangerous that a man would knowingly take his family back into persecution to avoid the perils of America?*

I had been taught from my youth to thank God regularly for the freedom and prosperity we enjoy, and I had learned to think of America as a blessed place to live. It was a place of spiritual and financial opportunity, a land of comfort, ease, and security. What was Andrei seeing that I was failing to observe? Why was he concerned about the influence our culture might have on his children?

Jesus told a parable one day about a sower who went forth to plant seeds.[a] He talked about seed that fell on stony ground, seed that landed by the wayside, and seed that fell on good ground. These three types of soil each had a direct impact on the harvest. Jesus' listeners would have understood this. Hard-packed soil and shallow topsoil are not good places to raise crops. Good soil is where seeds can grow and produce a bountiful harvest.

But Jesus went on to describe another place seed landed, and this time he said nothing about the condition of the soil. He didn't say if the soil was good, bad, stony, or shallow. The problem with the crop in this area wasn't the soil but the thorns. I think it is safe to assume it was good soil. This soil would have been capable of producing a wonderful crop—except for the thorns.

As I remember those discussions with Andrei, I believe the parable

---

[a]Matthew 13:3

of the sower explains the difference in our perspectives. As I looked at America, I was seeing good soil. I saw a place of complete religious freedom where a man could serve the Lord and raise his family without any hindrances. It was a great place to live!

Andrei saw all of this as well. He was aware of the amazing freedom and opportunity. But he also saw the thorns. And he saw the effect the thorns had on spiritual growth. Jesus said that the man who receives the seed among thorns "is he that heareth the word; and the care of this world, and the deceitfulness of riches, choke the word, and he becometh unfruitful."[b]

Survival to Surplus

Imagine a parent holding one end of a child's blanket while the toddler pulls with all his might on the other. All of his focus is on getting the blanket, and while it is all in fun, the battle lines are clear. The child wants the blanket, and every effort is centered on taking it from the adult. But what happens if the parent suddenly releases the blanket? Most children are so focused on getting it that little thought is given to how they would respond if it was suddenly theirs.

For many years our older generation focused on survival. Energy, effort, thought, and focus went into making ends meet. Suddenly prosperity came. And many, like the toddler who suddenly receives the blanket, have struggled to maintain spiritual balance.

We really shouldn't be surprised. God warned His people long ago that moving from survival to surplus is dangerous. As the children of Israel stood on the threshold of the Promised Land, they were cautioned about the result of coming affluence. They had lived out in the barren wilderness for many years, and it was all most of them had ever known. But now they were facing the prospect of receiving all the things they had been dreaming about during that long dusty plod. Plenty of food, homes of their own, great possessions, and more land than they would be able to use. It was a long list as Moses revealed the tremendous blessings that would be coming their way.

But interwoven throughout this lengthy list of blessings was a strong

[b]Matthew 13:22

warning. God knew man's tendency, and His admonition can be summed up in one sentence from Moses. "Beware that thou forget not the Lord thy God . . ."[c] Throughout history we have struggled to maintain a focus on God during times of affluence. It is hard to remember God when things are going well, and there is something about the shift from poverty to prosperity that destabilizes a man.

We see this played out with the lotteries that have swept the country. There is no question who is buying these tickets. The zip codes having the lowest incomes record the greatest sales, indicating that lottery tickets are being purchased primarily by the poor. Consequently, the individual who receives the prize is thrust into a scenario for which he is ill prepared. Newspaper articles abound telling of individuals who suddenly received a large sum of money only to suffer strained relationships, marriage conflicts, and long-term financial challenges as a result. Many people have lost millions within just a few years. As lotteries have become more popular and prevalent, counseling organizations have sprung up to help these "winners" deal with the myriad of pressing problems that follow the shift from poverty to prosperity.

> *. . . there is something about the shift from poverty to prosperity that destabilizes a man.*

Conclusion

In the majority of situations, our older generation has not suddenly become wealthy. Rather, the change has come gradually and almost imperceptibly. While a lottery winner knows the exact day the transformation occurred, many of those who have lived during the last seventy years have been almost unaware of the change. This has made the shift even more deceptive. Just like the parable that Jesus left to warn us, the thorns have gradually grown up, and slowly, ever so slowly, we have become entangled.

As wealth accumulates, our confidence in its ability to deliver increases as well. Where at one time we would have turned to our

[c]Deuteronomy 8:11

invisible God in adversity, we now turn to the visible checkbook. And subtly, with so many other things to lean on, we feel less and less need to depend on God. Jesus' words are still true today. We tend to become entangled and choked with the cares, riches, and pleasures of this life.[d]

It isn't impossible to survive spiritually in prosperous countries like America, and it isn't necessary that all of us try to relocate to a communist or impoverished country. There have been many godly individuals, men like Job, Abraham, and Joseph, who possessed great wealth and were still faithful to God. There is also no inherent righteousness connected with poverty. Many desperately poor men live very ungodly lives.

But Jesus was clear. Wealth is dangerous, and like weeds and thorns, it has a tendency to slowly choke out spiritual vibrancy. Our spiritual lives are much more likely to be vibrant and successful if we recognize that we are attempting to bring forth fruit in a thorn patch.

[d]Luke 8:14

Four

My
~~Thy~~ Kingdom Come

W ith a silent prayer for her little son, Anna sat down to write. It was January 1539, and she knew her time was short. The guards would soon come to escort her to the place of execution. Anna mentally reviewed her imprisonment. She remembered the cold nights in the stone prison and the loneliness, wondering how young Isaiah was doing. She thought of the hours she had spent praying for his spiritual welfare and the nights she had struggled with discouragement and disillusionment. It hadn't been easy leaving a nine-year-old son. Had she made the right decision? Was this really what God wanted her to do? As her weary mind had grappled repeatedly with these questions, she had always come back to the same conclusion. She must be faithful to her Lord Jesus.

Her mind turned to the future. Would her son survive the trauma of losing his mother at such a tender age? Would he grow up to be a man of God? Could he be faithful in this violent, evil world so intent on destroying truth and the people of God? Taking her pen, she began to write a final letter to her son.[9]

> *My son, hear the instruction of your mother; open your ears to hear the words of my mouth. Behold, I go today the way of the prophets, apostles, and martyrs, and drink of the cup of which they all drank . . .*
>
> *Love your neighbor. Deal with an open, warm heart thy bread to the hungry, clothe the naked, and suffer not to have anything twofold; for there are always some who lack. Whatever the Lord grants you from the sweat of your face,*

23

above what you need, communicate to those of whom you know that they love the Lord; and suffer nothing to remain in your possession until the morrow, and the Lord shall bless the work of your hands, and give you His blessing for an inheritance.

O my son, let your life be conformed to the Gospel, and the God of all peace, sanctify your soul and body, to His praise. Amen.

It isn't difficult to grasp the great longing Anna had for her son at the conclusion of this heartrending letter. "Don't let the things of this world distract you from following Jesus!" There is something about knowing you are just a few hours from death that simplifies life. It is much easier to clearly articulate your vision while listening for the executioner's footsteps. This letter was written in southern Holland in 1539. Many other letters and accounts of Anabaptist martyrs during this time echoed Anna's abhorrence of wealth and accumulation. These martyrs were determined to follow the Lord Jesus regardless of the cost, and they viewed the accumulation of wealth as a distraction sent by Satan himself.

> *There is something about knowing you are just a few hours from death that simplifies life.*

From Rags to Riches

But let's move forward in time. Within just one hundred years the picture in Holland had changed dramatically. Persecution was over, and prosperity had come. In the 1600s many of these Dutch Anabaptists were known for wealth and industry. Many had become involved in manufacturing, shipping, and silk weaving. They had built elaborate homes, and along one stretch of the Utrecht River was a string of Mennonite estates so lavish that they were nicknamed *Menistenhemel* (Mennonite Heaven)[10] by the locals. History records that these wealthy Anabaptists had, in a very short time, acquired a great fascination and penchant for collecting rare paintings and antiques.

This dramatic shift had a profound effect on the church. As they lost their desire to imitate the life of Jesus with regard to wealth and possessions, they also lost their burden for souls and their love for each other. As Hans de Ries, a Dutch Mennonite who lived through this transition, lamented, "When our houses were of wood, our hearts were of gold; but when our houses became golden, our hearts became wooden."

I cannot think of a more dramatic example of rapid theological shift in church history. In the mid-1500s the Anabaptists were actively teaching and writing on the topic of non-accumulation and were famous for their lack of interest in worldly possessions. Yet by the mid 1600s they had become well known in that area for wealth, elaborate homes, and big business.

> *When our houses were of wood, our hearts were of gold; but when our houses became golden, our hearts became wooden.*
> — *Hans de Ries*

But this scenario is not isolated to the Netherlands or to a particular time period. A similar change took place among the Anabaptists living in Russia around the turn of the twentieth century. These hard-working believers had moved into Eastern Europe in dire financial straits. They had focused their energy and work ethic on making the land productive, and the ground soon produced abundantly, making many of them rich. A visitor who lived among them during World War I found his hosts so focused on material concerns that he suggested they really should have been called Mammonites instead of Mennonites.[11]

How can such a dramatic shift take place in such a short time? How can believers change positions so rapidly? For the Dutch Anabaptists especially, the memories of martyrdom were still fresh in their minds. Many of them had grandfathers and grandmothers who could tell vivid, authentic stories of tremendous persecution and excruciating suffering. How could these people lose their footing so quickly? There are several possible answers to this question, but I believe there is one we should look at seriously. It has happened too often throughout church history to be ignored.

Acculturation

It isn't hard to sing "This World Is Not My Home" in the middle of persecution. When things are rough, we don't want to stay here anyway. But when the going gets smooth, we tend to acculturate and become more like our surroundings. When the world loves us, we tend to love it too. We lose our resistance in relaxation and begin taking our cues from culture rather than Christ.

A few faithful Christians raised the alarm in the 1600s. One of those was Thieleman van Braght, who compiled *Martyrs Mirror.* As he watched the church's focus shift toward materialism and wealth, he sorrowfully wrote in the introduction to his book, "These are sad times in which we now live; nay, truly, there is more danger now than in the time of our fathers, who suffered death for the testimony of the Lord."[12]

He warned fellow believers regarding their "large, expensive, and ornamented houses," and tried to point out the disturbing transformation the church had made.

So how could this have happened? Is acculturation this powerful? If so, is it possible we have drifted as well? Could we be guilty of shifting our gaze from the Lord Jesus to something else?

Following Culture or Following Christ?

As I have analyzed this question in my own life, I have found it enlightening to examine my view of success. Defining your criteria for success can help you discern whether you are following culture or following Christ. Analyze for a moment what success means to you. When you hear someone say, "That man has been successful," what comes to your mind? Do you first think of the fact that he has successfully avoided the entanglement of wealth Jesus warned so strongly against? Or do you think of a man who has amassed an earthly fortune? Remember, we are trying to discern whether our model of success is more like our culture's or like Christ's.

These two models are clearly opposed to each other. The rich man Jesus called a fool is the same man so highly esteemed by our culture. Earthly wealth is highly regarded by our society. Is it highly esteemed by you? Do you ascribe more value to a man who is known for his wealth?

Sometimes I hear myself describing the house another brother lives in by saying, "He's just renting." What does "just renting" mean? Where would I get the notion that renting is a less valid choice than buying? I am not denying that there are financial considerations to this question, but beyond that, I find myself ascribing some inherent value to being the owner. Where does that idea come from? Who teaches that we can ever own more than the use of an item? My choice of words when saying "just renting" reveals how much I have been impacted by my culture, and I am shocked at how normal this mindset has become in my life.

As you consider how the last half of your earthly life should be used, it is vital that you first examine what paradigm you are using to make decisions. What will your point of reference be in deciding how those years should be used? Are you going to be led by your culture or by the teachings of Christ?

> *Who teaches that we can ever own more than the use of an item?*

All About *Me*?

There are many articles on how to retire successfully. They can give you advice on how much to save, what retirement communities are best, and which medical facilities are rated highest. All of them assume your first priority is to enjoy life as long as possible. These writings are usually replete with enticing ideas and pictures of potential travel destinations and recreational activities. But examining your view of what it means to retire successfully can be revealing. It can help you discern whether you are being led by society or the Saviour.

Recently I was reading an article in a major news magazine regarding investing for retirement. What caught my attention was the unashamed, blatant self-centeredness of the article. There was no attempt to hide the end goal. The latter years of my life, according to the article, are all about *me*. In these articles, every aspect of those golden years is discussed from the viewpoint of how it affects *me*. Even as volunteering and giving are addressed, the focus is still on *me*. I am told how much I will enjoy these activities, how rewarding they will be, and how much better I will feel about myself. It's all about *me*.

Sociologists have labeled those born in the seventies, eighties, and nineties "Generation Me." While self-centeredness certainly isn't confined to those three decades, it does seem that humanity's focus is continually becoming more and more self-centered. As one secular author said, "Generation Me has never known a world that put duty before self."[13] Life has become a journey where self is preeminent and happiness of primary importance.

So how has this affected Christianity? Has this focus on self influenced us?

If we are honest, we have to admit it has affected us all. David Platt, in his book *Radical,* says:

> If you were to ask the average Christian sitting in a worship service on Sunday morning to summarize the message of Christianity, you would most likely hear something along the lines of, "The message of Christianity is that God loves me." Or someone might say, "The message of Christianity is that God loved me enough to send His son, Jesus, to die for me."
>
> As wonderful as this sentiment sounds, is it Biblical? Isn't it incomplete based on what we have seen in the Bible? "God loves me" is not the essence of Biblical Christianity. Because if "God loves me" is the message of Christianity, then who is the object of Christianity? . . . Me.[14]

In much of professing Christianity, it seems like the search is on for a church that cares about *me*, that has music that suits *me* or a youth program that is right for *my* family. At times it seems like a smorgasbord. People slowly walk along with furrowed brow surveying the options, intent on finding something just right for *me*.

Take a walk through the local "Christian" bookstore and notice how the themes tend to revolve around feelings and Christian experience. The shelves parade an endless selection of books about self-help, self-improvement, and self-esteem. Recently a publisher that markets books for mainstream Christianity said that if you really want a book to sell, there are two important things to remember. The title needs to reveal what it will do for the reader and how soon it will do it. Titles containing phrases

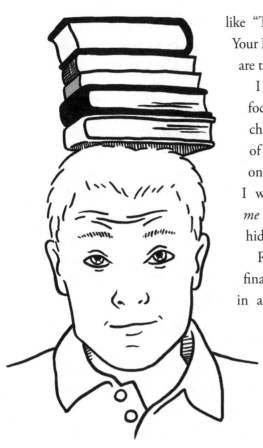

like "Three Easy Steps to Transforming Your Life" or "Thirty Days to a New You" are the ones that sell.

I wonder how much this *me* focus has affected our conservative churches. As I see the proliferation of counseling and the great emphasis on finding a church that is just right, I wonder. Sometimes it seems our *me* focus is just as strong, albeit well hidden behind a spiritual façade.

Recently I was asked to give a financial talk at a conservative church in a farming community. Afterward several men were discussing some comments I had made regarding debt. I had encouraged them to have an end goal of getting out of debt, but several of the local farmers vehemently disagreed. "You must not understand farming," one of them said. "I want all of my children to farm, and the only way to accomplish this is by taking on more debt, and that is what I plan to do."

I spent some time listening to this father's vision for his children. There was a lot of pressure in his community to farm, and it seemed his primary goal in life was to get his children onto farms of their own. He worked day and night to stay ahead of the banker, and he had no qualms about dragging his children into the same situation. He even viewed this as a spiritual pursuit. Really?

Something about the sight of believers bidding land up to unrealistic prices and competing against fellow believers at auctions sounds a lot like *me*-focused Christianity in spiritual skin. While giving my children opportunity can be a worthwhile pursuit, it can also become another way of promoting *me*. We are extremely creative in finding ways to advance the kingdom of *me*. To listen to this young father talk, you would think Christianity can hardly exist off the farm.

Make no mistake. Raising your family in a rural setting can be a great blessing. But surely we haven't bought into the idea that farming is an integral and essential pillar upon which Christianity must rest. I have seen vibrant congregations in the heart of huge Third World cities or meeting on the seventeenth floor of a housing complex in a persecuted country. So when I see the incredible push in some conservative communities to maintain certain lifestyles and livelihoods, I wonder if the focus hasn't strayed. Is this really about promoting the Kingdom of God? Or is it possible that under the guise of promoting and protecting our denomination, we are really attempting to build our kingdom rather than His?

God does love us, and there is nothing wrong with teaching our little children to sing "Jesus Loves Me." Let's keep singing this little song, but let's not forget—we were never intended to be the object or focal point of Christianity. Paul, after describing in great detail all that God has done for us, says, "That in the ages to come he might shew the exceeding riches of his grace in his kindness toward us through Christ Jesus."[a]

God reaching out to us is an exhibition of His grace, not to show how valuable we are, but how merciful He has been. And now that we have received this amazing grace, God has something for us to do as well. Jesus described our mission when He said, "This is my commandment, that ye love one another as I have loved you."[b] He has displayed His grace as a model for us, and we are to love others in the same way.

It is not about us; it is about God and modeling His character. The focal point isn't my family, farm, or church denomination; the focus must be the Kingdom and glory of God!

---

[a]Ephesians 2:7

[b]John 15:12

> *It is not about us;
> it is about God and
> modeling His character.*

Conclusion

Paul told Timothy that one of the characteristics of the last days is that men would be "lovers of pleasures more than lovers of God."[c] I have wondered about this verse. Has there ever been a time in history when this wasn't true? Hasn't this always been our problem? We are self-centered people, and our thoughts tend to revolve around ourselves. We just naturally find ourselves pursuing things that bring us pleasure.

Yet I think we all realize we are living in a time when this is intensifying. As the fear of God decreases, the passion for pleasure increases. "If it feels good, do it" is the theme of the day. Adding fuel to this prevailing tendency is the abundance of time and money. Man's nature hasn't changed; we just have more opportunity to do what we desire.

This is why it is so vital that we prayerfully scrutinize our desires. What is it you are pursuing? As we consider moving into a time of life when more time and money may become available, it is imperative that we examine our allegiance. Is it *thy* Kingdom, or *my* kingdom, that I really long to see?

---

[c] 2 Timothy 3:4

Five

When Desire Meets Opportunity

D ay after day he had faithfully walked. Explicitly following instructions, he had done his duty and silently marched. It must have been an amazing sight, masses of people marching on and on around the city. I can imagine them watching out of the corners of their eyes, scanning the massive structure and perhaps again looking at the scarlet cord hanging from the city wall. For six days this had continued, and Achan had marched along with the best of them. I don't know what the thoughts were in that silent parade, but I wonder if they didn't recount recent events as they marched around Jericho.

I wonder if Achan didn't marvel as he marched along at how the Jordan River had dried up miraculously so they could pass over. The Lord had done some wonderful things for them, and now He had promised to do something even more astounding. God had said that these massive walls were going to just fall down.[a] Can't you imagine the mixture of thoughts swirling around in the Israelites' minds? Giant stone walls don't just fall down!

I think Achan wanted to follow the Lord. I believe he had promised with the rest that he would faithfully do all that the Lord commanded. He may have even been known as one of the many God-honoring, faithful fathers in Israel. When the men gathered around their fires in the evening, perhaps he was known for encouraging the others. We don't know.

But one thing we do know. Achan was intensely interested in that

---

[a] Joshua 6:5

wall coming down. Like every other Israelite, his dreams depended on it. As the Israelites silently marched, their thoughts probably examined the possibilities. If these walls really came crashing down, the impact on the surrounding nations would be incredible. These men probably had visions of all their other enemies just standing in line with white flags of surrender. Who wants to fight against an army that can miraculously knock down city walls? Can't you just see those men marching with great expectation? If those walls really fell like God had said they would, life would be easy.

The seventh day finally arrived, and as Bible readers we know that the walls did fall. But as Achan entered the city that day, he found himself in another battle. Achan knew what God had said. All the men had been told that everything in the city was cursed, and nothing was to be brought out "but all the silver, and gold, and vessels of brass and iron," and they were to be "consecrated to the Lord: they shall come into the treasury of the Lord."[b]

Yes, Achan was well aware of what God had said. But as he eagerly scrambled over the rubble with the other Israelites that day, Achan carried more than just his sword. His fellow soldiers probably had no suspicions about him as they excitedly maneuvered through the mangled remains of the walls of Jericho. But deep down inside Achan was carrying something they couldn't see—something that would result in tragedy and heartache.

Secret Desires

Achan was carrying secret desires. I think he had faithfully complied with everything God had asked of him to this point. He had been circumcised, marched with the others, and tried to be obedient to God's commands. But deep inside Achan's heart was a secret desire. And when the walls came crashing down, Achan's desire met opportunity, and Achan fell.

All of us carry desires. We have inner longings, and it is possible for us to carry these desires for many years with few people being aware of them. I am amazed at our ability to wear masks. We are so good at saying the right things, looking right, and responding correctly that no one suspects what is inside. But deep inside of us these longings lurk, year after year, just waiting for opportunity. And when opportunity presents itself, our desires are usually exposed.

Desires can be good or bad. They can lean toward God or toward the flesh. But in either case it is usually opportunity that reveals where our desires lean. Do you suppose Achan was even aware of his own desires? The Bible doesn't say. When Achan finally was confronted and confessed his sin, he said, "When I saw among the spoils a goodly Babylonish garment, and two hundred shekels of silver, and a wedge of gold of fifty shekels weight, then I coveted them, and took them."[c]

We know little about Achan's thought life. Maybe it just seemed to him that all the other men had more than he did. Perhaps he had some fears about arriving in the Promised Land and not being able to finance all the improvements his property would need. Or maybe Achan had a discontented wife. Perhaps she was always reminding him that the other women had more fashionable garments. Possibly he was tired of hearing, "Why can't we have a nicer place to live like the neighbors have? I've about had it with this crummy tent!" We don't know. But this much we know. When those walls came down, Achan's desire met opportunity, and Achan fell.

Waiting for the Wall to Fall

Today our middle-aged, middle class Americans remind me of the men marching around Jericho. Day after day they march on, going to work and coming home. On and on they march, going through the motions of their occupations while waiting for the walls to fall. They are waiting for retirement, when the walls keeping them from doing what they really want to do collapse and they can finally live as they please. Our society longs for this period of life when the high walls of job, mortgage, and miscellaneous debt come crashing down and their longings can be fulfilled.

For many this is happening. The abundance of second homes, motor homes, travel trailers, water craft, and other recreational equipment owned by retirees, testifies that for many the walls have come down. They are finally realizing their long-held desires. For them, desire has met opportunity.

So what are your desires? Behind the spiritual niceties spoken at church or while sitting around the dinner table with other believers, what do you really long for? If you suddenly had an abundance of time and money at your disposal, how would you respond? Do you know your own desires? Do you regularly sit down with the Word of God and prayerfully analyze your heart? How much of your life as you march along day after day is simply being lived out because you have no other choice? Are you behaving as you do because you find yourself surrounded by walls—walls of debt, church requirements, or social obligations? What would happen if all those walls suddenly came crashing down?

Restraint Removed

I remember my father telling me that character is what you do when no one is watching. You find out who a man really is when all restraint is removed. This truth challenged me in my youth. I knew what it was like to listen to a powerful message and become convicted. I was familiar with that burning desire to live for God and be totally committed to Him. But I was also well aware how quickly I could miserably fail just a few hours after being so strongly convicted. Somehow when my parents were not there and restraint was gone, I wasn't always able to stand. We don't always know who we are until the boundaries are removed.

> *Character is what you do when no one is watching.*

We mentioned in the last chapter that, for many, there is an abundance of time and money in the last half of life. Money brings opportunity. Consequently, our older years are generally a time of great opportunity. How we use that opportunity reveals a lot about who we are. We learn much more about a man's theology by watching him in his older years than we do from all the nice things he said, sermons he preached, or even books he wrote. How a man responds to opportunity reveals who he really is.

When we are young, it is easy to be zealous and vocal regarding our beliefs. Life seems black and white, and conviction comes easy. It isn't difficult to see the problems and draw firm conclusions. We have clear ideas about money and how it should be used. But as we age and begin to deal with life's issues, we discover something. It is easy to hold strong convictions against certain things when we can't afford them anyway. It is obvious that expensive vacations, exotic cruises, or luxury vehicles are poor stewardship when little money is available.

But our desires have never met opportunity. The true test comes when a person has the ability to do whatever he wants. When restraint is removed, the heart is revealed. Sometimes this can be a beautiful thing.

On my desk is a letter from Harold. Harold worked for a company, driving a dump truck for many years. The company had a profit sharing plan, and when Harold was sixty years old, he was able to retire, drawing an income from this plan. Harold was still in good health, so he volunteered to help rebuild after a disaster. One rebuilding project led to another, and Harold has now worked on ten of these projects. In addition, his local congregation had a desire to plant more churches, so Harold offered to move and assist in starting an outreach congregation. Even though this means not seeing grandchildren and old friends as often as he would like, Harold has a desire to use his older years to help build the Kingdom.

But the most encouraging aspect of this letter is the obvious excitement with which Harold and his wife describe what God has done and is still doing in their lives. The handwriting gets smaller as you read down through this letter, and it is obvious they are trying to fit in all the exciting things they have seen God do. It is as if they keep thinking of more ways the Lord has blessed their lives.

Harold tells how several years ago his wife experienced health problems and they thought maybe it was time to slow down. But then she recovered miraculously, and they were able to head back out to another area that was in need of help. Their enthusiasm is contagious, and it is obvious what has occurred. Their desires simply found opportunity!

For years they had carried a longing to be of more service to the King. Now in their older years they are seeing that desire fulfilled. They have been able to help, both in planting a new church and in ministering to those who have experienced catastrophe. Desire meeting opportunity can be revealing. Whether it is beautiful or not simply depends on what you desire.

Conclusion

Maybe today you feel like those Israelites marching along day after day. It seems that you are constantly dealing with the mundane issues involved in providing for a family. Perhaps you long for the day when the walls that keep you from your desires come crashing down and you can do the things you have always wanted. Finally, after marching all those years, you will be able to go where you want and do what you have always longed to do.

Remember, Achan had similar ambitions. But when his day finally came, it brought disaster to him, his family, and his people. Examine closely the things you long for. Are you really ready for the walls to come down? Are you focused on the Kingdom of God and longing to serve Him with all that He has blessed you with? Or do you have other longings and desires, longings that could prove disastrous should restraint be suddenly removed? The last part of your life can be a wonderful blessing to your family, your congregation, and the Kingdom of God. But you will only bless the Kingdom then if that is your heart's sincere desire now.

Six

Who Is That Rich Man?

I remember reading the family Bible storybook as a boy, and I am amazed, years later, how the illustrations stick with me. One picture that firmly implanted itself in my mind was of the rich man and Lazarus. That rich man bothered me. The sight of him sitting there in his elaborately decorated home, dressed in a soft, flowing robe, and stuffing himself with yet another large helping of dinner was unsettling. It troubled me because just outside his kitchen window was skinny, sore-covered Lazarus with nothing to eat. Even the dogs roaming under the rich man's table were fatter and in much better condition than malnourished Lazarus.

"Hey, rich man," I felt like shouting, "take a look out your window! There is a man starving just outside." But the oblivious rich man just kept on eating, the portly dogs continued to lap up the leftover chunks on the floor, and Lazarus kept on gazing longingly at what he didn't have. The scene left me frustrated. How could anyone be so insensitive? How could that rich man even enjoy that mountain of food, knowing that Lazarus was just outside? And the dogs! If that rich man would have just glanced out the window and compared his dogs' health to Lazarus's, surely he would have jumped up in alarm. How could he keep stuffing his overfed dogs when Lazarus was in such need?

Am I That Rich Man?

Who is that rich man? I used to wonder. Who could possibly live such an uncaring, self-centered, and hardhearted life?

Years ago I was in Haiti with a work team, and after returning to Port-au-Prince from a building project, we took a day to see the city.

As we gained altitude, the neighborhoods began looking nicer, and soon we came to a wealthy neighborhood where the homes were large and expensive. These homes were magnificent, replete with sports cars in the driveways, satellite dishes on the roofs, and massive swimming pools in the backyards.

But what surprised me most was how close the rich and poor lived together. Right beside these mammoth, elaborate houses were people in rags who lived in tiny shacks. On one side of the fence were manicured lawns and Jaguars, and on the other, naked children. The contrast was stunning, and the sight stirred feelings within me similar to what I felt as a child gazing at the picture of the rich man and Lazarus.

This wasn't right. It made me angry just to look at it. How could you drive that car out through those electrically operated gates each morning, cruise comfortably past all those hungry people, and still feel good? What kind of a man could do that? How could anyone be so insensitive and self-centered they could even enjoy this luxurious living? How could they continually waste money on the unnecessary when just over the wall so many were in need?

But I hadn't traveled much farther up that road till I abruptly came to an unsettling realization. Those rich men might not be much different from me.

I have known all my life that poverty exists. I have read the statistics. I am aware that 25,000 people in my world die every day from hunger or hunger-related causes.[15] I know that millions of people die each year from preventable diseases.[16] I have often seen the statistics in the newspapers describing the great mass of humanity who still live in deplorable conditions and in great need.

As I sit down to yet another excellent dinner and again wonder how much of this food I can consume without gaining too much weight, I know all of this. Yet sometimes I continue as though this poverty doesn't exist. I have even found myself purposely overlooking certain articles. Some of this information seems overwhelming. Maybe, like the rich man in the Bible storybook, I don't really want any more information. Rather than addressing this massive problem, I keep stuffing myself and purposefully refuse to look out the window.

In the past I have spent a good deal of time writing about poverty.

I have tried to address proper and improper ways of dealing with it. I have tried to show what the Bible says about God's heart for the poor. But I don't think I have ever written about the rich man and Lazarus. I haven't neglected the story because it is complicated. No, even a child can understand the account. I tend to avoid the story because it messes with my theology.

The account ends with the rich man being thrown into hell and tormented by the flames. He sees Father Abraham in the distance and cries out for relief. And the only explanation given to the rich man is, "Son, remember that thou in thy lifetime receivedst thy good things, and likewise Lazarus evil things: but now he is comforted and thou art tormented."[a]

Now what is that supposed to mean? That everyone who is poor, destitute, and hungry in this life will be saved? That the final judgment will be based primarily on a man's tax return? That billions of people on the earth who live on less than two dollars a day will be saved and the rest won't? That the only way to be saved is to radically reduce your income?

> *I tend to avoid the story because it messes with my theology.*

If I stopped here with my analysis of this account, I would probably get a flood of mail. What kind of theology is this? Our minds immediately jump to a long list of Scriptures that explain the basis of salvation. We think of words like *grace, faith, and justification.* Scriptural phrases like "by grace ye are saved"[b] swirl around in our heads, and this little account that Jesus told quickly gets buried under a huge pile of verses. Relieved, we move on as though this account never existed.

What Was Jesus Saying?
But what did Jesus mean? Why did He take time to deliver this startling lesson, and what are we to learn from it? Normally when

---

[a]Luke 16:25
[b]Ephesians 2:8

we hear a minister refer to the story of the rich man and Lazarus, the lessons extracted regard the afterlife. There are few places in Scripture that give many details about life after death, so an account like this provides a welcome window into the next world.

But I believe Jesus' primary reason for giving this message wasn't to tell us about heaven and hell. It wasn't given just to enable us to sit around and speculate about life after death. No, the Bible says this lesson was given to the Pharisees who were covetous and trying to justify themselves.[c] It was given to warn them against comforting themselves in the midst of their materialistic pursuits. Since Jesus gave this warning to the religious people of His day, shouldn't we also pay attention? I think we can learn at least three basic lessons from this account. These lessons are pertinent to the latter part of life, the time when most of us will have more available resources.

1. God cares about the poor. This story says so little about Lazarus. We only know that he was extremely poor, he had medical issues, and he ended up in Abraham's bosom. We could assume he was a godly man because of his final destination, but the story doesn't say that. Maybe in reality Lazarus was a little difficult to get along with. Perhaps he had been a poor manager earlier in life, and there was a fear in the community that if you gave him more, he would just squander it. We don't know. The account just reveals that he was hungry, sick, and ignored.

In any case, Lazarus represents billions of people around the globe today, masses of people with little food, healthcare, or hope. But one important fact to notice in this account is that those who are ignored by people are noticed by God. He cares. God isn't looking at this world through the same lenses that our culture is. In fact, just before Jesus tells this sobering story, He says, "For that which is highly esteemed among men is an abomination in the sight of God."[d] We have a way of rating humanity. That is why we call some rich and others poor. Some people are at the top of the ladder, others toward the bottom. Jesus showed that God looks at things differently. God cares about the poor, and those who pursue the heart of God will have a deep concern for the poor as well.

---

[c]Luke 16:14-15
[d]Luke 16:15

2. With wealth comes responsibility. The Bible doesn't say much about the rich man either. Maybe he never attended the synagogue and regularly took advantage of his neighbors. We don't know, and evidently Jesus didn't think these details were pertinent to the story. But maybe this rich man wasn't like that at all. Maybe he had a nice family, was honest in the community, and was rich because he had worked hard and was a good manager. Perhaps he was always the first to get to the synagogue and was known for well-thought-out Scriptural answers to difficult questions. Jesus didn't say. All we really know about the rich man is that he had opportunity to help the poor and didn't use it. He may have worked hard for everything he had, but for some reason, he failed to open his eyes to the needs around him. It was in his power to relieve human suffering, but in the midst of all the daily activity that seemed so important at the time, he failed to respond. We also see that finally in hell he began thinking about others. He wanted desperately to send word back to his brothers. Even though it wouldn't help his situation, he longed to be able to tell them, "Hey, life isn't like you think it is. Change course before it's too late!" But his opportunity was over. He had been given great riches and opportunity. But with wealth comes responsibility, and he had failed to use it properly.

3. Wealth has a blinding effect. Picture for a moment the thoughts of the rich man as he was tormented in hell and thought about his brothers who were still alive. He knew what they were thinking. He knew the paradigm they were working within. The rich man knew all of this because he had been thinking the very same way—until just recently! He knew his brothers were likely comparing this year's crop with last year's. They were probably running some calculations on that piece of property adjoining theirs and wondering if they should go ahead and buy it. And they were also ignoring the poor.

It is easy to forget, in the middle of paying bills, how amazingly rich we are. There really is no precedent for the time in which we live. Historians tell us that during most of human history there was little economic growth like we have known and relatively little economic inequality between nations. In 1820, after thousands of years of human development, the average income per capita in the wealthiest countries was only about four times higher than the average in the poorest countries.[17] But then the Industrial Revolution came along. For some countries this brought amazing economic growth, but most of the world was left behind. As a result, individuals living in industrialized nations like the United States live high on the hog, raking in on average almost $100 per day.[18] Meanwhile, ap-

> *It is easy to forget, in the middle of paying bills, how amazingly rich we are.*

proximately one billion people in the world live on less than one dollar each day, and two and a half billion others survive on less than two dollars.[19] In light of these statistics, today's ratio between the rich and poor is staggering.

On the one hand, we are extremely connected worldwide through technology. At any given moment we can know what is going on in Tokyo, Mexico City, or Bangkok. Within a few hours we can even be there. We are truly living in a global neighborhood. Yet even though the world has grown closer through technological advancement, we are growing further apart in other ways. The rich are still getting richer, and the spread between those of us who are wealthy and the masses dwelling in chronic poverty continues to widen. Growing up in an extremely wealthy nation, we have no way to comprehend what others endure. While our ancestors may have been able to at least partially understand the ravages of poverty, we are so insulated that it is difficult to even grasp.

Wealth has a way of blinding us to the needs of others, and when affluence comes gradually, we find ourselves even more oblivious. But not only is the accumulation of wealth a self-centered pursuit, its preservation demands focus as well. Dom Helder Camara, the Catholic priest who for years championed the cause of the poor in Brazil, once said, "I used to think, when I was a child, that Christ might have been exaggerating when He warned about the dangers of wealth. Today I know better. I know how hard it is to be rich and still keep the milk of human kindness. Money has a way of putting scales on one's eyes, a dangerous way of freezing people's hands, eyes, lips, and hearts."[20] As the poor rich man endured the torment of the flames, I think this fact was clear to him. Earthly riches had blinded him to reality.

Conclusion

Today, as never before, many of us are surrounded with good healthcare, plenty of time, and an abundance of money. With these resources comes opportunity, and with opportunity comes responsibility. But I wonder. I wonder if too often we are so busy comparing ourselves among ourselves that we don't really feel all that rich.

Have you ever considered that maybe the rich man in the story of Lazarus didn't feel wealthy either? I suspect he had more than one window in his house. Is it possible that as he sat there at his table each day, downing yet one more good meal, he was just looking out a different window? Perhaps he stared at his other neighbor who wore finer linen and fared even more sumptuously every day? Sometimes we fail to see the Lazarus in our lives simply because we keep staring out the wrong window.

I don't know what all Jesus wanted us to learn from this story. But a day is coming when life will look different. What the wealthier neighbor might have owned will be of little importance. Whether or not we were able to keep up with the Joneses will not matter. But this story teaches that it *is* important to give thought to the poor people in our lives. As you begin planning for the last years of your life, remember the rich man and Lazarus. Remember how empty earthly wealth and pleasure will appear when this life is over. And be sure you are looking out the right window.

PART TWO
*A Time to
Reflect*

Seven

A Time to Reflect

Here in the Pacific Northwest where I live, salmon are born in small streams high in the mountains. After birth they swim many miles downstream, following each tributary as it dumps into increasingly larger streams that finally lead to the vast Pacific Ocean. The bodies of these fish have been created to transition from fresh water to salt, and they will live in the ocean for several years until an internal clock tells them it's time to head back toward fresh water, spawning, and ultimate death. But these fish don't just stay near the shore during their ocean years. A salmon may travel over two thousand miles out into the Pacific Ocean before returning to the mouth of the river where it entered the ocean and from there back to the site where it was born.

This incredible ability of the salmon to return to its exact birthplace is a tribute to the creative power of God. Along the Pacific coast many rivers continually dump vast quantities of fresh water into the ocean. Not only does the salmon have to choose from all these rivers, but then it must continue to choose each increasingly smaller stream correctly to finally arrive at its original spawning site.

Scientists have determined that salmon find their way using their incredible ability to smell. Researchers have determined that a salmon can detect just one drop of water from its home river out of almost two million gallons of water.[21]

But charting a course isn't the salmon's only dilemma. The adult salmon must also get there. This requires swimming upstream against strong currents for many miles, through swift rapids, and even up waterfalls. In fact, some of these waterfalls are so high and swift that passage seems impossible. It is not uncommon to see salmon propel themselves up over a six-foot or even eight-foot waterfall. Fighting against the current, crashing against sharp rocks, and jumping over waterfalls obviously takes a toll on these magnificent fish. This violent passage is hard on their bodies, and often they end their journey with deep wounds, scars, and missing chunks of flesh.

In spite of their great natural ability, salmon can become disoriented. They are known to become confused on this return trip and temporarily lose their way. Ironically, it isn't the turbulent rapids or the daunting waterfalls that confuse the salmon. It's the calm

> *The greatest threat to these incredible fish isn't the violent current but the peaceful pool.*

pools. Salmon have been known to valiantly fight their way through miles of rapids and waterfalls only to swim listlessly and become disoriented at the first quiet pool. Eagles and other predators prey on them there as well. Astoundingly, the greatest threat to these incredible fish isn't the violent current but the peaceful pool!

As I ponder the life of the salmon, I wonder if God hasn't designed them to teach us some lessons. I see men today accomplishing amazing things—devout men, fighting against incredible odds. They are attempting to raise godly children in an ungodly world. They labor each day to provide for their families in an uncertain economy and valiantly try to balance the time demands of church and social life. Some of the hurdles they face seem as intimidating as the rushing waterfalls that face the salmon. At times it seems the violent current will surely win. But they fight against this downward pull and bravely face each challenge that confronts them.

God put a natural desire within men to overcome obstacles. And though these obstacles at times frighten us and make us long for calmer waters, we actually feel most fulfilled when we are fighting and overcoming them. But there comes a time in most of our lives when things calm down. The mortgage is finally paid, the children begin to leave home, and survival is less difficult. We are a little like the salmon that, after fighting the miles of turbulent, crashing water, finally reach the calm, placid pool. There in the pool we may be weary and battered from the wild passage, but we have no rough rapids to fight, no strong current to overcome, and not a waterfall in sight.

The Danger in the Calm

We need to understand the inherent dangers in these calm pools. Men who have been courageous in the challenging current can collapse in the quiet calm. Surrounded by an unfamiliar abundance of time and money, they fail to sense the danger lurking in life's later years—the danger of becoming disoriented. We see examples of this in the Bible. We read about individuals who were great men of God in their youth but later lost their vision and purpose.

Consider King David. Do young men get any better than that? Slaying giants, writing psalms, and serving God with a passion and zeal we still marvel at. But the young man who could faithfully trust God while being chased as a fugitive from cave to cave later couldn't handle the temptation with Bathsheba. What Satan couldn't do in all the conflicts throughout David's life, he accomplished in one peaceful evening on a rooftop.

> *What Satan couldn't do in all the conflicts throughout David's life, he accomplished in one peaceful evening on a rooftop.*

Or what about Solomon? As a young man he exhibited strong character, wrote proverbs, chose wisdom over wealth, and zealously poured his energy into building the temple. But with the temple completed, no battles to fight, and peace and plenty surrounding him, he somehow lost his way. As I consider men like David and Solomon, I am sobered. If great men of God like that could be so valiant for the Lord while young, yet drift away when surrounded by peaceful prosperity, the warning is clear. It can happen to anyone.

How can we stay focused and vigilant in our later years as this transition occurs? How can we maintain a clear vision for serving the Lord? Is it possible to be useful to the Kingdom and accomplish anything worthwhile for the Lord when our flesh cries out for rest from the battle?

Yes, these years can be a wonderful time of building within Christ's Kingdom. In the latter part of this book we will address these questions.

But first we want to take some time to reflect. It is important for us to remember where we have been and where the Lord has brought us so far. It is important that we take stock of our lives and see what we can learn. All of us have unique strengths and weaknesses. As you look back at your life, how has God worked? Are there decisions you would like to reverse? I asked many older believers this question while writing this book. These individuals' names had been given to me as examples of godliness during their older years. But though they are living for the Kingdom now, that doesn't mean they have no regrets. Nearly all of them expressed sorrow over some part of their past.

"If I were to do it over, I would stay out of debt," admitted one.

"Looking back," said another, "I would have spent more time with my children."

"We thought we lived frugally," one older couple shared. "But living in a foreign country changed us more than any one thing in life—and we never forgot."

"When we decided to tithe, the Lord blessed us abundantly!" another exclaimed.

Some of the written responses were quite lengthy, almost as if the writers couldn't get done telling of the wonderful ways God had revealed Himself to them. One widower who had enjoyed a close spiritual connection with his wife wrote, "My wife and I nearly always prayed and fasted before making financial decisions, and I could share many experiences of how the Lord worked in ways we never realized were possible!" Today he looks back with fondness on the years of closeness he and his wife enjoyed.

These older believers learned to rely on the power of God during the heat of the battle and are finding fulfillment in serving Him to the end. In spite of scars from the past, in spite of their mistakes and weaknesses, they are determined to devote the rest of their lives to the Kingdom of Jesus Christ.

Wherever you are in life, take some time to reflect on your past. Where have you been and what have you learned from your experiences? How has God been preparing you for your later years? Looking back, we can often identify strengths and weaknesses God has given us. Understanding them can be useful in discerning how the Lord can use us during our final years.

The Lord has blessed some older men with construction skills, and we see many of them helping after disasters. I know of an older sister who has a gift for communicating by letters. Though few people are aware of her ministry, she regularly reaches out to individuals living many miles away, encouraging and exhorting them from the Scriptures. God has given you abilities that can be used to meet some of the many needs in our world. Take the time to prayerfully consider ways God has moved in your past. This may help you discern what He has for your future.

Conclusion

I have stood along mountain streams and watched adult salmon. These fish have fought their way bravely through miles of rugged water, and their bodies tell the story. They look tired, battered, and covered with scars. Some of their wounds are deep and the missing chunks of flesh reveal the pain they have endured.

Many of us, around the middle of our lives, feel a little like these salmon. We have been through some rough water. Things didn't turn out quite like we had hoped. Maybe we wish our spiritual focus would have been different, or perhaps we made financial choices we wish we could undo. Possibly not enough time was spent with a child, or maybe insufficient thought was given to a spouse. Some of us look back and wonder if we pursued the right career. Others look back with regret on church struggles. They wish for another chance to make peace with a brother or sister in their congregation. They wonder how much impact church conflict had on the current spiritual condition of their children.

It is important that we learn from the past. But it is equally important that we do not stay there. Those who fail to continue moving forward in faith are easy prey for the adversary. Wherever you are today, be assured that God has a purpose for the rest of your life. Take time to reflect, and then move on in faith, seeking His will for your life and His direction for handling the things He has entrusted to your care.

> *It is important that we learn from the past. But it is equally important that we do not stay there.*

Eight

Reality, Response, and Reaction

Some of the liveliest discussions in our family occurred in a place we called the North Room, a long, narrow storage area outside in an older barn. I have vivid childhood memories of some rather animated discussions there. This room was used for storage, and the discussions emitting from that room tended to revolve around the value of the items stored and whether or not these items would actually be needed again in the future. We all agreed that the room needed organization. It became a quick place to park a wide assortment of articles, and as the room filled up, it became somewhat useless.

There were two reasons why it became useless. First, the storage room became so full that a person couldn't see or even remember what all had been stored there. And second, even if we had a suspicion that what we needed might be lurking in the shadows, the difficulty of extricating it made it easier to go without.

Just opening the door and peering into the darkness was enough to discourage us. Going farther took more commitment and time than most of us possessed. The thought of trying to untangle all the items between us and the desired article was enough to discourage the most hopeful optimist. But if you did venture into the room, it wasn't uncommon to emerge from the battle with a few wounds. So once or twice a year, after one of my parents had attempted to fight their way into the murky depths of the North Room to retrieve an item, the proclamation would go forth: "We need to clean out the North Room this Saturday!"

This was welcome news to a young boy. I knew all the family was going to be together, and I knew it would be interesting. First, everything needed to come out of the room, so we would pile all the items out onto the driveway so we could evaluate our assets. This was generally uneventful, but after this mundane task was completed, things began to get interesting. For you see, while it was easy to agree that things needed to be cleared out, it was much more difficult to agree on what should go back in. Some would feel one item was important and should be saved, while others saw no potential in that item.

One thing was always obvious, however. My father and mother were the savers. They were the most reluctant to pitch any item of potential value. They would spend time imagining and discussing all the situations where the item in question might be the very thing needed. And generally, after much discussion, most of the items would go right back into the North Room. It was safer to just put things back—we might need them sometime.

Waste Not, Want Not

I remember being impressed by the fact that my parents were looking at life differently than I. Even though we ate at the same table and inhabited the same space, their life experiences had shaped them in ways I couldn't always identify with. While I liked to listen to stories of times when things were rough and enjoyed reading books about people who struggled to survive, those had been actual experiences for my parents. They had no guarantee that times like that would not come again. Therefore, throwing something away which had the slightest possibility of future use was absurd. I, however, would view the same item as nothing but a hazard to trip over.

Both of us were simply responding to our life experiences. They were responding to the realities in their lives, and I was responding to mine. To this day, if I can't think of a reason to keep something, I pitch it. Sometimes I regret that decision later, but my greater fear is clutter. I am responding to the reality of my experiences, and I am probably reacting to my parents' responses. People of each generation react in some way to the previous one, and I am no exception.

Obviously not all actions are a result of reaction. We are born with different personalities, and savers and wasters can grow up in the same home and environment. But in general my parents' generation tended to save due to the economic challenges of their era.

Most of us can think of examples of older individuals who saved in ridiculous ways. I heard of someone who had containers labeled with things like, "String too short to use." A grandmother I knew saved old subscription cards—those little cards that always fall out of each new magazine and have absolutely no value ten years (or even one year) down the road.

The older generation is famous for this kind of saving, but what will our generation be known for? What kind of a legacy, with regard to materialism, are we leaving to our children? When they look back at our waste, wealth, and general materialistic consumption, what will they say?

Fine Fare for Fido

In Chapter Six we looked at the story of the rich man and Lazarus. We considered the rich man's lack of interest in the poor man outside the window in contrast to the pampered treatment he gave the dogs that ate scraps from his table. That seems absurd to us. What a mixed-up value system!

But consider our own society. In 2010 we Americans spent 48.35 billion dollars taking care of our pets.[22] During that same year on the very same planet, 2.5 billion people were surviving on less than two dollars a day. Stop a moment and consider those figures. Statistics like this paint a picture not unlike Jesus' parable of the rich man and Lazarus. Even while we feed our animals well-balanced, nutritious meals, 22,000 children a day are dying from poverty.[23]

> *Even while we feed our animals well-balanced, nutritious meals, 22,000 children a day are dying from poverty.*

Statistics like this are familiar, and we tend to ignore them. But as our world continues to become even more interconnected, I wonder if our children will someday ask how we could have continued to ignore the great needs. Not only do we have access to more information, we also have access to more resources than any previous generation. We can't help this.

We didn't choose it, and we can't escape it. But the question is: how are we responding?

The Apostle Paul told the church at Corinth that we should live in this life as though we "possessed not . . . and use this world, as not abusing it."[a] How will our children say we used the opportunity we had? More important, what will God have to say?

An Equal and Opposite Reaction

In 1687 Sir Isaac Newton published what became known as Newton's laws of motion. One of these laws says that for every action there is an equal and opposite reaction. When Isaac Newton published this law, he was referring to natural forces and the way these forces and movements relate to each other. But we can see, even in the topic of saving, how the truth of this law exhibits itself. One generation focuses so much on saving that they become hoarders, while the next generation reacts, pitching useful items and becoming wasteful in the process of trying to be more organized. But this tendency to react is not confined to materialism and consumption alone. We can observe the same principle in our spiritual lives and churches.

Differences, Divisions, Modes, and Methods

When I was young, several books in my father's library intrigued me. They were thick books, and periodically I would take one off the shelf, trying to understand it. These books defended particular modes and methods in different church denominations. One book that particularly drew my attention was an account of a debate that happened back in the 1800s. The debate concerned how several Biblical ordinances were to be carried out and dealt with topics like the proper mode of baptism, feet washing, and procedures for a communion service. This debate lasted many nights, and a huge crowd assembled to see who would win. The entire book was devoted to recounting the event. It was almost like play-by-play action, as page after page explained the arguments given and the author's opinion on who had best presented his view.

---

[a]1 Corinthians 7:30-31

But more fascinating to me than the arguments was the realization that hundreds of people would sit night after night and listen to this debate. Not only would people listen, but there was enough interest in the event that someone had recorded each detail, a book had been published, and people had bought the book! Admittedly, these meetings were held before modern media, and I suspect that many in the crowd came because this was their entertainment for the year.

In recent times younger believers have grown weary of the constant debate on some of these issues. They have watched as church members took sides and congregations divided. They have listened to older believers argue the finer points of a particular method or mode. They have watched entire denominations split over issues that, in their minds, are not clearly defined in Scripture.

As a result, many young people have reacted. They have little interest in sitting and listening to a debate on a particular application of a Scriptural principle. If you ask some younger believers today for their opinions regarding a specific denominational detail, they may not even be able to explain their particular practice. Reaction to denominational debate is one of the reasons non-denominational church growth has exploded in America.

This dramatic change has not always been good. Believers should be able to explain to their children why they embrace a particular application of a Biblical principle. However, each generation should examine its emphases closely. By emphasizing the wrong things, we have the ability to cause unhealthy reactions. In the shift from saving to wastefulness, as well as the shift from intense focus on modes and methods to nonchalance, unhealthy reactions have occurred. How can we keep this from happening? In our older years, how can we live in a way that will not cause negative reactions in future generations?

One answer frequently given to this question is moderation. The reasoning goes that if people would be a bit more moderate in their approaches and opinions, things would go more smoothly. But is moderation alone really the solution? A lot of lukewarm Christianity is justified under the heading of moderation. And while moderation in how we use this world's goods is Biblically correct, moderation was never to be the church's primary focus. The Apostles were not known by the world around them as a group of moderates. They were known as radicals. They were interested in following and imitating the example of Jesus Christ, even if it called for radical change in their lives.

Following or Just Studying?

I am convinced that this is also the need in our generation. God is calling us to follow the example and teachings of Jesus, even if it requires radical change in our personal lives and churches. For too long we have compared ourselves among ourselves. We have defined radical Christianity as following our particular group's understanding of practice. We have focused on why our way is better than their way, and over time Jesus begins to look an awful lot like us. Instead of conforming to His image, we subconsciously transform Jesus to ours. The Bible can become just a pool of verses that we occasionally dip into to carefully extract a verse that supports the lifestyle or group we are defending.

Stop for a moment and analyze your life. Jesus' teachings are revolutionary, and they speak to almost every part of our daily lives. Yet how many times have you radically changed your behavior simply because of His teachings? You have told your children that you are a Christian, but how often do they see His words make you stop in midstride and head in a different direction?

> *Instead of conforming to His image, we subconsciously transform Jesus to ours.*

In describing the tendency to have a head knowledge of Christ's teaching that does not affect practice, David Bercot wrote, "The focus changed from follow Me to study Me."[24] If we are going to leave our children a path worth following and help them avoid the error of reaction, we need to give them an example, not only of studying, but of following the teachings of Jesus.

We tend to forget as we study the early Anabaptists that the Protestant reformers were the ones who were known as Biblicists. They were the men who emphasized a focus on proper theology and understanding of the Scriptures.

While the Anabaptists desired proper theology, they wanted much more. More than just having the proper understanding of Biblical words and Greek tenses, the Anabaptists insisted on actually living those Scriptures out. They believed it was most important to imitate the life of Jesus and follow His teachings.

Many of us, I think unknowingly, have become theologians. We have become very adept at defending the path we are on. We become more focused on proving our path is correct than on correcting our path.

Almost every church professes to follow the Bible, and each can point to Scriptures that support its major doctrines and practices. But our world and our children are crying out for more than just debate and defense. They are looking for believers who are willing, even toward the end of their lives, to make radical choices.

Conclusion

For too long we have tried to walk a straight path by zigging where our parents zagged. They focused on one ditch, so we steer for the other. Wouldn't it be better to show by our life choices that we are focusing on the changeless teachings of Jesus? What if our children saw in us more of a desire to address and confess our own deficiencies, and a passion to order our lives by Jesus' teachings? What kind of a legacy could be left to those coming after if they saw in us a willingness to make radical changes in midlife, simply because we have been convicted by the Holy Spirit and the Word of God? As I grow older, I have two fears. One fear is that I will be unwilling to change—that I will gradually slip into a pattern of life and assume that I am doing things correctly.

> *For too long we have tried to walk a straight path by zigging where our parents zagged.*

A few years ago I spoke with an unbelieving neighbor regarding his need for the Lord. He was in his eighties, divorced and remarried, yet he seemed to have no fear of death. He had simply lived this way long enough and justified his position often enough that he couldn't imagine being wrong. He was unwilling to consider the possibility that he was on a wrong track. I fear this tendency in my own life.

But the other fear, which is the burden of this chapter, is that when I do make changes, I will make them for wrong reasons. I fear that my changes will occur more out of reaction to others than out of response to Christ. May the Lord help us as we age to remain open to the possibility of being wrong and to change out of response to His call, not in reaction to the failings of others.

Nine
An Inward Look

Many of us can remember a time when the road stretched out far ahead of us and life seemed like it would never end. Of course, we knew it would, yet that time seemed so far off it was barely on the radar. So many concerns, challenges, and exciting events kept us occupied that it was easy to forget the brevity of life. But suddenly, about midlife, the end of the road comes into view. Lack of energy, a few gray hairs, and the frequent funerals of friends not much older than us come like sober warnings along the path. Like "Road Closed Ahead" signs, these things awaken us to the reality that time is short, and life will not continue forever.

We often jokingly speak of being "over the hill." I am not always sure what we mean. Perhaps we are acknowledging that the first part of our lives, the uphill part, has been a struggle. Maybe raising a family and financial dilemmas brought strain during the first part of our lives, and as our children leave home, some of these stresses are relieved. Or we could be referring to the fact that time seems to speed up during the last half of life, just like speed increases when we go down a hill. Whatever the logic, the hill provides a picture of life that can be helpful. Imagine yourself stopping briefly at the top of life's hill, and think of this time in midlife as an opportunity to reflect and refocus. Take some time to look back over the road you have traveled. There are probably some choices you would like to reverse and some decisions for which you thank the Lord.

It has been interesting interviewing aging believers and trying to discern what has shaped their older years. Many spoke of godly parents, a spiritually minded spouse, or a trip that had a great influence on their lives. But all of them arrived at the places they are today because of a series of choices they made.

For just a little while, we want to look beyond those visible choices. In fact, we really want to look *behind* them. Let's think about ourselves. Why did we make the decisions we made? What was driving us, day after day, to make choices that changed the course of our lives and the lives of our families? Some were little choices that seemed insignificant at the time. But what motivated us to choose those paths? And finally, if we were to identify our primary motivation in the past, what would it be?

"One Thing"

I recently read a newspaper interview of a famous basketball player. In the course of the interview, he was asked how he maintains such intense focus during the game. The athlete replied, "Because winning is the one thing that matters." Winning basketball games was his passion and source of fulfillment. He made winning his "one thing."

What is the "one thing" you have been living for?

Jesus said, "I am the true vine."[a] He went on to explain that those who follow Him will receive their nourishment from their connection with Him. Jesus will be their source of life and fulfillment. But take another look at these familiar words of Jesus. He didn't say He is the only vine; He said He is the true vine. In fact, His words imply that there are other vines. We can be connected to other things and draw our nourishment from them.

We see examples of this all around us. Recently I spent some time with a neighbor man who is heavily involved with rental property. This man owns many pieces of property in our city and is constantly purchasing more. As I talked to him about his life, he never let the conversation stray far from his properties. He loved to talk of great buys in the past, the best ways to leverage, and the art of finding good renters. It didn't take long to understand that rental property is his "one thing." It's not that he isn't involved in other things. He has a family and a nice home. He attends his church and is well thought of in our community. But rental property is obviously his source of life and fulfillment. It is the

---

[a]John 15:1

primary focus of his words, energy, and resources.

We have all met people like this. Actually, we all *are* people like this. All of us have a primary focus in life from which we draw our joy and fulfillment. So what is yours? As you pause at the top of the hill in midlife and look back, what has been your focus? What have you been drawing life from? Try to honestly examine the things you have focused on and drawn fulfillment from and write them down. Include things you enjoy thinking about when you are tempted to become discouraged and subjects that, though you might not tell others, give you a feeling of worth when you reflect.

Maybe taking the time to examine and write down these other potential life sources seems like a waste of time or a little too radical. But evidently the Apostle Paul didn't think so. He not only wrote his list down, he shared it with the church at Philippi. Paul listed the areas that had been a source of life and fulfillment to him in the past. He listed his family lineage, personal zeal, and faithfulness to the law. He even included things like circumcision, which although he had no choice in it, gave him value and standing in his society. Before finding Jesus, all of these accomplishments had been his source of life. I think there was a time Paul would have loved to talk about them. Just reflecting on them made him feel good and gave him a sense of worth.

Notice that these items on Paul's list were all good things. He wasn't saying he had been receiving his satisfaction from immorality, gambling, or theft. He had lived an upright life, and the things on his list were proof. But notice these words at the end of Paul's list. "But what things were gain to me, those I counted loss for Christ."[b] At one point in Paul's life, these things were important to him. They gave him value. But at the end of his life, he counted all those things as worthless in light of his relationship with Christ. Paul had made a midlife correction.

Let's go back to the illustration Jesus gave using the grapevine. I picture a time in Paul's life when he was drawing nourishment from several vines. There was the vine of the tribe of Benjamin, and Paul liked to reflect on that one. This connection was a source of life to him. And there was the Pharisee vine. I think he received great fulfillment

---

[b]Philippians 3:7

from this. Paul was doing things right, and his connection to the Pharisees proved it. We could go on down his list and see how each item was a source of life to him. I suspect he received encouragement to go on when he reflected on these things.

So, what would your list look like? Maybe it includes possessions. Perhaps you have worked hard, accumulated some assets, and enjoy thinking back over your accomplishments. Maybe the list includes a place of leadership in your church or community. While you would never mention this, you find your self-worth bolstered by the position you hold, and reflecting on it brings you joy and encouragement. Or maybe you would list your church denomination. Perhaps your church is well known in your area, and your membership in it has become a life source to you. You enjoy telling others how your group does things and why. Maybe your occupation gives you fulfillment. You find your mind continually circling around your daily activities, and gradually your work has become more than just a source of income. Instead, it has subtly become the vine that sustains you.

There is nothing wrong with having possessions, being a leader, belonging to a good church, or enjoying your occupation. These are good things. But have they become your source of nourishment? Where has your satisfaction in life been coming from? Before you begin thinking about how you want to use your remaining years, take time to identify what has been motivating you. Take an inward look and prayerfully examine who you really are.

Conclusion

I have found that taking a serious inward look can be painful. I would much rather focus on where I want to go than reflect on where I have been. But prayerfully examining who we are can provide a starting point in determining where we want to go. The goal is not to remain focused on the past. After the Apostle Paul had looked back and identified all the vines he had attempted to draw life from, he said this: "But this one thing I do, forgetting those things which are behind, and reaching forth unto those things which are before, I press toward the mark for the prize of the high calling of God in Christ Jesus."[c]

[c]Philippians 3:13-14

Paul had learned from his past and was determined to move on. More than that, he was determined to now focus on just "one thing." Men who have accomplished great things have been men of focus— men with the ability to zero in on the target and pour their energy and resources into that "one thing." This is what inspires us as we read accounts of the martyrs. They were men and women who successfully turned their backs on all the competing vines that surrounded them. Jesus Christ became their "one thing," and everything else was simply a distraction.

> *Jesus Christ became their "one thing," and everything else was simply a distraction.*

Ten

A River or a Dam?

I n the Pacific Northwest few issues incite opinionated responses like the topic of dams and rivers. For many years we have enjoyed the blessing of irrigated fields, vast recreational lakes, and inexpensive hydroelectric power due to the dams that harness the energy of our rivers. Thousands of acres of dry wasteland have been successfully transformed into productive farmland because of these dams. For many years little was said regarding the environmental impact that dams have on rivers, but recently many individuals, organizations, and Native American tribes have asked that the dams be removed.

Environmentalists argue that dams have devastated the natural habitat. Consequently, millions of dollars have been spent studying the impact these dams have had on fish and other wildlife.

The issue of dams has increasingly pitted farmers, naturalists, and Native Americans against each other as each side attempts to persuade the voting public that its view is correct. Tempers have flared, harsh words have been spoken, and the ongoing issue continues to plague the courts. Both sides understand you can't have it both ways. You can't have the blessings that result from hydroelectric projects without a dam, and you can't have the advantages of free flowing water while blocking the flow.

As you continue to take an inward look at the use of the resources God has placed in your care, is it possible you have been restricting the flow? Do you, like a river, freely pass on the unneeded blessings you receive, or do you find yourself building self-centered dams? Do you forget that God is the owner of all, and that resources beyond your needs should flow on to others? Do you find yourself desiring to dam up the flow and use more than necessary for personal enjoyment? Or maybe you struggle with fear of the future and have a tendency to hoard out of concern for what might occur?

As you consider these questions, let's look at a familiar verse in Paul's letter to the church of Ephesus. This little passage is like a window into the heart of God as we consider His will for us. "Let him that stole steal no more: but rather let him labour, working with his hands the thing which is good, that he may have to give to him that needeth."[a]

This verse contains several powerful and concise statements that demonstrate clearly God's intentions for our lives, occupations, and resources. Let's look closer.

"Let him that stole steal no more." This tells us that He desires that all we do be ethical. I am saddened as I see older individuals in our society chasing money using any available channel. There seems to be an unquenchable thirst for easy money among many of America's senior citizens. Sweepstakes, bingo, and various financial scams prey on the elderly due to their continued desire to get rich quick.

In the western United States, mammoth casino parking lots are full as a result of older retirees involved in gambling. The slot machines and other gaming devices hold such an attraction for them that you can see elderly individuals being pushed through the doors in wheelchairs fitted with oxygen tanks. Their health has departed, but they have retained their thirst for money.

"But rather let him labour, working with his hands the thing which is good." God intends that we work at something useful as long as we can. Later we will discuss some options for occupying our time,

[a]Ephesians 4:28

but let this passage speak to you. God wants us to be involved in good things—things that bless our communities. There is nothing wrong with working to obtain an income, but this shouldn't be the only goal. Be sure whatever you are involved in is not only ethical, but a blessing to your neighborhood. I can think of one older brother, well into his nineties, who works at a store carrying out groceries for the customers. In addition to making a small income, he is also contributing to the community. He has a wonderful opportunity to develop relationships and reach out to individuals needing friendship. It is just a simple job, but he is using his time to do a "thing which is good."

"That he may have to give to him that needeth." While the first part of this passage deals with how money is to be earned, this sentence reveals why. God obviously expects that we produce more than we need, and He has a purpose for the extra. He intends that it flow on to those in need. The Bible is clear that we are to provide for our own households.[b] But this passage reveals that God also doesn't intend for us to use more than we need.

I get a picture of God pouring resources into our lives. He continually pours financial resources, time, and various abilities into our lives. Visualize a river—let's call it Resource River—that contains the abundance that flows from God to you. This verse tells us that God expects us to take what we need from Resource River as it passes. He intends that we provide for our families, but He also expects the extra resources to flow downstream to others who lack.

Which Am I?

So, are you just a "dipper" from the river, or a builder of dams? Are you allowing Resource River to continue its flow, or do you find yourself damming it up? I think most of us in capitalistic America will have to admit we have built some dams. Our greed-centered culture coupled with our self-centered hearts is a powerful combination. But it is important at midlife that we address this tendency. As these abundant resources flow past us, the enticement is great. Sometimes we succumb to the temptation to build little dams and begin indulging in just a

---

[b]1 Timothy 5:8

little more than we really need.

Often we have good intentions. We assume God will continue to increase the supply, and we plan to eventually let the flow go past us to the needs downstream. But God is not asking us what we will do with future flow. He is calling us to wisely use the resources within our control right now.

We hear the cry of needs from downstream, and yet we also hear competing cries. Our culture says to us that there is nothing wrong with damming the flow and using a little more than we need. We look around at what is normal in our society and almost subconsciously we begin restricting the flow. We find more and more of Resource River simply sustaining an affluent lifestyle and less and less trickling on downstream.

Midlife is an excellent time to examine these dams. How much do you really need? What percentage of the resources God is pouring into your life does He really mean for you to use for yourself, and how much does He intend to flow on to those in need? These questions call for personal and prayerful soul searching. But don't wait till the end of life and then wish you had demolished the dam. Get a vision for letting go and allowing more to flow on to the needs below.

The Smell of Stagnation

Resources are a lot like water—they begin to stink when they become stagnant. God gives these resources, intending that we use them for His Kingdom. But sometimes, amid pressure both from inside and outside our church communities, we lose sight of God's best. My own journey in this area has been no exception. I have found myself damming up Resource River and using more of God's blessings for my own use than necessary. But I have noticed something else about these dams. As my personal consumption goes up, my level of inner peace and joy comes down, and I begin to feel uneasy. For example, I may know there are individuals in my community or church family who need someone to spend time with them. As I indulge myself with a hobby or one more good book, the cry of need downstream penetrates my conscience. Deep inside I know that instead of passing on my extra time, I am consuming more for myself than is necessary.

Maybe I read of a desperate need in some far-off country. I know resources are needed, and as I waste money on some item that was not really necessary, something churns within me. The cries of need from downstream rob me of anticipated pleasure. The tall dam I have constructed begins to bother me. I have allowed so many blessings to stay on the "me" side and so little to flow on to the "need" side. I become more and more miserable as the pressure builds.

> *Resources are a lot like water—they begin to stink when they become stagnant.*

Conscience-Relief Holes

Finally I can't handle the pressure anymore. The guilt becomes too great, and I find it destroying my peace. But rather than dismantling or lowering the dam, I find myself drilling little "conscience-relief holes." I might commit to volunteering for some church project or sign up for a twenty-five-dollar-a-month sponsorship to a charitable organization. I am looking for relief from the guilt, something I can draw comfort from the next time I hear the cries coming from downstream.

Sometimes we feel justified in building dams due to an improper understanding of ownership. We forget that we are only stewards, and we ascribe more value to items than just their use. God intends that we use the items within our control, but we need a proper understanding of ownership. When we begin to think of ourselves as owners of our possessions and attribute unwarranted value to them, they become a curse in our lives. We can make ourselves miserable and even lose the pleasure God intended we have in their use.

Our family has been involved in foster care for several years, and at one point we kept a little boy named Adam. Adam was just two years old when he came into our care, and he was about as nice a little boy as you could find. He was especially good at sharing. If another child wanted what

73

he had, Adam would freely give up the toy and go find something else to play with. But there came a time in Adam's life when we saw an abrupt change. As is typical in children, Adam suddenly began to think of himself as an owner. He wasn't interested in just using a toy; he wanted to own it as well.

One evening as we visited a friend's home, Adam spied a new John Deere tractor among the toys. Adam loved John Deere tractors and immediately made a beeline across the room to claim it. The look on his face told the story. This was now Adam's tractor. And for the next couple of hours, Adam just about sat on that tractor. He warily watched around him, scowling all the while, concerned that someone else might take his tractor. In fact, he was so serious about protecting what was "his" that he couldn't really use or enjoy it. Ownership was consuming his life!

But the humorous part of the story is that the only other children there that night were two little girls. These girls had no interest in tractors and played with their dolls all evening, oblivious to Adam's great mental anguish. We have laughed about this story many times in our home. Adam's obsession with ownership was ridiculous. It made him unable to even use the tractor, and what is a toy tractor for if not to use? Besides, Adam couldn't take the tractor home at the end of the evening anyway. It wasn't his to start with.

But even as I have laughed at this little event with the family, I must admit there is something about this story that makes me uncomfortable. Unfortunately, I have found a little of Adam in me as well. I have found myself ascribing more value to things than just the value of their use. I have taken pride in thinking about the fact that I "own" something and have worried that "my" things would be damaged. I have to remind myself that the only value any earthly item has, whether it is property, a bank account, or a piece of equipment, is its use. Beginning to think of ourselves as owners causes us to build dams in our lives. And this mindset ultimately brings grief, fear, and anxiety.

Conclusion

I cannot imagine that removing existing dams here in the Pacific Northwest makes either economic or ecological sense. But I do believe we need to each take a look at some of the dams we erect in our personal lives. I am not able to tell anyone else how much God intends for him to consume from the resources provided. We each need to humbly take this question before the Lord in prayer. But two divergent voices call out to us today.

One is from our culture. This voice says, "You have worked hard and earned what you have. You really owe it to yourself to sit back and enjoy the fruits of your labors in your latter years. Others may not have been as diligent as you and may not be able to relax. But you are different. You have been industrious, and you deserve the best. You have earned it!"

But another cry comes from the very heart of God, and I believe He is telling us to tear down our dams. He asks us to let the resources we are tempted to hoard flow on downstream to the needs. God isn't asking us to live in misery. He isn't calling us to a life of unhappiness. No, He made us and knows what actually brings joy in our lives. He well understands that the truly joyful are those who release "their" resources back to Him.

Even unbelieving researchers are discovering this truth. Recent experiments monitored brain activity while individuals were involved in various activities, including giving. One conclusion these neurological researchers came to was that when "you give from the heart . . . it satisfies the brain."[25] This should come as no surprise to believers in the Lord Jesus. Being the Creator, He understood this concept long before these researchers, and He stated it like this: "It is more blessed to give than to receive."[c]

> *The truly joyful are those who release "their" resources back to Him.*

---

[c] Acts 20:35

Eleven

How Much Is Enough?

I
n the last chapter we discussed our inclination to consume more than we need. Humans are selfish by nature, and our modern capitalistic society has encouraged this tendency. We know God wants us to share, but just how much does He want us to give, and how much should we keep? Under the Mosaic Law, the Israelites were commanded to bring their "tithes into the storehouse."[a] Much of Christianity today has interpreted this to mean that they gave ten percent of all their income. However, it wasn't quite that simple. One writer has described God's method under the law like this:

> There was not just one standard tithe for the people of Israel, but three tithes. One of those supported the priests and Levites (Numbers 18:21, 24). Another provided for a sacred festival (Deuteronomy 12:17-18; 14:23). The third tithe was given to support the poor, orphans, and widows (Deuteronomy 14:28-29; 26:12-13). The first of these tithes is often called the Levite tithe, the second the festival tithe, and the third the poor tithe. The Levite and festival tithes were ongoing tithes each year, but the poor tithe was taken only every third year. This meant that the three tithes actually amounted to an average of 23 percent per year.[26]

Israel was not only a spiritual community, but a nation as well. This means that part of this revenue was used for basic national upkeep, similar to our income tax today. So what does this mean for us now? What changed after the coming of Jesus? Are citizens of His Kingdom to give in the same way?

Irenaeus (A.D. 120-205) was a prolific writer of the early Christian church and an overseer of the church in Gaul. He was also a student of Polycarp, so he would have had a good understanding of even earlier Christianity. In one of his writings, Irenaeus describes the difference between the Jewish tithe and early church giving. Notice how he describes the difference:

> The class of oblations in general has not been set aside. For there were both oblations there [among the Jews] and there are oblations here [among the Christians]. Sacrifices there were among the [Israelite] people; sacrifices there are, too, in the Church. Only the outward form has been changed. For the offering is now made, not by slaves, but by free men . . . [The Jews] had indeed the tithes of their goods consecrated to Him. In contrast, those who have received liberty set aside all their possessions for the Lord's purposes, bestowing joyfully and freely not the less valuable portions of their property, since they have the hope of better things.[27]

Notice what Irenaeus is saying. The Israelites were required to pay their tithe. Similar to our taxes, it was a requirement if you were going to be a part of the nation. The tithe could hardly be classified as giving. You don't give your income tax; you pay it. Today we are free from the obligation to tithe. No longer do we need to pay a certain percentage on what we possess, because we no longer possess anything. As believers, we acknowledge that we have freely given everything to our King. It is His, and as Irenaeus said, it is for the Lord's purposes.

How Much Is for Me?

So what do we do with this? We can agree that everything we have is actually the Lord's, but what does that mean? We still have to live. Even though the assets are God's, don't we need to use some of them for survival? And how much does He want us to use? How much is enough?

In the last chapter I suggested that resources from God are like a river, and we have a tendency to dam their flow. But let's consider that concept with another illustration.

Imagine you are driving down the road and you see a large fuel truck ahead. It pulls out of a distribution center and heads out to deliver fuel. You follow for a few miles, and suddenly the truck pulls over along the road. You watch as the driver gets out, pulls a hose from the large tank in the back, and starts filling the small fuel tank supplying the truck's engine.

Now, you have never seen anything like this before. Most trucks carry enough fuel to get to where they are going. But there are several logical explanations. Perhaps the driver forgot to fuel his truck or thought someone else had refueled it. This is understandable.

The goal is to get the fuel in the large tank to the intended destination, and it would be foolish to abandon the mission due to a lack of fuel when there are thousands of gallons so close at hand.

So you watch the driver fill the smaller tank, hang up the hose, and continue down the road. Now just suppose you continue following this truck, and a few miles down the road the exact same thing takes place. The driver pulls over, gets out, pulls fuel from his large tank, and puts it into his smaller one. *Something is definitely wrong here! Either that small tank has a hole in it, or this truck is consuming much more fuel than it should.*

Imagine that this little scene repeats itself over and over, until finally the truck pulls into its destination with only a few gallons of fuel left to deliver. The entire situation seems bizarre, and you would like an explanation, so you decide to ask the driver. But to your surprise, the driver doesn't seem too concerned. In fact, he is defensive about his truck. He admits that it does consume a terrific amount of fuel, but it really is a delight to drive. The truck has all the latest features, and driving it brings him great enjoyment. Maybe he can even point to other fuel trucks that are consuming more.

In spite of all these explanations, how long do you think the fuel distribution plant would continue to use that truck? Their goal is to transport fuel to the many waiting customers. Regardless of how much enjoyment the driver was receiving from his driving experience, the truck would have to go. Fuel distribution plants are not in the business of creating happy driving experiences. Their goal is to deliver fuel.

Our lives can resemble that wasteful truck. The Lord loads us with resources. He gives us abilities, time, and financial resources, and He intends that we deliver them to those in need. But so often I regard the resources I am transporting as mine. I begin thinking about the enjoyment they could bring to me, so occasionally I find myself pulling the hose around and redirecting some of the resources to myself. As a result, very little actually gets to the intended destination.

> *Fuel distribution plants are not in the business of creating happy driving experiences. Their goal is to deliver fuel.*

Now, make no mistake. God does intend that we use some of these resources for ourselves. A fuel truck without fuel will never make a delivery. The owners understand this. But the question is, how much is enough? How much does God intend for us to consume in the process of delivering His resources?

I have struggled with this question and will probably wrestle with it until I am gone. I am not alone in this. I think most of us have given this issue some serious thought. We are in a much different situation than many of our forefathers. Many of them focused on survival. They were just trying to keep food on the table and clothes on the children. But today many of us can choose the level at which we are going to live, especially as we come to the latter part of our lives. How will we decide how much we should use for personal consumption?

Of course, we want to always turn to the Scriptures for guidance, but when we do, we find that different passages seem to point us to different lifestyles. Some of Jesus' teachings seem to suggest a more radical approach to finances, while other passages in the epistles have a slightly different emphasis. I believe it is critical to address these differences and understand why both are included in the Bible. Rather than being contradictory, the different emphases complement each other and show that God's purposes for His children can vary from person to person. It is important not only to find a God-honoring lifestyle for ourselves in our older years, but also to have understanding and charity as we observe the choices of others. Let's begin by looking at two types of callings we find in the New Testament. The first we will call the Forsaker Who Goes.

The Forsaker Who Goes

We have all been called to forsake.[b] But it seems clear that Jesus called some men to literally walk away from everything they had in their service to Him. The Apostles were obvious examples. Jesus told them to follow Him, and they literally got up and walked away from their occupations and ways of life. These were men with a special calling, and to fulfill that calling, they had to travel. But the Apostles weren't the only ones. We find Jesus sending out seventy more men with specific instructions regarding possessions. They were to totally divest themselves of personal assets on their journey. Again, these were men with a specific calling, and the Lord gave them specific instructions regarding how this mission was to be carried out. These men needed to rely on others to survive. They were told to take nothing with them. Nothing! Not even extra clothes or a wallet. Their total focus was to be on the task at hand, and possessions would have distracted from this mission.

Several years ago I met a believer in China who lived very much like this. Traveling from village to village, he met with various house

---

[b]Luke 14:33

churches. As he went, he encouraged the believers and provided much-needed Biblical teaching. With the authorities always just behind him, he had to stay on the move, and he rarely knew where he would be eating or teaching next. Even a suitcase would have been a burden to him. God had given him a calling to serve his people in the underground Chinese church, and he was attempting to follow the Lord's leading. This man, like the Apostles, was a Forsaker who went.

The Forsaker Who Stays

But it is also evident that God didn't call all His people to walk away from their homes and occupations. I suspect that when Jesus selected the twelve, there were others who would have liked to have been chosen. But Jesus chose only twelve. Later we find Jesus casting out demons and healing a man in the country of the Gadarenes. This man pled with Jesus. He wanted to leave his home and travel along with Him. But Jesus wouldn't let him. Jesus said, "Go home to thy friends, and tell them how great things the Lord hath done for thee, and hath had compassion on thee."[c] Here was a man who really wanted to leave everything he had, but Jesus said no. God had something else for him to do. If you follow this account, you will find that this man did just what Jesus told him. As a result, the people of his village marveled; in other words, they were moved by the power of Christ. This man obeyed Jesus' command to stay home, and God blessed his ministry there.

In other places in the New Testament, we find encouragement and instruction to those who are called to stay home. Paul addressed the believers at Thessalonica in this way: "And that ye study to be quiet, and to do your own business, and to work with your own hands, as we commanded you."[d] In other words, work diligently so you don't need to be dependent on anyone else. This teaching is radically different from the instructions Jesus gave to the seventy He sent out. He told them to take nothing along and to eat what was provided by others.

Obviously, God has not called everyone to the same lifestyle. Some have been called to literally walk away from everything to fulfill their

---

[c]Mark 5:19

[d]1 Thessalonians 4:11

mission, and others are commanded to stay home and work in their occupations. This is not to say there are only two categories. Often we find the Apostle Paul traveling, yet stopping at times to work and provide for himself,[e] and I believe there is some overlap in these callings. God has clearly called individuals within the body to different tasks.

But it is equally important to note that, although there may be some overlap in these callings, they both have the same ultimate goal. We find some going out and some staying home, but both are focused on building the Kingdom of Jesus Christ. We do not find anyone being encouraged to just relax and focus on enjoying this present life. We don't find disciples of the Lord Jesus doing whatever they please with the resources they have been given and ignoring the ultimate goal of building the Kingdom. While many today may be living self-centered lives while calling themselves Christians, they cannot be called disciples.

Why Does It Matter?

Why is it important to address and acknowledge these callings? There are two reasons I feel this is vital. First, as you attempt to chart a course for your older years, you must discern what God is asking of you. Some of you will be called to walk away from the lifestyle you have come to regard as normal.

One older brother told how his wife's passing changed his outlook on life. At first he was devastated and couldn't see good coming from her death. But as time passed, he found opportunity to bless others in ways he never could have while he was married. He spends his days and nights on call. Individuals with spiritual and emotional problems are directed to his cell phone, where he is able to pray with them and share with them in their struggles. Approaching eighty years of age, this elderly brother is using his final years to reach out to others and bless them. It is important for us to understand that God has different callings, and that though these callings can change during our lives, there will always be something for us to do for God.

But the second reason it is important to address callings is because of our tendency for misunderstandings. There is still a need within

---

[e] Acts 18:3

the body of Christ for both the forsaker who goes and the forsaker who stays. The challenge we face is that when we feel called to one of these roles, we tend to see little need for the other. In our zeal to follow the Lord's leading, we become persuaded that everyone else within the body should feel the same burden, and we can't understand why others don't share our vision.

Imagine the Kingdom of God as a cornfield. God has placed you in one of the rows and has asked you to hoe. Since you are focusing on the need in your row, it is easy to wonder why others are not working there as well. The work seems overwhelming, and from your vantage point there is more to do in your row than anywhere else. It becomes easy to suspect that the need isn't nearly as great in other rows and to imagine that others are not as busy as you are. Consequently, many times much energy is expended in the church trying to convince others that our row is the one with the greatest need.

What would happen if every member in the body focused on the row given him and blessed others as they labored in theirs? What would a church be like where every believer felt affirmed in his labors instead of feeling the need to constantly defend his row?

Youth especially need to feel some affirmation as they begin laboring. Often their ideas may seem wild or immature, but it is important to encourage them instead of immediately throwing cold water on ideas that seem outside of the box. Hoeing is hard work, and the body of Christ needs the enthusiasm and energy of youth. Young people also need the maturity of those who have been hoeing longer. This combination of enthusiasm and maturity will never take place, however, unless older believers come alongside the younger ones and the two groups work together.

As you consider what God may have for you in your older years, you may find that He is calling you to come alongside younger believers and hoe with them. There is a time to speak the truth in love and explain how to hoe more effectively. But make sure you are hoeing before you speak.

> *Make sure you are hoeing before you speak.*

Conclusion

How much does God expect us to consume, and what kind of lifestyle does He expect us to live? It is obvious that God doesn't have just one calling for everyone and that these different callings will affect our lifestyles. The brother in Asia, for example, who travels from village to village by night encouraging the churches, will have needs much different from another individual who frequently uses his home for large gatherings and hospitality. Both are blessing the Kingdom, but in entirely different ways. There are some basic Biblical principles that transcend personal callings, and it is important to use these truths as reference points. One of those universal truths is found in the Gospel of Luke, where Jesus said, "Whosoever he be of you that forsaketh not all that he hath, he cannot be my disciple."[e]

This passage in today's vernacular could literally be rendered, "Anybody who doesn't give up his rights to everything he has cannot be my disciple." Now apply that to your latter years. Do you feel like you have some rights? Do you secretly feel you have earned the right to do what you want with "your" resources?

One of the amazing paradoxes of Kingdom living is that those who have relinquished all rights to personal fulfillment are the ones who are really fulfilled. But this truth should not surprise us. It was Jesus Himself who once said, "He that loseth his life for my sake shall find it."[f] Many believers around the world have discovered the truth of this

---

[e]Luke 14:33
[f]Matthew 10:39

statement. As we forsake the pursuit of our own happiness and share the resources He has given us to deliver, we discover the joy and peace we had been craving.

Twelve
Without Hypocrisy

I t was June 1992, at a gathering unlike the world had ever seen. Held in Rio de Janeiro, Brazil, the conference was referred to as the Earth Summit. Heads of state from one hundred and eight countries gathered to discuss solutions to the world's environmental concerns. In addition to the leaders, over 2,400 representatives from various organizations participated. All these special-interest groups came with their own concerns and looked for opportunities to share their solutions to the environmental issues at hand.

There had been political wrangling for years. Laws had been passed around the globe in an attempt to address the myriad ways countries were polluting the environment. Yet in spite of these laws, political infighting, corporate profits, and governmental corruption effectively kept real change from occurring. In some developing countries, like China, the air quality in cities was so poor it was having a direct impact on citizens' health. But this wasn't just a local problem. Pollution from one nation affected surrounding nations, and it seemed clear that something needed to happen on a larger scale.

Many years have passed since the Earth Summit in Brazil, and most of the things that were said have long been forgotten. In fact, most people feel nothing really significant happened there—except one six-minute speech.

A Six-Minute Speech
There was one speech during that twelve-day event that stands out to this day. People still talk about it, quote excerpts from it, and watch videos of it. It has been called the speech that silenced the world for six minutes.

This simple yet stunning speech was given by Severn Suzuki, a twelve-year-old girl from Canada. For six minutes she pled with this large group of dignitaries to consider what they were doing to the world. She rebuked them for ignoring poverty and pollution while continuing to engage in needless fighting. Severn reproved them for not being consistent.

"At school," she said, "even in kindergarten, you teach us to behave in the world. You teach us not to fight with others, to work things out, to respect others, to clean up our mess, not to hurt other creatures, and to share and not be greedy." Then Severn continued with this penetrating question: "Why do you go out and do the things you tell us not to do?"

The vast audience of dignitaries sat spellbound in uncomfortable silence. They were all well-paid representatives of their countries and organizations, attending the conference with their travel expenses paid. But this twelve-year-old girl had worked hard and saved enough to travel thousands of miles to speak from her heart and fight for her future. She reprimanded the crowd for their foolish political skirmishes, shortsighted profit taking, and greedy self-centeredness, and then finished by saying, "You are what you do, not what you say. And what you do makes me cry at night. You grown-ups say you love us. I challenge you; please, make your actions reflect your words."[28]

It's What You Do, Not What You Say

The transcript of Severn's speech has been published, quoted, and passed around for years. Environmentalists and activists have used it as a rallying point, but as I have read the words and tried to listen to the cry of her twelve-year-old heart, I have found a sobering parallel. Her words remind me of the cry coming from the younger generation in many of our churches. As they see continual church splits, materialistic mindsets, cold formalism, and sometimes an obvious love for the world, they get discouraged. I have listened to young fathers who are concerned about the future when they see few older role models in their congregations. I have heard them, like Severn Suzuki, speak of the great difference between what is taught and what is actually lived. The young are longing for older believers they can emulate. They are searching for battle-hardened warriors they can look to for advice and courage. And they are looking for honesty.

Honesty?

There is no question that churches today are struggling. And often as we look at the difficulties the church is experiencing, our primary concern is with the youth. Why do they ask so many questions and challenge ways we have been doing things for years? Why can't they just be a little more content and not quite so radical? Why must they be so idealistic and unrealistic with their expectations?

Without question, there are reasons to be concerned about the coming generation. They are growing up in a society that questions everything and seems to rebel against any type of authority. This cultural trend has had its impact. But before we lay all of the current unrest on the younger generation, let's back up for a moment and take a look at ourselves.

Is it possible that the older generation has contributed to the problem? Have our lives really been examples of godliness, separation from the world, and spiritual vitality? How much has the prevalent culture affected us and our way of thinking? Are we really consistent in what we profess and what we practice? Most of us would agree that we have also been affected by our culture. We have made mistakes. We haven't always been the spiritual leaders in our homes and churches that we should have been. But are we willing to openly confess this?

As I look in churches today, I see older men who are good men. Many have been godly examples for years. So what more do younger believers want from the older generation? Why do they at times seem discontent with the lifestyles and suggestions of those of us who are older?

As I listen to many younger believers, I don't believe they are looking for perfection. But they are looking for older believers who are honest about their strengths and weaknesses. They are quick to detect hypocrisy and don't feel comfortable following those who are not completely honest about their failures. Let's look at a few areas where perhaps our generation hasn't been as honest as we could have been.

1. Honesty with our past. Most of us move into midlife with some battle scars. We started out raising our families with high hopes and expectations. As we look back, we see times when we should have done things differently, and some of these poor choices can be sore spots we would rather not discuss. But desire for Kingdom growth needs to be stronger than our fear of damaged reputations. Our young families need to hear more admissions of failure from the older generation.

> *Desire for Kingdom growth needs to be stronger than our fear of damaged reputations.*

There is a lack of confession in many churches. Perhaps this is because we sense a general lack of respect, and we fear that the younger generation would have even less respect if more of our deficiencies were exposed. But the truth is, our weaknesses are already observed. We could greatly bless those who are younger if we would be humble enough to let them learn from our failures.

2. Honesty regarding church fellowship. In my work I interact with a variety of different conservative fellowships, and most groups that are seriously trying to apply the Word of God seem to be doing some things well. But each also has areas of weakness. Regardless of your particular fellowship, if it has been in existence very long, there are areas of difficulty. Satan does not give the church that is trying to aggressively fight his domain any rest. But there is a difference in how fellowships address these weaknesses and difficulties.

Some seem willing to openly and humbly discuss problems and prayerfully seek solutions. They begin by honestly admitting they don't have all the answers. But others are reluctant. There is a tendency, especially as we grow older, to become fearful of open dialogue. Open discussion regarding our practices can bring criticism of cherished methods, and sometimes we are unwilling to risk such conflict.

But few things build frustration in zealous youth like obvious problems that are ignored in a fellowship. This frustration increases when it is perceived that we are focusing on others' weaknesses while ignoring our own. When we attempt to divert the focus to the failings of others rather than openly acknowledging our own weaknesses, we confirm the suspicions of our youth and may be giving them reason to justify their lack of respect.

Most of us who are older are loyal to our fellowship, and we want those coming behind to share this appreciation. There is nothing wrong with supporting and having an appreciation for our heritage and local fellowship. This is Biblical. But when out of balance, this good trait can evolve into another form of self-centeredness, and it is very possible as we grow older to become focused on our fellowship rather than on the Kingdom of Jesus Christ. When this occurs, we find ourselves trying to explain why our own church group's faults aren't as serious as the weaknesses we observe in others. Instead of praying for and honestly seeking the good of other fellowships that are also fighting against sin and Satan, we focus on their inconsistencies, using this as a diversion from our own. Not only is this process uncharitable, it is not honest. We need more honesty as we humbly examine our own failings, and we need churches that value and encourage both personal and collective repentance and confession.

3. Honesty about the battle. Recently a young father told me, "Few things alarm me more than having a leader encourage us just to trust him." He went on to explain that he would much rather hear a leader openly confess that he doesn't have all the solutions and request a season of prayer and fasting while seeking direction. There is a tendency among those of us who are older to rely solely on precedent. We have already lived for quite some time. We have made many decisions. Some have turned out well, while others have yielded less-than-desirable results. But most of us have found that certain choices tend to produce favorable results. Consequently, we tend to feel less and less need for external guidance, and we begin to rely more and more on past practice. There is nothing wrong with using this to help guide us. In fact, any wise leader will learn from history. But if the past becomes our primary reference point, it is easy to drift off course. When the early church faced the crisis of Peter's imprisonment, they immediately met for prayer. There was no precedent to fall back on. Their only hope was to cry out to God. When we graduate to a level where we no longer feel the need to gather for focused prayer, we are moving in the wrong direction. We all like to think we are trusting in God. But to really find out where our help is coming from, we need to examine where we go to get it. When faced with a question, do you go to God first? How often is your congregation called to prayer for a specific need? How frequently are times of fasting announced, and is your entire congregation expected to participate? These questions will reveal what we are actually leaning on and whether or not we are being honest about the battle.

Conclusion

Jesus lived on this earth over thirty years. He witnessed many injustices, saw the oppression of the Roman government, and quietly observed as day by day the powerful abused the poor. When confronted with the blatant sin of the woman taken in adultery, Jesus responded calmly with forgiveness and grace. When frustrated with His self-centered disciples who argued over who was the greatest, He responded with a gentle reprimand. Even when Herod killed His cousin John, an act of extreme injustice, Jesus didn't respond with anger or force. It seems that Jesus could put up with quite a lot of injustice and wrong.

But one thing Jesus could not tolerate was religious hypocrisy. The most scathing comments Jesus ever uttered were directed at men who were not being honest. They were proclaiming one thing with their lips yet demonstrating something totally different with their lives.

All of us struggle with hypocrisy. I find it easy to tell others they need to pray more. But I find it much more difficult to keep the fire of fervent prayer alive in my own life.

This chapter is not intended to give license to youthful zeal that rebels against spiritual authority. Our zealous young people need to humbly offer their insights only if they are first under the godly authority in their lives.[a]

> *I find it easy to tell others they need to pray more. But I find it much more difficult to keep the fire of fervent prayer alive in my own life.*

[a]Hebrews 13:17

But I do want to call us, regardless of our ages, to humility and honesty regarding our weaknesses. I am convinced that the only way we will increase the spiritual fire in our lives is if we are first humble and honest about our faults. This is true both personally and collectively. Revival begins with repentance. And as we openly share our failures, I believe God will rekindle the fire in our lives and in our churches!

Thirteen
Wanted: Older Active Warriors

S everal years ago I sat around a campfire and listened as several young fathers shared inspirational thoughts, Scriptures that had blessed them, or concerns they had for the Kingdom. Toward the end of the evening, one young father shared an article he had recently written. This was a gathering of primarily younger families, but the writing he shared was a call to those who were older. It was the heart cry of a younger father to older men, pleading with them to be the warriors God has called them to be. I have included his article because it speaks to the hearts of many men today. As you read this, I challenge you to hear the cry from the younger generation. Some of the young men in your own congregation may have similar burdens that they have never expressed.

How Can We Inspire Our Men to Fight?

Old men are supposed to dream dreams. So what happens when they don't? What happens when the only things old men think about are retirement funds or paying off that second or third mortgage? What happens when their focus is to retire to Florida so they can fish and play shuffleboard, cards, or checkers? What happens when a man's entire life vision is to attend a church, get married, have a family, and own a plush house that's paid for? Is that all there is to life? Is there no nobler calling? What happens in the minds of young men when they see this?

God made man in His own image. God is a warrior, and He made men to fight. In God's Kingdom, the fight does not call for weapons that take men's lives. Rather the fight is against Satan and his kingdom of darkness.

Young men have to fight, or they die. Not a physical death—at least not at first. But if they don't fight, they become increasingly frustrated. Eventually, if they are not given a cause to fight for, they become disillusioned and seek to fill the void in their hearts with amusements.

But imagine young men listening as old warriors recount stories of past battles, of raids deep into enemy territory, or of buddies who died in combat. The faces of the young men are intent as they breathlessly hold on to every word, sitting on the edge of their seats, eyes and ears intent. Moved and inspired, they eagerly await their own opportunity to engage in battle.

To give one's self for a worthy cause is the ultimate sacrifice. So what would keep a young man from fighting? What would rob him of his strength and spirit, bringing him to disillusion and despair, making the ever-beckoning lights of the world look attractive? Could it be that our young men have never heard of past battles, that we have a generation of older men who have never fought and don't even know how? Could it be that these men's fathers didn't fight either? Is it possible we are ineffective at teaching our sons to fight because we ourselves have never been taught? What will it take to wake us up, to rouse our troops from their drunken stupor, this lethargy that permeates the church of Jesus Christ?

What if those of us who are older would rise to the challenge and really start dreaming? Dreaming of reaching the thousands of souls going to a Christless eternity every hour. Dreaming of rescuing even one of the murdered millions of helpless unborn children. Dreaming of helping our children and grandchildren who are moving toward the world and becoming part of the problem instead of the radical solution. Dreaming of communities of brothers—warrior brothers—who will acknowledge their own hearts as their strongest enemies and will unashamedly open their hearts to confess their sins to the brotherhood.

What if those of us who are older began to show the way, organizing the charge, rallying the troops, and actually moving forward in offensive engagement instead of just talking about the glory of the church? What if we sent men out two by two to encounter the enemy and scout out the land for souls who are open to the Gospel? What if we would recognize the good in other conservative camps, stop stealing sheep from each other's pastures, and encourage straying sheep to return and build in their own congregations? Are you beginning to dream with me?

What if we took more risks? What if we ordained more men and planted more communities of first-generation churches? What if we stopped all this rhetoric of defense as we sit around carving and sharpening our arrows (our children), without a vision for sending them out? What if we stopped encouraging them to amuse themselves by organizing play activities that inoculate their warrior hearts and create a generation of spineless, passionless, but hopefully good, church members? What if we repented, grieved, and apologized to the hundreds of young men who have left our congregations and gone someplace else (usually some liberal camp if anywhere) looking for meaning in life? How would it look to abandon some of our methodology, our defensive ball playing, and play the ball directly into Satan's court? Isn't it insanity to continue to do the same thing over and over, hoping against hope that our children and grandchildren will turn out different?[29]

Hezekiah Syndrome

Sometimes I think those of us who are older have become infected with Hezekiah Syndrome. You remember the account of King Hezekiah in his later years, when the prophet Isaiah told him he was going to have fifteen good years before he died. Isaiah warned Hezekiah, telling him that terrible destruction was coming upon his children and the entire country of Israel. Hezekiah listened to this prophecy and then made this assessment. "Good is the word of the Lord which thou hast spoken . . . Is it not good, if peace and truth be in my days?"[a]

Hezekiah makes me think of our tendency. He was no longer young, and perhaps battle fatigue had settled in. Things were peaceful around him, and he had fifteen good years ahead of him. What else could a man want? Good food, abundance of wealth, and all the personal comfort he could desire. Surely that was enough for any man.

[a]2 Kings 20:19

But what had happened to the warrior Hezekiah? Where was the Hezekiah who, just a few chapters before, had valiantly made a clean sweep, destroying the idols and groves that had plagued the nation? What happened to the Hezekiah who, when faced with a powerful adversary, had rent his clothes, sought the Lord, and emerged victorious over the enemy? In fact, the Bible says that this Hezekiah, as a young king, was so passionate for his God "that after him was none like him among all the kings of Judah, nor any that were before him."[b] This man was a fighter!

What had happened to the warrior Hezekiah? The same thing that had happened to David and Solomon. In their old age, surrounded by wealth and plenty, they surrendered their passion for the Kingdom and lost their desire to fight.

Warriors From the Womb

Within the heart of a man is an inborn desire to fight. As men, we are warriors from the womb; God made us that way. As new believers, we not only have this desire to fight, but we also have a desire, inherent in our new nature, to see people get right with God. This involves battling with the enemy and helping others escape his grasp. We want to see the Kingdom of God prevail in people's lives, and we want to defeat the foe.

> *When our aim is no longer to be a reconciler of the lost, we tend to become evaluators of the saved.*

But sometimes in our zeal we forget who the enemy is. And when we fail to fight the real enemy, we tend to fight each other. When our aim is no longer to be a reconciler of the lost, we tend to become evaluators of the saved. Our energy and desire to fight evolves into continual analysis of our brother or fellowship. Instead of helping the hurting, we hurt the helpers, and sadly, the lost remain unreached and the hungry unfed.

[b]2 Kings 18:5

I wonder if this tendency to become analyzers of the saved is a learned trait. Do our youth learn to scrutinize other believers and fellowships by listening to those who are older? What if these younger warriors observed a continual interest and strong desire within the older soldiers for the salvation of the lost? What would happen if they were surrounded by older men whose prayers and actions demonstrated a love for the unsaved and a burning desire that Satan's kingdom be destroyed? What would happen then?

The church desperately needs more older believers who are willing to risk their fortunes, their reputations, and even their lives for the sake of the Gospel. Our youth need to see examples of men and women who are still willing, in old age, to take risks and fight for the Kingdom.

There is a time to defend doctrines and even specific practices we have agreed to embrace. Yet it is possible, in our great zeal to preserve a particular practice, to lose something of even greater value. Jesus said, "By this shall all men know that you are my disciples, if ye have love one to another."[c] Love and humble service are the hallmarks of a New Testament church. Yet unfortunately Christendom is famous not for love and humility, but for church splits and divisions. Fellowships divide over an amazing array of issues, and it must burden God's heart as He observes infighting among His children.

Sometimes our churches become identified primarily by our restrictions. As some have observed, the church in America may be the only organization in the world that defines its success more by what it doesn't do than by what it actually does.

But warriors must have a higher vision than just safe, defensive warfare. Our young soldiers are searching for more than that. They are looking for older active warriors who are frequently found in prayer and fasting. They want to see men and women who recognize that they are involved in a spiritual battle and who know that nothing short of aggressive spiritual warfare will win the war. They want to see older believers who care about more than peace and prosperity and risk-free ways to coast out of life. This doesn't mean that every older believer must be visible and outspoken. I am privileged to know quiet, stable older men whose personalities keep them in the background,

[c]John 13:35

but whose love for God enables them to encourage young soldiers to press on. These older men can give excellent counsel when the battle is intense. We need more of these godly examples among us.

Conclusion

On the day of Pentecost, when the Holy Spirit filled those early believers, Peter quoted a passage from the book of Joel prophesied hundreds of years before. I think there is a great need to reexamine this passage in our day. "And it shall come to pass in the last days, saith God, I will pour out of my Spirit upon all flesh: and your sons and your daughters shall prophesy, and your young men shall see visions, and your old men shall dream dreams."[d]

I see many young men with spiritual vision. They have a strong desire to aim even higher than their parents in holiness and commitment to the Kingdom. We need these young men with their energy and idealism. But we also need old men who can dream! We need older men who can see the whitened harvest fields, yet provide the needed stability that comes only with age and experience. Our young men are longing for faithful older men who are willing to lead in the battle. As you visualize living out your final days here on earth, resolve to be that kind of warrior for the Kingdom!

[d]Acts 2:17

Fourteen
The "Right" to Retire

One of my challenges is getting enough exercise. Most of my work must be done while staring at a computer, and consequently it is possible to forget to get outside and move around. To combat this tendency, I try to take regular walks. I set a timer to remind myself, head outside for a fifteen-minute walk, and then go back to squinting at the machine. But sometimes these fifteen-minute walks stretch into longer periods of time. And when they do, it's because of Spike and Jim.

Spike and Jim are two older men who live around the corner. They are healthy, retired, and bored, and getting past their houses can be a challenge. Spike is generally puttering around in the yard or garage looking for something to occupy his time. When I appear on the horizon, his eyes light up. In me he sees a diversion, something to focus on for a few minutes in the midst of another long day.

Jim, who lives just a few houses down from Spike, spends his day differently. He has a little retiree refuge set up in his garage, where he spends most of each day sitting in an older Lazy-Boy in front of a television. To his right, and within reach, is a small, well-stocked refrigerator so he can refresh himself in the middle of watching the ball game. Jim's garage door is usually up in warm weather, and in my many walks past his house, his profile in front of the television has become a familiar scene. With a cold drink in his right hand and the remote in his left, Jim passes the day in his garage. Like Spike, he seems to welcome the diversion of chatting with me when I walk past.

Both Spike and Jim are living out the American dream. They have spent a good part of their lives on the job, longing for the day when they wouldn't have to work anymore. Now, after all those years of planning, hoping, and saving, they have finally arrived. They are at the pinnacle of their lives. Spike and Jim are retired!

In preparation for this book, I immersed myself in information regarding retirement. I read books, newspaper articles, and retirement planning guides. The sheer amount of information on the topic is astounding. Almost everyone, it seems, either is retired or wants to be. According to government figures, 38,385,000 Americans are over sixty-five and receiving Social Security benefits.[30] And if the articles and books are any indicator, another 150 million Americans are going to work each day and eagerly longing for the day they don't have to.

Retirement has captured the imagination of the American people. Everyone, we are told, needs to be actively saving and planning for that day when he can tell his boss he's not coming back. Retirement is purportedly the time when you can finally do what you want, go where you want, and be the person you have always wanted to be. Retirement has become so normal and expected that there is something wrong with the man who isn't longing, planning, and saving for it. But where did all of this come from?

During the years I was involved in commercial construction, most of our jobs were government projects. Consequently I spent a good portion of my time working with individuals who were on government payroll. Government jobs have pros and cons. The good part is that your income is predictable and you are rarely affected by recessions. And once you are hired, it is difficult to lose your job. But the downside is that you are surrounded by politics and insider bickering, and if you are too energetic, you can get yourself into trouble. Pointing out ways tasks could be accomplished more efficiently isn't always appreciated.

To survive, many exert no more energy than necessary. They come to work, do the minimum required, and go home as soon as possible. This creates the least concern for upper management and ensures a long career. This same stifling atmosphere pervades many large corporations as well.

Day after day, bored workers line up early at the time clock, just waiting to punch out the minute the bell rings.

Obviously, this type of atmosphere isn't very efficient or productive. These workers are capable, healthy, and intelligent. They desperately need an outlet for their energy, and since new ideas that focus on production and efficiency are discouraged, they typically zero in on the weekend's activities, upcoming vacations, and retirement.

Retirement seems to be the favorite of all the topics, and workers discuss the subject endlessly. Many of them know, even down to the number of days, exactly how long it is to retirement. The pros and cons of 401(k)s, IRAs, and different pension plans are hot topics. Stories of others who have retired, where they moved, and what they are doing (or aren't doing) fill the day. It seems the hope of retirement is what gets these employees through each long, boring week. Retirement becomes the carrot dangling out front.

This Is It?

But I have thought about this as I walk past the homes of Spike and Jim. Is this all that bored workers are longing for? To aimlessly putter around the yard or sit in a garage watching TV? Jim has a large home, and the fact that he prefers the garage, even in colder weather, tells a little about how things are going between Mr. Jim and Mrs. Jim. It is said that good marriages get better in retirement and bad ones get worse.

So why does our society long for this kind of existence? Why do many finally arrive at this place only to discover it isn't what they thought it would be?

And where did this idea of retirement come from? Have people always retired? What does God think about retirement? Are there any Scriptural principles that address this topic? Let's begin by looking at the history of retirement.

The topic of retirement is noticeably absent in the Bible. In fact, there is only one place where retirement is directly mentioned, and this is where God speaks to Moses regarding the Levites. "This is it that belongeth unto the Levites: from twenty and five years old and upward they shall go in to wait upon the service of the tabernacle of the congregation: And from the age of fifty years they shall cease waiting upon the service thereof and shall serve no more."[a]

The Bible doesn't say why the Lord asked the Levites to stop serving. The next verse insinuates that there was still some work for them to do, but God asked them to stop serving in the tabernacle at the age of fifty. Maybe we can learn a lesson from God's instructions to the Levites. Although God desires every believer to remain active and productive throughout his life, our abilities change. Our bodies weaken, mental alertness diminishes, and sometimes we are not aware of our reduced capabilities. There may be a time for church leaders to pass on the baton before they really sense the need themselves. I can think of leaders who have successfully passed on their leadership role to younger ones while remaining active in preaching and in lower-profile avenues of service. This selfless acknowledgment that others have the capacity to lead can bless a congregation. Knowing when this should occur requires prayer, humility, and communication.

Beyond this instruction to the Levites, we find nothing in the Bible encouraging individuals to stop working at a certain age. We find plenty of instruction regarding helping those who are not capable of providing for themselves. But it is safe to say that retirement, as our culture promotes it, is not based on Scripture.

Where Did Retirement Come From?

Retirement as we know it is a very recent innovation. Some older people living today can still remember a time when retirement was almost unknown. During the first half of the 1900s, very few people had enough wealth to just stop working and begin playing. Extra money was scarce, and everyone worked who could. The thought of healthy people just sitting around was preposterous. But in the 1950s, as the postwar economy picked up steam, labor unions bargained with large corporations to increase workers' incomes and benefits. These companies were much more agreeable to concessions that resulted in long-term

> *Retirement as we know it is a very recent innovation.*

[a]Numbers 8:24-25

benefits, such as pension plans that cost them little at the time, than to immediate increases in wages.

Suddenly, for the first time, retirement was a possibility for the common laborer. Now employees of these large corporations could imagine staying home in their older years with a steady flow of income supporting them until they died. Smaller companies soon felt pressured to offer similar plans, and it wasn't long till retirement became a supposed right.

It was a rapid and amazing shift. Just a few years before, in the 1930s, millions of workers had been out of work during the Great Depression, and it had been almost impossible for older Americans to find employment. This had created major hardships for many older couples. In 1935 President Roosevelt, in response to this need, set up the Old Age, Survivors, and Disability Insurance program, which today we know as Social Security. This program was originally intended as a supplement for those who were disabled or had no means of support in their older years.

But after World War II, politicians, in a bid for public favor, began to rapidly expand Social Security benefits. As the benefits escalated, little thought was given to the future costs of funding this massive program. No one imagined just how large Social Security would become. Elected officials tend to gravitate toward programs that offer instant rewards and delayed consequences. This program offered both.

With the private sector increasingly offering retirement benefits to employees and a government guaranteeing income in old age, the nation's mindset changed rapidly. As financial counselor and author Larry Burkett has said, "By the late sixties, most Americans viewed retirement as a foregone conclusion."[31]

As the years progressed, more and more emphasis was placed on retirement and planning for it. Today financial planners are aghast if you don't have some kind of retirement plan. But for centuries older people worked until they were physically unable, and then family members, churches, or even neighbors in the community assisted the elderly until they passed away.

There is nothing inherently wrong with some planning for retirement. But it is important that we understand the impact our culture has had on us in this area. Our tendency is to ignore Scriptural teaching on caring for the weak and elderly, and our culture can become our reference rather than the Word of God.

Conclusion

During my teenage years, one of the ministers in our area made a timeline. It spanned from the creation of the world to the present, and each foot of the timeline represented one hundred years. It took around sixty feet to get from the beginning of time to our day. All along the way he had drawn pictures representing events that happened during each period. At the very beginning was a drawing of Adam and Eve, and about fifteen feet down the timeline was a drawing of Noah's ark. About forty feet from the beginning was the cross, the empty tomb, and the beginning of the church age. Then, almost twenty feet later, he portrayed current events.

That timeline helped put history in perspective. It also revealed how many of the things I viewed as normal were actually recent inventions. Consider for a moment how transportation would look on this timeline. For almost six thousand years, or sixty feet on the timeline, little changed. You either used an animal, a boat, or your legs. Then, in the last hundred years, or only twelve inches on the timeline, man went from those three modes of travel to automobiles, airplanes, and spacecraft. Astounding changes took place in an extremely short period of time!

But we forget this. It often seems that things have always been this way, and we forget how recent and revolutionary some of our everyday conveniences are. Retirement is the same. On that timeline, retirement as we know it would span only about six inches of the entire sixty feet. Yet in the minds of people like Spike and Jim, retirement is a nonnegotiable right and relaxation a goal worth striving for—in spite of the fact that many retirees spend day after meaningless day vegetating and wistfully longing for some diversion.

But is this what God has in mind? Does He intend for healthy men and women to coast out of life without vision or purpose? The Bible is clear that God has a much higher vision, and we have many examples like Moses, Abraham, and the Apostles who served God until the end. Whatever your age, God has something for you to be involved in. As you continue reading, open your heart to what that might be.

PART THREE
A Time to Refocus

Fifteen
The Rest of My Time

It was June of 1980 when Ervin and Martha first visited their local jail. For some time they had prayerfully considered reaching out to the inmates there, but they could not have anticipated how this small step of faith would affect their lives and the lives of many prisoners. This first visit increased their interest, and it wasn't long until they were visiting inmates each month. The first few times were a little stretching for Ervin and Martha, since the jailor would lock them into the cells with the prisoners. But over time they developed relationships. Several of the prisoners were transferred to larger prisons, and Ervin and Martha stayed in contact by mail, sending letters of encouragement and Christian literature.

Time passed, and one of the men who had been transferred asked for a good study Bible. So Ervin sent him one with his name printed on it so it couldn't easily be stolen. Another prisoner heard about it and also requested a Bible. Word quickly spread and more requests came, as many as several hundred a year. In response, Ervin and Martha began providing a basic Bible correspondence course. Prisoners who completed the course received a free Bible and additional material to assist them in studying the Word of God. Ervin and Martha started this program near their home in Ohio, but today their Bibles and correspondence courses are shipped to prisons as far away as Los Angeles. They still grade the courses and personally respond to prisoners from their home. Many of these prisoners have been abandoned by their families, and the letters, tracts, and cards they receive from this older couple provide hope.

A brother in Ervin and Martha's congregation shared with me about their work, and I contacted them, asking a little more about their ministry. The sheer simplicity of their program impressed me. Few are even aware of what they do, but they are quietly using the opportunity that God provided.

At the conclusion of a letter describing their correspondence ministry, they said, "We praise the Lord for opening doors along the way. We appreciate being able to do this in our sunset years, grading courses and corresponding with those who want to."

After commenting on the shortness of time, they finished with, "So we seek to work while it is still day. To God be all the honor and glory."

In this brief statement they acknowledge that their time is short. Yet instead of allowing this fact to discourage them, they are letting that reality spur them on! A sense of excitement fills their letter. After all, they aren't aimlessly meandering from one day to the next. They have chosen to labor for the Kingdom and are on a mission for the King of Kings Himself!

As I think of people like Ervin and Martha, I am reminded of the words of the Apostle Peter. After recounting Jesus' amazing sacrifice for our sins, Peter encourages the reader to get involved in the battle just as Jesus did. Notice the forward focus of his words. "Forasmuch then as Christ hath suffered for us in the flesh, arm yourselves likewise with the same mind: for he that hath suffered in the flesh hath ceased from sin; That he no longer should live the rest of his time in the flesh to the lusts of men, but to the will of God."[a]

In the first half of this book we have reflected on who we are and where we have come from. Sometimes that inward look is painful. But the above passage was written by a man who understood failure. This man actually walked with the Lord, witnessed miracles firsthand, but then walked away when things got a little hot. Don't you suppose looking back was painful for Peter? Can't you see him wishing things could have been different?

But what impresses me is Peter's willingness to move on. He was willing to accept the forgiveness offered by the Lord and not let Satan use past failures to immobilize his future. Resolve to do the same! All

[a]1 Peter 4:1-2

of us have things in the past we wish we could change, but continually dwelling on them can make us ineffective. Peter's message to the believers of his day is also for us. He encourages us to be of the same mind as Jesus and serve Him with the rest of our time.

The Same Mind

Peter says that we should arm ourselves with the same mind that Jesus had when He suffered for us. What was that? What kind of mindset did Jesus possess as He went to the cross? As I examine Jesus' life and focus, the word that comes to mind is "selfless." All of His actions were inspired by a desire to bless others regardless of the cost. We see that same mindset in His followers immediately after the resurrection. Men who just a few days before had been trying to protect their reputations, possessions, and lives were suddenly filled with reckless abandon. They abruptly lost interest in self-preservation, and their sole desire was to tell others about Jesus.

Peter encourages us to have that same mindset. The goal is not to see what we can get out of each day and event, but rather to use our lives to promote the Kingdom of Jesus Christ.

The Rest of Our Time

Peter goes on to describe how this change in mind will affect our use of time. I like his choice of words when he says, "That he no longer should live the rest of his time in the flesh to the lusts of men, but to the will of God." He subtly acknowledges the possibility that in the past we have not used all of our time for the glory of God. As the chapter continues, Peter openly acknowledges this. Much of our past has been focused on selfish, fleshly pursuits. But that doesn't mean we need to continue on that path.

Everything in a believer's life has been given back to God, who owns it anyway.

We have been redeemed, and the only appropriate response is committing everything we have to the Lord Jesus. We have chosen to relinquish all rights to our possessions, our families, and our finances. Everything in a believer's life has been given back to God, who owns it anyway. Maybe over time we have failed to acknowledge God's ownership of "our" possessions and wealth. We can rectify this by openly choosing to commit these items to God.

Time Has No Reverse

When it comes to time, we can't back up. We can repent, but opportunity to use past time correctly is gone. All we can do is commit our remaining time to God. That is Peter's message. As you consider the rest of your time, from this moment on, what are you planning to do with it? How are you going to use this resource that God has placed in your care?

What would your life look like if you made a conscious choice to openly commit the rest of your time to the Kingdom of Jesus Christ? What changes would need to occur? Consider this question as we proceed. As I have read about retirement and listened to people who are pursuing personal pleasure in their retirement years, I have felt depressed at times. So many talented, healthy, and capable people are futilely searching for something that is missing in their lives. The chase is on for the right vacation home, the perfect restaurant, the ideal cruise, or a memorable experience in some exotic locale.

Free But Not Needed

But they come back from these pursuits, and by their own admission, something is missing. I have noticed this especially in men. Men are in a great predicament. We desire to be unencumbered, yet we also long to be needed. We desire to be free, yet we also desire to be important. This places us in a dilemma, for the more we try to free ourselves from being needed, the less important we feel. This truth is evidenced all around us.

I have talked to many men in the prime of life who wish they didn't have to go to work. They don't necessarily mind the work; they just don't want to be required to go. They long to get up when they want to get up, do what they want to do, and go where they want to go. They are tired of employers or fellow workers giving them directions or always coming to them for answers. They want to be free from all that. But they fail to realize that what they long to be free from is the very thing that provides them with a sense of fulfillment.

Many retired men find themselves in this quandary. They free themselves of the yoke they despised for years only to feel miserable and unfulfilled. Many men who have realized this continue working. After puttering around the house and finding it a miserable existence, the workplace doesn't look like such a bad place after all.

Another Option

Others have chosen a different path. They have found a cause to live for, something they can pour themselves into, which in turn helps them feel needed and significant. I have talked to men who have left full-time employment and focused on environmental concerns, growing produce to share with their neighbors, or a particular need in the community. These men are primarily seeking personal satisfaction and enjoyment in life. They are searching for fulfillment.

But the Apostle Peter calls us higher. He calls us to imitate the Lord Jesus Himself. He calls us to give up our selfish desires and use the rest of our time to build the Kingdom of Jesus Christ. Are you ready for that? As you contemplate the incredible sacrifice Jesus has made for you and the history of martyrdom that believers before you have endured, does committing the rest of your time to the Kingdom seem too costly?

Conclusion

All of us have read accounts of individuals such as Hudson Taylor or Amy Carmichael. These believers stand out like beacons in history. Some of their experiences and the testimonies that came from their lives are remarkable. I have read many stories of men and women like them who, against impossible odds, were faithful to God and accomplished wonderful things.

But I also confess that I have felt a little intimidated by their testimonies. Some of them prayed for hours each day, endured great affliction for the Gospel, and fasted for long periods of time as they sought the Lord's will. When I compare their stories with my own pitiful attempts at sanctification, holiness, and love for the souls of men, I feel overwhelmed. The story of my life just doesn't read like theirs.

That is why the testimony of believers like Ervin and Martha is needed among us. They are just ordinary people who are willing to be used by the Lord, individuals like the Psalmist described who "shall still bring forth fruit in old age."[b] Testimonies like theirs remind us that God can use anyone, regardless of ability or age. God is just looking for men and women who are willing to consecrate the rest of their time to Him.

[b]Psalm 92:14

Sixteen
An Amazing Opportunity

All of us have experienced times when a chance meeting, an inspiring writing, or a convicting sermon has changed our direction and influenced our lives for good. Some time ago I met an older brother named Joe who inspired me.

I had been researching retirement and the best ways to live out the last half of our lives. I had read books and articles directed toward seniors and listened to dinner table discussions as older individuals talked about their lives. Frankly, I had found it all a little discouraging. There seemed to be little to look forward to. I began to wonder. Does getting older just consist of waiting for the Social Security check, occasionally checking on mutual funds, comparing warm places to go in the winter, and discussing physical ailments with other senior citizens? Is it a game where whoever has the nicest RV, the best fishing story, or the greatest travel plans for next winter wins? Does it primarily consist of sitting around chatting about the best restaurants, problems in other congregations, or how much better life was in the Good Old Days? Is this all I have to look forward to?

During the time I was pondering these things, I met Joe. The event we had both attended was over, and as I stood and prepared to leave, I met Joe in the aisle. We didn't talk long that afternoon, but in just a few sentences Joe radically impacted my outlook on the retirement years. I don't remember how the discussion started, but somehow we got onto the topic of needs within the Kingdom. We compared some of our experiences, and then Joe said, "This is such an exciting time to be alive! There are so many needs and opportunities. We are able to communicate globally like never before, we are able to travel anywhere

117

we choose, and we have the financial resources to bless others in so many ways. It's just a fantastic time to be serving the Lord!"

Joe went on to describe the marvelous blessing our older generation has with excellent healthcare and the privilege of living longer. But while the words Joe spoke were encouraging, it was the way he said them that arrested my attention. His facial expression and tone of voice were what you would have expected from a Forty-Niner who had just discovered an untapped vein of high-grade gold. He was as excited as a four-year-old at Christmas who has unwrapped the very thing he has been dreaming of for months. Joe had a gleam in his eye you wouldn't have expected from a gray-haired man near the end of his life. His level of excitement was contagious. He made me long to reach that place in life where I could more fully pour myself into living for the Kingdom and reaching out to those in need.

The dark, discouraging backdrop of so many retirees living meaningless lives made Joe's bright testimony even more encouraging. While thousands of retirees aimlessly meander through their final years and unconcernedly watch the last grains of sand slip through the hourglass of life, Joe was a man with a vision. Whereas many, even as their bodies begin to fail, see retirement as a time to wring the last bit of pleasure from life, Joe saw it as a wonderful opportunity to serve the Lord in ways he hadn't been able to before.

Purposeless Living

Even in the secular world people are recognizing disillusionment among retirees. Recently I was reading a financial adviser's observations on retirement, and I noted some points from his study of retirees in America. Notice the emotional toll that "finally getting to do what they always wanted to do" is having on many people:

- Retiring is as stressful as getting married, losing your job, or having a close family member become ill.

- The highest suicide rate in the United States, for any segment of the population, is men over seventy (50 percent higher than the suicide rate for teenagers).

- One-third of all men over sixty-five are depressed within one year of retirement.

The study showed that work had been the retiree's primary source of meaning and the biggest occupier of his daytime hours. Replacing that time with activities that are both mentally challenging and emotionally fulfilling doesn't happen automatically.[32]

This financial adviser went on to say, "Ten thousand Americans are retiring daily. And the sad truth is that most people spend less time planning for retirement than they do for a vacation." This is a sad reality in our Western world. Many are entering this time of life unprepared. Individuals have lived self-centered lives and longed for the day when they can finally do whatever they want. But when they arrive, they find self-focused living to be a greater burden than they anticipated. There is a nagging fear that life has passed them by and they have missed out on something.

Harold Kushner, a Jewish rabbi and author, in his book, *When All You've Ever Wanted Isn't Enough*, described another problem with living for ourselves. "I am convinced that it is not the fear of death, of our lives ending, that haunts our sleep so much as the fear that our lives will not have mattered, that as far as the world is concerned, we might as well never have lived. What we miss in our lives, no matter how much we have, is that sense of meaning."[33]

Many people are meandering out of life without a purposeful vision. We see aimless, meaningless living around us daily, and in an unbelieving, self-centered world, we have come to expect it. But when these same attitudes manifest themselves among people professing to be followers of Jesus, it is alarming. When people who claim allegiance to the Lord have no greater vision than the unbelievers who surround them, it becomes discouraging.

Contagious Enthusiasm

I have become better acquainted with Joe since that first meeting, and I am convinced that his vision for living out the last part of his life is within the reach of everyone. Joe doesn't have perfect health. He actually has some major disabilities that most of us will never have to endure. He doesn't have a financial portfolio providing him with a secure, steady income. The retirement experts whose articles flood our newspapers, magazines, and mailboxes would shake their heads at Joe. He doesn't have anything they say is required for a fulfilling retirement experience. It seems all Joe has is a desire to be used by the Lord in his last days.

The effect of this passionate desire in Joe's life is impossible to miss. I have talked to many older people about their retirement experiences. Neighbors have told me about their new RVs and second homes. I have visited the shuffleboard courts in some of America's retirement spots. I even spent a morning with a neighbor who flies his private airplane once a week just for the fun of it. But I haven't discovered any of them who are as fulfilled as believers like Joe who are pouring their lives into the Kingdom.

Joe isn't alone. Like him, many others are using the final years of their lives for the Lord. Many could afford to live for self. They could take cruises, travel around Europe, or buy another home and enjoy the winter in a warmer climate. But they are choosing, instead, to dedicate their lives to those in spiritual and physical need. In short, they see this time of life as an amazing opportunity to be the hands and feet of Jesus.

Conclusion

About ten years ago I was traveling with one of my children, and we stopped for the night in an area where many older retirees were spending the winter. That evening several of these older folks got together to play games. As the evening progressed, it was obvious to us that this group had spent a lot of time playing games together. At one point my teenage daughter leaned over and whispered, "They remind me of a bunch of teenagers."

I have thought about that comment over the years, and I've concluded that she was right. Teenagers and the older generation have a lot in common. Both tend to have more time and money than they need, and both sometimes forget the opportunity and responsibility that those resources bring. Whether we are young or old, we can use these resources on ourselves and waste a tremendous chance to bless others, or we can recognize the precious opportunity the Lord has placed in our hands and dedicate these resources to Kingdom building. The choice is ours.

Seventeen
Imagine the Possibilities

Even now, many years later, my wife and I still occasionally reminisce about our financial condition in our first few years of marriage. It seemed like regardless of how we tried to scrimp and tighten the screws on our budget, there was always more month than money. It really wasn't because of insufficient income or the high cost of living, however. Most of the difficulty was self-inflicted, and we kept ourselves financially strapped as we tried to pay off debt. We had bought a small house, and the mortgage from that purchase, coupled with debt I had previously incurred, troubled me. Neither of us liked debt, and we put a lot of thought, energy, and focus into eliminating it as quickly as possible.

Whenever we sat down to plan for the future, the debt hung over us. Any enthusiasm regarding potential trips, new furniture, or a better vehicle was always tempered by the constant reminder of that debt. It was like an ominous cloud that shadowed every movement, and I longed to be free from it. Any time there was a little extra cash, it went toward the debt. If we saved a little here or made extra there, it was headed for the debt. It was an unhealthy preoccupation since we didn't focus on giving like we should have, but it did reduce our indebtedness quickly.

As I look back over those years now, something troubles me. Why was it easier for me to focus so intently on eliminating debt than it has been to develop that kind of focus spiritually? Why did I find it easier to give up personal comforts during those early years because of my drive to pay off a loan, than I do to deny my flesh in order to bless the Kingdom of Jesus Christ?

Out of these times of self-examination, another question has surfaced. What could the Lord do with a man who was as passionate about serving the Lord in his later years as I was about paying off debt when I was first married? What if a man entertained no thought of personal gain and possessed no motivation other than the glory of God? Can you imagine the possibilities? What could God do with a man like that? What could He do with a church filled with believers like that?

> *What if a man entertained no thought of personal gain and possessed no motivation other than the glory of God?*

Sometimes we look back to the early church with spiritual nostalgia. Those believers seemed to possess something that we sense is lacking in our congregations. We long for the vibrant, enthusiastic, single-minded focus that seemed to permeate their lives. In our minds we see rows of early Christians all itching for the opportunity to take on the lions. In contrast, we glance at the brother yawning beside us on Sunday morning and become frustrated.

But were the early Christians actually that different? Notice these words of the Apostle Paul as he analyzed the early church. "For all seek their own, not the things which are Jesus Christ's."[a] If this were all Paul had ever written, we could assume that the early church was in a deplorable state. This statement sounds like a disheartened sob from a discouraged old warrior. Maybe the early church wasn't as different from the church today as we sometimes imagine.

But let's look a bit more carefully at Paul's observation of the church. This is part of the letter to the church at Philippi, and the passage is found right between Paul's commendations of two excellent role models. Of Timothy he said, "But ye know the proof of him, that, as a son with the father, he hath served with me in the gospel."[b] Paul was holding Timothy up to the church at Philippi as an example of

---

[a]Philippians 2:21
[b]Philippians 2:22

a saint and a godly role model, and Paul says there was no one quite like him.[c] A little farther on Paul speaks of Epaphroditus. Again Paul describes the kind of man Epaphroditus was when he said to "hold such in reputation: because for the work of Christ he was nigh unto death, not regarding his life."[d]

Can you see what the Apostle Paul is doing here? Even though the church may have had many who seemed halfhearted in their pursuit of the Lord Jesus, Paul was holding up two men as role models. In effect he was saying, "Look at these men. Look at what the power of God has accomplished in their lives, and then visualize what God could do in yours! Imagine the possibilities!"

Battle Fatigue

One of the struggles we face in midlife is battle fatigue. We feel like we have seen about all there is to see and heard about all there is to hear. It takes something pretty astounding to make us perk up and take notice. When we were young, we had high ideals and strong convictions. We stood up for them, debating and defending our positions. But as the years pass, it becomes easier to not get too emotional about anything. When some enthusiastic, spiritually minded young man comes along trying to reform our congregation by next Sunday, we quickly label him an unrealistic idealist. We give him little encouragement and predict that his optimism and energy won't last long, and generally we are right.

But I want to ask something. Do you still believe in the transforming power of the Gospel? Really? Do you still believe that God can take a man off the street in your hometown, completely transform him from the inside out, and make Him a new creature in Christ Jesus? One of the great challenges most believers deal with in midlife is the ability to imagine the possibilities, to retain an unshakable faith in the miracle-working power of God. So when you find older believers who are able to imagine what God can do, I encourage you to make them your role models.

[c]Philippians 2:20
[d]Philippians 2:29-30

Godly Examples

My father was an active minister throughout most of my parents' married life. They traveled frequently, and my mother, an energetic woman, enjoyed this active lifestyle. But in their later years my father was afflicted with dementia, and the life of preaching and traveling they had enjoyed came to a halt.

Suddenly my mother found herself confined at home with a husband who could no longer communicate intelligently. This had a dramatic effect on her. Years went by, and my mother spent her life, day after day, taking care of my father's needs, attempting to make his life as comfortable as possible. Care for him became more and more intense until her life revolved around watching him as one would watch a small child. The shift was traumatic, yet she adjusted to it without complaint.

Then suddenly my father passed away. Again my mother's life changed significantly. My father had become her focal point, and now he was gone. But she again adjusted her focus, volunteering at a local hospital, helping at the church school, and visiting shut-ins. Through all these life changes, she was an example to me of steadfastness and service.

But while her dedication and faithfulness were wonderful, another quality in her life impacted me even more. It was her ability to visualize change—to imagine the possibilities. To her dying day, my mother still believed that people could change, and she wasn't afraid to exhort them to do it. Many times I saw her speak to people in town about their need for the Lord or about what the Bible says regarding divorce and remarriage. She really believed there was hope for them—that they could change. Up to the time of her death, she wasn't afraid to point out weaknesses in my life and give me specific admonition or encouragement. She still believed there was potential for me to improve.

This willingness to speak the truth in love and really believe that God can still effect change in the lives of others is rare. Too many of us lose hope in our older years. We need people who are willing to share the ways that God has transformed their lives and who still believe God can change the lives of others.

Bill has been another powerful role model for me. I first met him about ten years ago, and since then Bill and I have spent many hours together in the country of Haiti. Bill raised his family in America, but later in life felt called to live among the Haitian people. For many years he has lived in a remote area of Haiti, trying to bring change to these impoverished people. From his little house high on a steep mountain hillside, Bill can look down to a lower hilltop where voodoo sacrifices and rituals are conducted. Daily he works with the Haitian people, encouraging them to renounce the demonic powers that surround them and turn to the Lord Jesus.

But there are few places on the globe more discouraging to work than Haiti. Hopelessness and futility hang heavy in the air. Missionaries experience burnout, and after a few years of seeing little change, many become discouraged and are tempted to look for work elsewhere. Nevertheless, Bill has plodded on, year after year. His faithfulness has encouraged many. But again, the element in Bill's life that has blessed me most is his ability to envision what God can do.

To this day, if you come up with an idea that might bless the Haitian people in some way, Bill is willing to try it. When we first began experimenting with a microfinance program in Haiti, few individuals thought it would succeed. Since Bill had as much experience with the Haitian culture as anyone, I asked him for advice. Bill voiced a lot of concern, but he was willing to try. Even though he had reached an age where few people are willing to take risks, Bill could visualize the tremendous impact this program could have on the spiritual and physical lives of these people, and he was willing to give it a try.

Conclusion

The Gospel of Luke tells of a man named Simeon who was alive at the birth of Jesus. The account doesn't say just how old Simeon was, but he must have been very old, because the Bible says, "it was revealed unto him by the Holy Ghost, that he should not see death, before he had seen the Lord's Christ."[e] He was a man still longing for spiritual awakening, and he hadn't given up hope. Simeon still believed that change was possible and that it was just around the corner. The description of this man says that he was "just and devout, waiting for the consolation of Israel."[f]

---

[e]Luke 2:26
[f]Luke 2:25

That verse is inspiring because it tells us that Simeon wasn't just looking back at how things used to be. He wasn't just praying without real belief that change was coming. Instead, he was eagerly waiting for the Lord to perform what He had promised. I wonder if he didn't expectantly pick up each child who was brought into the temple, hoping it would be the one. I wonder if he didn't get up each morning suspecting that this might be the day. Simeon was living in anticipation—he could imagine the possibilities. I wonder if that steadfast faith isn't the reason God chose Simeon to fill this role in the story of Jesus.

As we grow older, we tend to become less idealistic. Our tendency is to view radical change, whether in our life or in someone else's, as increasingly impossible. But it doesn't have to be this way, and thankfully we have some inspiring examples to follow. Don't be afraid to imagine the possibilities!

Eighteen
Who Are You Seeing?

J esus spoke of two groups of people who will stand before Him someday. After describing these groups, Jesus said that the assembly on His left will be doomed to everlasting punishment. The ones on His right, however, will be rewarded with life eternal. He will separate the two groups "one from another, as a shepherd divideth his sheep from the goats."[a]

We are all familiar with this passage, and there are various opinions as to how and when all this will come to pass. But it is interesting to notice in this account that neither group appears to have been seeing things correctly. The one group was chastised because they had failed to feed the hungry, give drink to the thirsty, and house the stranger. They had also failed to clothe the naked, assist the sick, and visit those in prison. Jesus rebuked this group and condemned them to everlasting punishment. They had failed to see how much God valued the needy and unfortunate.

But the other group didn't have perfect vision either. Although they had assisted the needy, there was something they hadn't been fully conscious of. I have heard people try to explain that this group of people hadn't even been aware they were helping. But while helping the hurting can become so natural that believers are hardly aware of all they are doing, it would be difficult to imagine them totally unaware of this amount of activity.

But we don't need to speculate. Jesus didn't say these believers were unaware they were helping; rather, they were not conscious of who they were helping. They were unaware it was the Lord they had been

[a]Matthew 25:32

assisting. When you see the poor and hurting in the world, who are you seeing?

Agnes Bojaxhiu was born in 1910 in Skopje, Macedonia, to a Catholic family, and she became a nun at a young age. While on a trip to India, she was appalled at the living conditions. Agnes visited the slums of Calcutta and felt God was calling her to spend the rest of her life there. Years later she became known as Mother Teresa, and her example of caring for the hurting became legendary. During one of the interviews she gave later in life, a reporter asked why she had chosen to live her life in this way. She responded by saying, "I see God in every human being. When I wash the leper's wounds, I feel I am nursing the Lord Himself."[34]

> *When I wash the leper's wounds, I feel I am nursing the Lord Himself.*
> —Mother Teresa

While I have questions regarding some of Mother Teresa's theology, her perspective on helping the poor was correct. Jesus explained it like this: "Inasmuch as ye have done it unto one of the least of these my brethren, ye have done it unto me."[b] How do you see the poor? How would your response change if you could literally see the face of Jesus as you look at them?

I wonder what the priest and Levite saw as they traveled between Jerusalem and Jericho and came across that man who was half dead. In this parable of the Good Samaritan, Jesus said the priest passed by on the other side of the suffering man. It sounds as though he didn't even want to look. The Levite came along, and at least he took some time to look. But what did he see? How would he have responded if he had seen the Lord instead of a dirty stranger?

Finally the Samaritan came along, and the Bible says he had compassion on the wounded man. Even more than that, it says the Samaritan "went to him, and bound up his wounds, pouring in oil and wine, and set him on his own beast, and brought him to an inn,

---

[b]Matthew 25:40

and took care of him."ᶜ

I don't know if he saw God in the wounded man or not, but he saw opportunity. This man lying along the road had a need, and this Samaritan had the resources to help. I suppose the other two had some good reasons to pass by. They may have even had good religious reasons why they weren't obligated. But this Samaritan wasn't looking at this as an obligation. He was looking for opportunity, and he saw what the others missed.

What Would You Have Done?

We all like to identify with the Samaritan. The priest and Levite seem so cold and calloused. How could anyone see great need like that and just walk on? I don't know how many people were on the road that day, but I have always pictured a desolate setting. How could you just walk off and abandon a man without doing something? But have you ever read this account and seriously thought about how you would have actually responded? Did you ever wonder which of the three really typifies you? How would you have reacted on the road between Jerusalem and Jericho that day?

In December of 1970, psychologists John Darley and Daniel Batson conducted an experiment inspired by the parable of the Good Samaritan. They wanted to find out what determines whether a person will stop to help or keep going in situations like these. Before the study began, each student was given a questionnaire to assess his beliefs regarding stopping to help those in need.

To conduct the study, the researchers gathered a group of forty Princeton University seminary students. They gave half of the students a copy of the parable of the Good Samaritan, telling them they would need to give a talk on this parable in a few minutes. The other half of the group was told they would be giving a short presentation regarding potential employment opportunities for seminary graduates. Both groups were informed they would be giving this presentation in a building a little ways away. Some students were told they needed to hurry to the location where the talk was to be given, and others were

ᶜLuke 10:34

told they had plenty of time.

As each student walked to the building where the presentation was to be given, he passed a poorly-dressed man slumped in a doorway. The man's head was down, his eyes were closed, and he was not moving. As the students passed, the man coughed twice and groaned. During the experiment, the researchers tried changing the situation somewhat, with some students actually needing to step over the groaning man on their way. But in all the scenarios, the results of the study revealed that only one particular feature seemed to matter. It didn't make any difference whether the students were preparing to talk on the parable of the Good Samaritan or not. It didn't even matter how strong their personal convictions were regarding stopping to help the unfortunate. The only factor that made much difference was whether or not they were in a hurry. The results of the study revealed that 63 percent of those who thought they had plenty of time stopped to help. Of the students who were told they needed to hurry, only 10 percent responded to the needy man.

> *The only factor that made much difference was whether or not they were in a hurry.*

Now remember, these were students preparing for the ministry, and half of them were even thinking about the Good Samaritan as they walked. Yet the study revealed that whether or not you are in a hurry has a far greater impact on how you will respond than what you are thinking or your personal feelings on helping others.

Similar studies have been conducted, and they reveal that most of us believe we would do better than average. We know most folks wouldn't stop to help, but somehow we think we would. As our lives speed up, however, our responses become much more self-serving. As one of the researchers commented after the Princeton study, "Ethics becomes a luxury as the speed of our lives increases."[35]

So how would I have responded that day between Jerusalem and Jericho, and how much effect would my full agenda have had on my response? Our lives can become almost breathless as we scurry from appointment to appointment, and frankly, there just isn't time for the man along the road.

Sometimes even our structured church life becomes a distraction to serving. We are so busy responding to the urgent business within the church that there is little time for the needs without. In the rush to be at the next function or meeting, there just isn't time to help the man with the flat tire along the road. Like the priest and the Levite, we pass by on the other side.

Does It Get Better?

As I listen to those who are older, it doesn't sound as though aging eliminates this tendency. Not having regular employment doesn't always reduce a person's hurriedness. Some retired people will tell you they are busier now than ever. So what will help us respond properly to the hurting along the way? What will it take to wake us up to the needs that confront us daily? As I have listened to older believers, a reoccurring theme emerges. Those who see needs and respond to them understand that what they have is not their own.

In the parable of the Good Samaritan, the characters viewed life in different ways. Analyze briefly the different viewpoints that emerge in the story. Then, as you consider them, see which one best describes your view of life.

- **What's yours is mine**. The account says that this man fell among thieves. The thieves were out to get whatever they could in the easiest possible manner. If they thought they could get away with something, they would try it. Do you ever act differently when no one else knows? Would you be more honest on your tax return if your congregation were aware of all the details? Are you ever tempted to take advantage of another in a business deal simply because the other party doesn't have all the facts? If so, maybe this first category fits a certain part of your financial life.

- **What's mine is mine**. The priest and Levite in this account demonstrated this mindset. Legally, there was probably no reason they needed to respond. They chose to view their time as their own, and consequently, there was no good reason to stop. This attitude hits a little closer home. I work hard, and it is easy to believe that what I have earned is mine. My time, money, and abilities are for my benefit. I suspect the priest and Levite could easily have explained why they couldn't stop. Maybe they could have even produced a list of Scriptures to support their position. But the bottom line was that they viewed their time and money as their own, and they saw no need to share with a stranger.

- **What's mine isn't really mine**. The Samaritan demonstrated a totally different paradigm. The first two men's attitudes were self-focused, but the Samaritan understood something that they didn't. He realized he didn't actually own anything, and as he viewed life from this vantage point, everything looked different. He didn't just see an interruption in his day or a problem for his schedule. In this man lying along the road, he saw a fellow human, a man just like himself, created by God and in need. And the great length he went to in responding tells us something else. This wasn't an obligation for him. Instead, it seems the Good Samaritan saw one of God's children and responded as though God Himself was in need.

Conclusion

Who do you see when you observe hurting people? When you bump

WHO ARE YOU SEEING?

shopping carts with the unkempt in the supermarket or see the poorly dressed mother with several scruffy children from uncertain parentage, what are your thoughts? How do you feel as you follow the dilapidated car belching blue smoke and overflowing with trash? Sometimes I wonder if one of our greatest challenges is seeing the poor correctly. It is easy to notice poor hygiene, poor planning, and a poor work ethic; but do we see God's children? It isn't hard to recognize poor choices, lousy parenting skills, or emotional struggles; but can you see Jesus?

> *It's easy to notice poor hygiene, poor planning, and a poor work ethic; but do we see God's children?*

What could our communities look like if we really believed that our resources are not our own? How much could we accomplish in our older years if we actually saw Jesus in the faces of those who struggle and opened our hands to minister to them? I wonder if there won't be an abrupt awakening as we stand before the Lord on that final day. Suddenly it will dawn on us that we had been surrounded by opportunities—many wonderful opportunities—to bless the Lord Himself. Take some time now to reflect on whom you have been seeing when you look at the poor. Seeing the poor correctly has the potential to transform our older years. As Mother Teresa once said, "Each one of them is Jesus in disguise."[36]

Nineteen
A New Focus

While discussing the subject of this book with a brother, he said, "You really need to meet Dale and Betsy!" Just a few days later another person mentioned them, so I knew I needed to hear their story. I had never met Dale or Betsy, but after I talked to them on the phone and explained my project, they agreed to write out their life story. It joined the growing pile on my desk.

A couple months after I had reviewed their story, I tried to contact Dale and Betsy again. Betsy answered the phone, but Dale was unavailable. In fact, he would be gone all day. He was out with his truck and trailer visiting motels and collecting used bedding to send to Third World countries. I hung up even more intrigued. How many eighty-nine-year-old men maintain a truck route and are still focused on blessing the Kingdom like this?

A Super Farmer
Dale was born on a farm in 1921, and since childhood he knew farming was for him. But Dale didn't want to just farm. He longed to be the best. His goal was to have the nicest farm in the area. In his own words, he wanted to be a "super farmer."

Dale and Betsy were married in 1943, and things didn't start out quite as planned. Betsy's father died in June of that year, and since Betsy's mother had a large family and needed help, Dale and Betsy moved in with her family immediately after the wedding to help with the fall harvest. Dale still carried his dream of being a super farmer and continued to watch for an opportunity to get started. World War II was in progress, and many young men were being asked to leave their farms and head for the battlefield. For Scriptural reasons, Dale was opposed to going to war, but he knew the volatile world scene could disrupt his long-term farming plans. If he received a draft notice, he might have to leave the farm and perform alternative service as a conscientious objector.

But in January of 1944, a local farmer offered Dale the opportunity he had been looking for. During those years the government offered what was known as a deferment. If an individual was needed on a farm or involved in some industry deemed important to the war effort, the government exempted him from military service. This local farmer offered Dale a position on his farm along with deferment from the war. This was extremely attractive to Dale, not only because of the deferment, but also because of the farmer who had made the offer. This farmer was a super farmer! Working with this man would be a step toward Dale's goal.

For the next ten years Dale and his young bride worked feverishly. Finally they were able to purchase their own farm, and Dale's feeling of satisfaction grew. His plans were finally falling into place. But Dale and Betsy also wanted to be builders in their church. If someone would have accused them of focusing too heavily on material things, Dale would have objected strongly. They attended church regularly and were well thought of in the community. People regarded them as an up-and-coming Christian couple.

But a series of events forced Dale and Betsy to stop and reevaluate their lives. After ten years of marriage, they lived on their own farm and were experiencing yearly financial growth. They assumed it was God's will for them to continue in the same course. But the Lord had another path in mind for them, and He used some traumatic events to get their attention.

Plagued With Problems
It began when a sudden hailstorm totally destroyed their wheat crop, and their free-range broilers were stolen. Then one of Dale's dangerous Ayrshire bulls got him down in a pen, and although he survived, it was a powerful and sobering wakeup call. Why had he been spared?

Was God trying to get his attention? But these disturbing events didn't end. Four times in quick succession he faced narrow escapes, sometimes almost losing his life.

At the same time, Betsy was involved in a fire and burnt badly. With third-degree burns over a third of her body, she was forced to lie in a hospital for twelve weeks. With both Dale and Betsy recovering from injuries, neither could help the other, and sober thoughts began to penetrate their minds.

Reading their story is like reading the account of Job. Problems came at them in such rapid succession that they were forced to closely examine their goals and ambitions. Was being a super farmer that important? Was this really what God had in mind for them?

Reaching Out

When Betsy returned from the hospital, she and Dale began to review their past and reconsider the future. They began to look beyond themselves and consider needs in other parts of the world. Ultimately, they decided to make a career change. They sold their farm and started a small business that gave them more contact and interaction with the public. They began using their business facility as a place to can food for other countries. Soon they found themselves working on various projects that focused on helping others, both locally and abroad.

Although Dale and Betsy had a growing desire to visit other parts of the world and see the needs there, they also had older parents to take care of. They felt this responsibility was more important than traveling, so they continued serving from home as they assisted their parents through their older years.

But the Lord finally opened the door for them to travel. For many years they had carried a burden for the little country of Haiti, and in 1983 they were able to visit. They had seen the pictures and heard the stories, but Dale and Betsy were totally unprepared for what they experienced. Actually seeing the incredible poverty moved them. They hadn't planned on additional trips, but how could they not respond once they knew about the needs? The next year found them heading back down to help build a school. More trips followed until finally in 1989 they decided to make another major change. Their business had been very successful, but Dale and Betsy decided to sell it to enable them to do what they had been longing to do. The super farmer was moving to Haiti.

A Time of Learning

The next decade was a time of learning for Dale and Betsy. They learned a lot about the Haitian people, but they learned more about themselves. They had thought they were frugal, but they discovered that they really weren't. They witnessed firsthand the difficulties new believers in Haiti have in living out a life of holiness. They realized how easy it had been to draw strong conclusions about individuals across the water when they hadn't had to deal with the struggles those individuals faced.

Dale told of problems they created as they tried to help. They learned that giving free gifts wasn't always beneficial but could in fact be harmful. Many of the lessons they learned would bless them later when they returned to the States and continued trying to assist these struggling people.

During those years they also met people whose examples would change their lives forever. One was a faithful Haitian pastor who was very careful not to live at a higher economic standard than his congregation. Even though he could have afforded a better lifestyle, he didn't want wealth to hinder the Gospel in his desperately poor congregation.

Dale and Betsy moved back to the States transformed. Wealth, possessions, and earthly status had less attraction, and they saw America from a different perspective. To this day Dale marvels at how resources are wasted in pursuits that have no eternal value. On the phone recently he spoke with concern of our selfish focus in this country. He addressed the need many countries have for a Christian witness, and spoke of how much could be accomplished if we could get a vision for using our resources for the Kingdom. Dale also talked of the need for creating more sustainable businesses in these countries. He reminisced about a small food-grinding business he had helped start in Haiti. A Haitian family is still being blessed as they operate this business today. In other villages, small guttering and welding businesses began, allowing young men to provide for themselves and their families.

I hung up the phone inspired, not only by Dale's Kingdom vision, but also by how united Dale and Betsy were in that vision. She wasn't on the phone with us, but he would stop and say, "Betsy said to make sure and tell you this," and he would share something she had mentioned regarding the topic. Both of them know they don't have much time left, yet their joint desire is to exalt the Lord and expand His Kingdom to the very end of their lives.

A Midlife Correction

Dale started out with a selfish vision. He was complying with all that his church and community demanded. He was well thought of, and none of his dreams were considered unacceptable. But God allowed Dale and Betsy to see themselves in a different light. They began to compare their lives to Christ instead of to their culture, and God gave them the opportunity, in midlife, to change course.

Through the series of events that hit them broadside, Dale and Betsy were blessed with the opportunity to deeply examine their lives. God gave them new desires, and when they were finally able to sell their profitable business and live however they wanted, they knew how they wanted to live. They had discovered the emptiness of self-focused living and had found that living for the King was all that really satisfied. The Lord, by His grace, had changed their longings.

Conclusion

Dale and Betsy had no idea the effect their choices would ultimately have on others. They were simply trying to find God's will for their lives day by day. But many lives have been impacted. They could not hide a profitable enterprise, and everyone in their community was aware that upon selling their business they had the means to live however they wanted. Dale and Betsy's choices openly demonstrated their desires. Their neighbors watched them live frugal lives and focus their resources on the Kingdom, and so did those within their church fellowship. Young men and women in their church also have had dreams of accumulating wealth and being successful by society's standards. One young man shared with me how their godly example had changed his life's vision and goals.

Another group of people who have been blessed by Dale and Betsy's choices are the Haitians. They saw Dale and Betsy give up lives of ease in America to live Kingdom-focused lives among them. This example of self-denial wasn't lost on the Haitian people.

As you consider your future plans, don't settle for less than God intended for you. Don't assume the best years of life are gone and all that is left to do is coast to the finish. Many years ago the prophet Habakkuk cried out to God, "O Lord, revive thy work in the midst of the years."[a] Today we need more people like Dale and Betsy who are willing to make midlife changes. We need men and women who still cry out to God for revival and renewal, even as they approach the end of their lives.

---

[a]Habakkuk 3:2

PART FOUR
A Time to Demonstrate

Twenty
Is This Really Worth It?

D uring long winter evenings while our children were growing up, we would discuss potential backpacking trips. We had books telling of the wonders of high mountain lakes, and it was enjoyable to hike from the armchair. It seemed the more difficult the hike, the more attractive the pictures and descriptions of the potential locations. And so we were always torn. We had been on enough hikes to know the reality of sore legs and backs, yet the descriptions sounded so compelling. Phrases like "the sound of crashing water cascading over sheer granite cliffs" would draw us in, and sitting by the fire, it was easy to commit to hikes that were probably a little out of our league.

Some of those hikes are still etched in my memory. One such hike was to Robin Lake. Robin Lake is perched high in the Cascade Mountains a little over six thousand feet above sea level, and the trail that snakes up the side of the mountain to it is designated as strenuous. Of course, as mentioned, none of this looks too difficult when everyone is excited, the pictures in the book are impressive, and the author is an optimist. Somehow, sitting in a comfortable chair by the fire, the fish in the lake get longer and the trail becomes flatter.

> *Somehow, sitting in a comfortable chair by the fire, the fish in the lake get longer and the trail becomes flatter.*

The day finally arrived for the hike to Robin Lake. There are always a few sobering moments when backpacking. One is when your pack starts to feel overweight and your shoulders begin to ache, but your vehicle is not yet out of sight. I have never yet completed a hike without, at some point along the rugged trail, doubting my sanity.

And traveling with small children only increases the challenge. You not only must carry your own pack, but you also must feed the children a steady stream of encouragement lest you be required to carry theirs as well. About every five minutes comes the inevitable question, "Daddy, how much farther is it?" I would try to make confident comments to spur them on, but after a few hours of, "I don't think it's that much farther," the children have lost confidence in Daddy's ability to judge distance. But when we finally crest the last hill and see the campsite, the pain of the trail is forgotten. It is worth it all!

What children (and fathers) really long for while hiking is the opportunity to meet other hikers. There is nothing like meeting someone on the trail returning from the place where you are headed. It is even better if they say, "You're just about there, and it's a wonderful place to camp!"

As we hiked toward Robin Lake that morning, we knew the first portion was the easy part. We also knew the last two hours of the hike would be totally different. The book said this last section was unmaintained and very rugged. Now, as we approached that final leg, we were somewhat apprehensive. We stopped to rest, and frankly, we were already tired. We had left the truck three hours before, and the realization that the worst was yet to come was a bit overwhelming. But it was too far to go back, and the day was getting hotter, so we again shouldered our packs and prepared to attack the rugged path that seemed to climb straight up the mountain.

Just as we were preparing to climb, we saw some movement up ahead, and to our great joy we spied a fellow hiker coming down the very path we were preparing to ascend. This was good news. Not only could we get firsthand information about how bad the trail really was, it also gave us a few more minutes to rest.

As we waited for the hiker to descend, I could see the anticipation on my children's faces. Hope flickered across their faces. Maybe the trail wasn't as hard as they imagined. Possibly it was even shorter than the book said. Their hopes were pinned on this approaching stranger's report. As he got closer, it was clear that this man was an experienced hiker. From his lightweight sleeping bag and expensive hiking shoes to the spandex outfit and aluminum walking stick, the message was clear: he took hiking seriously. I am sure we looked like a ragtag crew with our borrowed gear, regular clothes, and overweight packs. Unlike us, this man was equipped to hike.

The children began to pepper him with questions while he was still a good distance away. "So, what's the trail like? Is it steep all the way?" The man didn't respond until he had come all the way down, and then he stopped, caught his breath, and looked the children in the eyes. They anxiously scanned his face, hoping for some ray of hope. "That trail," he replied slowly and deliberately, "is brutal!"

Brutal

I suddenly understood what Moses must have felt like with the Egyptians behind him and the Red Sea ahead. I watched as the last remaining molecule of enthusiasm for hiking departed from my children's faces. They had already suggested that areas we were hiking through would be good places to stop. And who wants to lug overweight packs up a mountain during the heat of the day when the trail ahead has been described as brutal?

But fortunately, the man on the trail didn't stop with that comment. Maybe seeing the children's faces caused him to commiserate with us. Or maybe it was the look of sudden panic that washed across the face of their weary father. Thankfully, he went on to say, "The path is very difficult, but when you get to the lake, it will be worth it!" This was just what we needed, and we were ready to go again. That trail was brutal, and we had to stop several times during the next couple of hours to remind ourselves of the man's encouragement. But we did make it, and it was worth the hike!

Many young families feel a little like my children on the trail that day. They are in the heat of the battle, and the day seems long. Mothers grow weary of the daily grind. They are dealing with laundry to wash, a house to clean, and clothes to mend. They constantly have to play referee in the midst of childhood squabbles. On top of this, they feel the pressure of knowing that they should be spending more time teaching Biblical values to these children who will soon be gone. The magnitude of the task and the abundance of pressing needs can be overwhelming. Sometimes they stop in the middle of a busy day and ask, "Is this worth it?" Like my children, these mothers are sometimes tempted to give up, to abort the original plan and just stop at a quiet place along the trail. Secretly they long to lose themselves in some novel that allows them to escape the reality of their responsibilities. They wonder if the battle is worth it.

Our young fathers are also tempted at times to give up the fight. Attempting to provide enough income for the family, do general maintenance around the house, and encourage a tired wife can seem overwhelming. And then there are nagging fears that they are not the spiritual leaders they should be. They know the importance of a vibrant family devotional time and how essential it is for children to be taught from the Word. Yet when they sit down with the family for times like these, they feel inadequate.

They suspect other fathers are doing a much better job of teaching and training, and they are tempted to become discouraged. Sometimes they wonder if all the effort is really worth it. They toy with the thought of escape. Some seek relief by pursuing a hobby or sport. Others are tempted to buy that boat or take that trip, subconsciously hoping for relief from the battle. In the heat of fighting for the Kingdom, they wonder: *Is this really worth it?*

These embattled, weary young warriors limp into church Sunday morning needing to refuel and reconnect with the Lord. The battle between the spirit and flesh is fierce, and these young parents long to be victorious. Society and their own flesh tell them, "Relax and retreat with a novel," or "Go ahead and buy that boat." When they come to church, they are searching for spiritual nourishment and reinforcement that can help them overcome these temptations.

But these young fathers and mothers are doing something else. They are watching those who have been on the trail longer, scanning the faces and lives of those of us who are older, and they want to know. Is it worth it? Is it worth giving up present pleasure to live for the Kingdom? Is it worth passing up all these enticing diversions? There are less difficult paths with more inviting places to stop along the way. Why stay on this rougher path when there are so many easier options? The trail looks long and hard. Is Kingdom living really worth the fight?

I wonder sometimes if we understand the impact our decisions have on our young families. When a grandfather reaches the time in life when he can do whatever he wants, and he chooses to pour his time and money into some hobby or travel for pleasure, what is he telling those looking on? When a grandmother chooses to while away her time reading novels or doing crossword puzzles, what kind of message is going out to young struggling mothers? Do our actions tell the younger generation that the battle is worth it? Does our lifestyle reveal that Jesus is enough for us and that the world around us has nothing to offer?

Conclusion

You need to ask yourself a question as you look ahead to the final years of life: Is Jesus enough? Are you really finding your fulfillment in Him? You will not be able to fool the generation that follows. They are watching where you go, what you drive, and how you furnish your home. You may have the correct theology and a keen understanding of church history. But what those observing really want to know is this: Is Kingdom living worth it?

Do you understand the pressures our young parents feel? Can you comprehend how difficult it can be for them to consistently make counter-culture choices? Can you remember that time in your life? While they experience many of the same difficulties you endured, today there are additional pressures. Affluence coupled with electronic gadgets, instant communication, and an increasingly godless society has turned up the heat.

These young parents know the trail is rough. You won't need to remind them that the path is steep and difficult. They are well aware of the weariness of the way. What our young families really long for are older ones who say, by word and by example, "Yes, the trail is brutal, but it's worth it!"

Twenty-One
A Single, Sanctified Vision

Soon after my wife and I were married, we began occasionally visiting Joyce. Joyce was an older single sister, well known in our community for frugality and an interest in spiritual things. She always parked her ancient car in the exact same spot at church, and it was hard to miss. By the time I was a teenager, the vehicle was a relic almost forty years old. To the young boys standing around after church, who had no appreciation for antiques, her old clunker was nothing to be desired.

But as I grew older, I learned to appreciate something about Joyce, and that was her love for the Word of God. The first time we went to visit her, she described her reading schedule. It was something like three times through the entire Bible each year with several more times through the New Testament for good measure. She did confess, with an embarrassed shake of her head, that recently, due to health issues, she hadn't been keeping up. If I remember correctly, the reason for her shame was that she had dropped from three to two annual readings through the Bible!

In addition to her love for the Word, Joyce was known for her views on prophecy. She had her very own unique twist on end-time events—so unique that she didn't know of one other person on the globe who agreed with her. Not one!

On our second visit to her home, Joyce had a little table set up in front of her fireplace with three chairs and three Bibles. The evening's agenda was clear. After discussing several Scriptural topics, I asked a question regarding prophecy. That was all it took. She started back in Genesis and walked us through the Bible, explaining her viewpoint as we went. We didn't stop until we got to the maps in the back. She knew her Bible!

My wife and I thoroughly enjoyed the evening, and we came away with a great respect for this older sister. It wasn't because we agreed with her view of prophecy. In fact, I couldn't even explain it today. And it wasn't due to a charismatic personality or her persuasive defense of her opinion. Rather, it was because of her single-minded focus. Her mind was obviously on her Lord. She loved Him and was attempting to follow Him with everything she had. And in spite of her strange conclusions regarding prophecy, there was something refreshing about a single sister who hadn't been reading or following anyone else's prophetic views. Joyce had just continued to read her Bible until future events were clear in her mind. She had cheerfully ignored all the opposing views and stuck to what she believed.

When individuals finally begin to slow down, it is interesting to observe what they cling to. I have seen older people hang onto a few little trinkets that remind them of a trip or a special event in their lives. Some people surround themselves with family pictures, cards from grandchildren, or cherished items belonging to a deceased spouse. But with Joyce it was different. When her health began to fail, she made a conscious choice to dispose of almost everything she had. In fact, she confided in another older sister that she wanted to keep only three things. All she wanted was her bed, her phone, and her Bible. At the end of her life, she didn't want distractions. She wanted to focus on what was most important to her, and she became a shining example of the effects of a single vision. There is something extremely powerful about watching older saints with this single vision. Watching them focus on the approaching harbor gives courage to those who are still battling the storm.

Recently a young brother was traveling through our area and wanted to talk, so we met at a local restaurant for lunch. We chatted about a few things, and then,

> *Watching older saints focus on the approaching harbor gives courage to those who are still battling the storm.*

after a moment of silence, he looked me in the eye and asked, "Gary, is fasting a part of your life?" Now, the question was a little unusual. Many of us have grown up trying to take Jesus' warnings literally, and we don't normally go around talking about how much we fast. But this brother went on to explain the reason for his question. He had been asking older brothers in his church whether or not fasting was part of their lives, and their responses had been discouraging. Some had said fasting was practiced more in Bible times, and others had tried to avoid the question altogether. This young brother was reading Jesus' teachings. His words indicate that fasting will be part of the believer's life in the last days. In three of the Gospels Jesus explicitly said that in the days after He was taken away, His followers would fast.[a] As my friend compared this with the lack of fasting among the older members of his congregation, he was concerned.

As I listened to this young brother over lunch that day, one thing became clear to me. Fasting was not really the issue. His real concern was much deeper. This young brother was searching for genuine, authentic Christianity. He wanted the real thing. He had a young family, and he wanted to make sure the people he was following were actually following Christ. He knew it was possible for a church to become so preoccupied with its history and culture that it loses sight of the Lord Jesus. He was searching for older believers whose lives demonstrated a single vision—a focus on the Lord Jesus Himself. As he looked at those ahead of him, he wasn't sure whom they were following.

I don't know how old a person needs to be to sound an alarm or to admonish those who are older. Most of us probably never reach a point where we feel comfortable doing this. But there are a growing number of young, serious-minded believers among us, and I believe a warning needs to go out to the older generation. In the words of Job, "Great men are not always wise: neither do the aged understand judgment."[b] There are many illustrations of this truth, not only in the Bible, but also in life. Most of us have observed those who were zealous for the Lord in their youth but in old age lost their courage, zeal, and eventually even their faith. If you are one of the older ones in

[a]Matthew 9:15, Mark 2:20, Luke 5:35
[b]Job 32:9

your church community, I ask that you humbly consider the following four issues.

1. A focus on Jesus' teachings. I see a great interest in our young families in returning to a focus on living out the basic teachings of Jesus. They want to use those teachings not just to support their practices but as a source of guidance for daily life. The young brother's question regarding fasting is a prime example. I think most of our churches would say fasting is a good idea. But is it actually practiced? Today emotional needs abound, and our first response seems to be a search for the right pill or a counseling center that has an opening. There is a place for both medicine and counseling, but could we start with fasting, prayer, and anointing with oil? Where in the Gospels or the early church do we find that medicine was the first remedy to be tried? Perhaps we should begin addressing specific needs by times of prayer, anointing, and public fasting.

2. Appreciation for tradition. There is a tendency in our culture for youth to disparage tradition, and sometimes this creeps into our churches as well. Some seem to be eagerly looking for new ways to do just about everything. Sometimes this is driven by a hidden desire to embrace more of what the world has to offer, and this is rightly alarming to those who are older. But before you condemn the young person in your congregation who

> *There is a place for both medicine and counseling, but could we start with fasting, prayer, and anointing with oil?*

desires to make some changes, take time for prayerful discernment. Many of the young families I have listened to are not just on a quest for more freedom. They aren't looking for an opportunity to pitch everything from the past. They recognize the value in some of the traditions handed down to them. But neither are they interested in hanging onto a practice simply because it has always been done. Tradition can be a great stabilizing force in the church, but it can also be a hindrance to spiritual growth. The Bible addresses both of these truths. Paul encouraged the church at Thessalonica to keep the traditions they had been taught,[c] yet Jesus gave strong warning to the Pharisees regarding the traditions they were keeping.[d] Obviously there are traditions that help and others that hinder. The value of some worthwhile traditions is not always immediately clear, and younger people should be cautious about recklessly dismantling them. On the other hand, spiritually minded young families sometimes have legitimate concerns, and the validity of certain traditions may need to be prayerfully reconsidered. Some may object to messing with a structure that seems to be working. But if its supporters are no longer seeking God's face by prayer and fasting, is it really working?

3. Respect and appreciation for other Bible-believing fellowships.
At some time or other almost every conservative church verbally attacks the positions of other groups in order to substantiate their own. For some reason we decide that promoting truth is not enough, and we resort to identifying flaws in surrounding fellowships. It is true that heresy must be exposed. The Bible is clear that church leadership is to be vigilant in warning against ungodly teaching and practices. Much of Paul's writing attempts to refute heresy that had already crept into the church. But there are many ways to live out Biblical principles. Younger members of our churches often grow concerned when the focus in preaching shifts from Biblical truth to attacks on other believers who are practicing Biblical principles slightly differently.

We need to teach the principles behind our practices. Our children and grandchildren need to be taught why we have chosen the particular methods we have for living out Biblical teachings. But can we do that without tearing others down? Can we humbly admit that we are not superior but simply doing the best we know? Even more than this, can we be humble enough to ask advice of other fellowships? Can we admit that our understanding may not be complete?

Make no mistake. This is not a call to blindly accept anyone walking around under the banner of Christianity. We are in a time of insidious deception, and we need to be extremely vigilant. But in the

[c]2 Thessalonians 2:15
[d]Mark 7:13

battle, let's make sure we are fighting heresy and not different parts of the body of Christ!

4. Separation from the world is all-inclusive. It is sometimes easy for a fellowship to select easily definable criteria to indicate separation from the world. These criteria might be things like certain cuts of clothing or particular types or colors of vehicles. While the rationale for making these choices may be valid, over time these items can become "separation-from-the-world indicators." If a person fits the criteria, they are deemed to be separate from the world and vice versa. When young people begin to question this method of ascertaining separation, they may find that these questions alone label them as a troublemaker or lover of this world.

As I have listened to and observed many in this younger generation, however, I have concluded that they are interested in a higher level of separation from the world, not lower. They have seen too many individuals in conservative settings who have learned how to comply with a few baseline rules while living worldly lives. Such individuals tend to obey the required criteria to prove their sanctification, but then, as though their tithe has been paid, they feel free to live the rest of their lives for themselves. But I see a new generation emerging that wants more. They are searching for older people who believe in a separation of heart that affects every part of life, not just a few arbitrary areas. It is not that they are afraid of standards, but they are looking for more than strict adherence to a code. They want to follow older believers who desire to unite every part of their lives with one single, sanctified vision.

Conclusion

Henry Varley, the well-known evangelist, inspired Dwight L. Moody to give himself more wholly to the service of the Lord. They were sitting on a park bench in Dublin when Varley said, "The world has yet to see what God will do with and for and through and in and by the man who is fully consecrated to Him."[37] Those words greatly influenced Moody. Varley hadn't said that God needs great men or educated men; He just needs men who are fully consecrated to Him. Moody resolved that day on the park bench to be that man.

Henry Varley was a mentor who challenged Moody to higher ground. I hear a cry for such mentors coming from our younger generation. While youth are often idealistic, I don't think they are searching for perfection. Instead, they are looking for mentors who have purposed in their hearts to finish well and to demonstrate a single, sanctified vision until they're gone.

Twenty-Two
Potential to Influence

Mark scanned the rows ahead of him again. He knew he should be listening to the sermon, but his mind was preoccupied. Up and down the rows his eyes wandered, searching and analyzing as he went. Finally he forced his eyes back to the minister, but his mind was far from the message.

For several weeks now Mark had been troubled by a thought, and today his mind just wouldn't let it rest. He had been thinking about the reality of aging. His children were getting older, and as he contemplated the future, he wondered what life would be like after they were on their own. What effects would aging have on him? How would it affect his spiritual life?

In response to his ponderings, Mark decided to take a look at the older men in his congregation. He specifically considered those who had not been called to positions of leadership. Mark had a high regard for his leaders, but since he himself hadn't been called to lead, he wanted to look for good role models among laymen like himself. And so, as Mark scanned the older men around him, he was trying to discern what was ahead for him. Somehow he found himself discouraged.

The men he observed were all good men. They were men you could trust for advice on farming or business. They were men you could deal with and know they would be honest. And they were friendly men. In fact, most of them were fun to be around. They enjoyed a good story, and most of them were fond of practical jokes. But Mark was after more than that. He could think of a good many unbelievers in the community with those qualifications. No, Mark was searching for men who were aware of the spiritual warfare around them and were actively engaged in the battle. He was looking for men who read their Bibles and carried a verse or an encouraging thought to share with fellow believers. Actually, he would have been satisfied to find older men who just wanted to be like this even if they hadn't yet attained it. But Mark left the service that day disappointed. He saw men who were in good favor with their church but who seemed to have little interest in spiritual vibrancy and growth.

Perhaps Mark was unfair in his assessment. He admitted these were good men. Maybe they had hidden qualities he hadn't seen, and he was just stuck in Elijah mode, foolishly supposing he was the only one left.

I don't know Mark or the men in his congregation very well, and as I listened to him, some of these possibilities went through my mind. Maybe he was being uncharitable and too critical in his analysis. But regardless, two things were clear. Older men were being analyzed, and it was affecting those who were younger.

Unrecognized Sway

We each have the potential to encourage or discourage others in the battle. I remember, as a young man, holding a high opinion of a particular couple in my local congregation. This brother seemed spiritually stable and confident in what he believed. He and his wife demonstrated what I wanted when I became older. As a young man, I had many questions, felt insecure, and longed for the day when I would no longer find myself wavering on so many issues. The fascinating thing about this memory is that the couple I admired was probably only in their thirties at the time. Unknown to me, they probably had as many questions as I did. They had no idea that anyone was looking to them as an example of stability and strength.

I was in my mid-thirties when I suddenly realized that someone could be watching me in the same way. I remembered my youth when I had admired the older couple, and I realized that, although I was now the same age as they had been, I didn't feel the confidence I had assumed they possessed. But that didn't change the fact that others could be looking to me as an example.

For better or worse, others are looking up to you. As you approach the latter years of your life, it is important that you consider this. But

> *For better or for worse, others are looking up to you.*

don't just consider and marvel at this truth. Resolve to use the coming years to influence others for the Kingdom. Let me share a few examples of role models that either discouraged or encouraged those who were observing their lives.

I hadn't known Ivan very long when I began to work with him. Ivan was much older than I and a leader in a local church, so I looked forward to the opportunity to learn from him. Our job provided plenty of opportunities for discussion, and for several days I asked Ivan about particular Scriptures or his opinion regarding some spiritual issue of the day. I was trying to raise a family, so occasionally I asked for advice in training children. But I soon found that Ivan had little to say. It seemed no matter how hard I tried, I never could get him to give much of an opinion. He just didn't seem interested. After a few days of attempting to start conversations, I concluded that Ivan was just a quiet man, and I was asking too many questions.

Soon after that another event complicated my conclusion. A visitor walked onto the jobsite one day, and as he talked to me about the project, he made a passing comment about his interest in collecting toy tractors. Ivan was quietly working nearby, seemingly paying little attention. But the remark concerning toy tractors instantly brought his work to a stop. He soon came over and got involved in the conversation, and I learned two things.

I learned that Ivan also had a great interest in collecting toy tractors, and I learned that Ivan could talk. Personally, I had little knowledge regarding the topic, and I could never have guessed that two adults could talk so long about antique toy tractors. I wasn't even aware there was enough information available to keep a discussion going, but there was. Not only was there enough information, Ivan became very excited and animated in sharing his opinions.

I don't remember just how long this discussion continued, but it was enlightening. My failure to start a discussion with Ivan had nothing to do with his inability to talk. It wasn't because he didn't have opinions or things he could share. I just hadn't hit the right topic. Even though Ivan was a leader in his church and was occasionally called upon to preach from the Bible, the Word of God didn't really seem to be his primary interest. Ivan seemed to be a good man, and I enjoyed working with him. But his passion was toy tractors.

A brother once hosted an older couple in his home. This couple had traveled a couple thousand miles to visit, and the host asked his guests what they would enjoy doing during their time together. The guests said they really enjoyed looking for dolls, so the next day they shopped all day. The host took them from one antique store to another as they hunted for dolls. He shared later how it would have been easier to take the day off work if the dolls were at least something the couple's grandchildren could have played with. But these were expensive dolls, the kind displayed on glass shelves for others to admire. This older couple had amassed quite a number of these and were excited about expanding their collection.

While incidents like this can be discouraging, I have also had the opposite experience. I spent a couple of days, years ago, with an elderly Hutterite man. He was visiting from a colony on the East coast, and I asked about the spiritual vitality of the older saints in his community. His answer has encouraged me many times. "As believers in our community grow older," he said, "their interest in spiritual things grows much stronger. The closer you get to heaven, the less this old world has to offer!"

> *The closer you get to heaven, the less this old world has to offer!*

What a testimony from an old soldier! It has been many years since I spoke with him, but I can still visualize the look on his face and picture the way his eyes lit up as he talked. It was evident this world had less pull on him every day. He was drawing closer to the harbor, and as the end drew nearer, his vision was getting clearer. He was going home!

This short discussion made a lasting impression on me. This man had something I wanted. I wanted to end my journey with that same level of excitement and joy. I wanted to be that confident that turning my back on the worthless tinsel of this world was the right thing to do. The man had used this opportunity to influence and encourage me in Kingdom living.

These incidents have made me ask some soul-searching questions. When I am older and younger ones are looking to me for guidance, what will they conclude that my passion is? What will I enjoy talking about, and what subject will excite me?

A Passing Comment

Fred grew up knowing his family was probably the poorest in their church. From time to time the church needed to help Fred's family financially due to a medical or business situation. It seemed like no matter how hard his father worked, there was never enough money to go around. One day Fred overheard one of the men from his church make a negative comment regarding his father's ability to provide for his family. Fred was engulfed in shame and embarrassment. As he related this experience to me many years later, the pain was obviously still very real. "Hearing that comment made me so mad," Fred said, "that I resolved then and there that someday I was going to be richer than that entire congregation put together." He was determined to show that someone in his family could be successful. And Fred did it. He was a millionaire before he was thirty. But now that he had arrived financially, Fred was discovering how foolish he had been. He had put too much emphasis on proving the assessment of that older individual wrong, and his reaction had almost destroyed his spiritual life. A passing comment had changed his life's direction.

In 1964 a young man named Don Stephens was on a mission trip in the Caribbean with a program called Summer of Service. He went with typical youthful zeal, hoping to change the world in one trip. Don was just nineteen years old at the time, and he had no idea his team was heading right into the path of a hurricane. The hurricane hit with a vengeance, and Don found himself hunkered down in a British World War II airplane hangar, hoping the creaking structure would survive the storm.

After the storm subsided, Don and the other young people went outside to survey the damage. They were shocked. These youth had come expecting to improve the lives of these poor people, but they hadn't expected to witness anything like this! As they viewed the devastated homes and the desperate need for medical help, Don overheard a teenage girl make a passing comment that changed his life and the lives of many others. As she observed the lack of emergency facilities, the girl commented, "Wouldn't it be wonderful if there were a ship with doctors and nurses that could come in after such a disaster?"[38]

Don knew nothing about ships. He was from the mountains of Colorado, far from the ocean. For some reason, however, that little observation kept circling in his mind. Years later Don founded Mercy Ships. His organization provides medical care, relief aid, and training to developing nations. Today Mercy Ships operate in Third World ports around the world. Yet just a brief observation by a teenage girl planted the idea in Don Stephens' mind. She probably never knew the tremendous impact of her passing comment.

Your life is going to influence others. It may be through just a thoughtless comment. But the question you need to ask yourself is this: Will the rest of my life point others toward the Kingdom of Jesus Christ or lead them closer to the kingdom of this world?

Conclusion

A passage in the seventy-first Psalm inspires me as I ponder my potential to influence others as I grow older. The writer says, "O God, thou hast taught me from my youth: and hitherto I have declared thy wondrous works. Now also when I am old and grayheaded, O God, forsake me not; until I have shewed thy strength unto this generation, and thy power to every one that is to come."[a]

I love the focus of this passage. The burden of the Psalmist was that he could still proclaim God's faithfulness even as he grew older. His eyes were not on his own wellbeing. His primary concern wasn't whether or not his older years would be enjoyable and fulfilling for him. He was focused on blessing the Kingdom and the generation following. What an encouraging example of Kingdom living!

---

[a]Psalm 71:17-18

Twenty-Three
Not Many Fathers

"Gary, could you come in here? I want to talk to you." These words from my father were normally followed by a sober silence. Toys, games, and books were suddenly forgotten. Being summoned to my father's study usually meant I had crossed a line and something serious was to be discussed. I wish I could say that my life was so upright and infractions so rare that I knew which rule I had disobeyed when the summons came. But the truth is that I could usually imagine several possibilities on my way to the study. The study was just off our living room, and my father spent a good deal of his time there, reading and preparing for sermons. It was a small room, and the close proximity added to the solemnity of these occasions.

A lot of teaching occurred in that little study. This wasn't just a time when my father shared a general lesson or casually mentioned that I might try to improve a little in my behavior. No, the teaching I received in the study was to the point. When the door was shut, my father didn't beat around the bush. He informed me quickly why I was there, and when I departed, I was well aware how things should be done differently in the future. I knew my father loved me and cared about my direction in life, but I also grew up knowing he wasn't afraid to give a loving rebuke.

Rebuke

Rebuke isn't a popular topic today. Tolerance seems to be the current buzzword. You can believe whatever you want, do whatever you wish, and live however you please. There are no absolutes. No one has the right to determine what is right or wrong, and each person determines

165

his own standard for what is acceptable. But strangely enough, there is one exception. Somehow the same culture that declares there is no absolute standard of right and

> *Somehow the same culture that declares there is no absolute standard of right and wrong has developed a standard of its own.*

wrong has developed a standard of its own: No one has a right to impose his paradigm on another, and it is wrong to rebuke others. This seems to be one of the only absolutes remaining in our society.

The end result is that rebuke has fallen into disgrace. What right do you have to tell anyone else what he should or should not do? After all, the logic goes, each of us has the right to determine for ourselves what is right and wrong. This logic pervades our society. The Bible is no longer the standard, and consequently, our daily newspapers read like the book of Judges where "every man did that which was right in his own eyes."[a] I am concerned that this logic doesn't only exist in society. The church at large has also lost its ability to rebuke.

The Apostle Paul, in an appeal to the church at Corinth, said, "I write not these things to shame you, but as my beloved sons I warn you. For though ye have ten thousand instructors in Christ, yet have ye not many fathers."[b] Obviously, Paul noticed an astounding ratio between the two, but what is the difference between an instructor and a father?

Maybe Paul was saying many men will tell you how things should be done, but few will actually live out what they teach. Or maybe he was saying that a father has stronger love than an instructor. When a son chooses a dangerous path, a father keeps loving him and reaching out to him. These are good explanations, but I wonder if Paul was also pointing to another way in which fathers differ from teachers. Perhaps he was saying that a father loves enough to rebuke.

This passage precedes Paul's rebuke of the church at Corinth for their tolerance of open immorality. He seems to be pleading for them

---

[a]Judges 17:6
[b]1 Corinthians 4:14-15

to consider that a father loves enough to address and rebuke sin. Many are willing to make general statements about how things should be. But few care enough to confront you, look you in the eye, and lovingly point out an error in your life.

Abundant Teaching

Never in the history of Christianity has so much instruction been available. In addition to good teaching in most of our churches each Sunday, we have Christian bookstores full of "how to" books. Professing believers go to great lengths to attend another seminar that promises to provide the missing ingredient in their Christian experience or marriage. Our mailboxes bring a flood of religious magazines, newsletters, and periodicals. There is no shortage of teaching and instruction.

Technology has brought even more resources. Hours can be spent listening to spiritual messages, Christian music, and even the Word of God itself. Thousands of websites offer religious teaching and try to help believers find victory in Christ. A person can go online and find teaching on just about any subject. While at times it seems people turn to Google rather than God, for some people, technology has been a tremendous blessing. Muslim seekers around the globe are connecting with Christians and finding answers to their questions. And while there is plenty of erroneous teaching online, it cannot be denied that there is also good teaching available to the discerning seeker.

But I wonder if the ratio between instructors and fathers is any better today. As the Apostle Paul concluded his instructions to Titus on godly conduct for believers, he said, "These things speak, and exhort, and rebuke with all authority."[c] Most of us are accustomed to good speaking and exhortation from willing and capable pastors. They can take the Bible each Sunday and capably apply Biblical teaching.

But I wonder sometimes where the mature believers are who care enough to rebuke. It is easy to lay this responsibility on leadership, but maybe all of us are partly to blame. Generally, my failure to rebuke isn't because I love my brother too much, but too little.

Recently I heard a young brother say, "I don't like being reproved.

---

[c] Titus 2:15

In fact, I am scared of it. But I am absolutely terrified of living in a community where no one cares enough to rebuke."

Examine your own congregation for a moment. What would happen if you became covetous and started acquiring more and more unneeded possessions—not items that violate a church standard, but just unnecessary things? How long would it be before someone came to you and lovingly addressed the issue, not in a casual, joking way, but seriously, out of concern for your soul? Or what about time spent seeking personal pleasure? How far could you go in pursuing a hobby before someone cared enough to speak up?

Turn this around. How soon would you speak up if you observed a dangerous trend in a brother or sister? As you grow older, are you planning to be only an instructor? Will you be content to just share an occasional devotional when called upon or a public prayer now and then when asked? Or are you willing to help fill the void in the church today and be a father?

> *Generally, my failure to rebuke isn't because I love my brother too much, but too little.*

Warriors Welcome Rebuke

Several years ago I was working on a construction project in a large jail. Working in a jail can be challenging. Guards go to great lengths to make sure the inmates do not have access to anything that could be used as a weapon. Yet we started each project by dragging all kinds of potentially dangerous tools into this secure environment. We were involved in several projects there, and at the beginning of each one, the guards gave us some training, reminding us of the importance of keeping our tools close and accounted for. But after hearing the same instructions many times, it was easy to forget the seriousness of the situation.

One day as we left for lunch, I neglected to return a screwdriver to the locked toolbox. When I returned, I was severely scolded for my negligence by an angry guard. He was all but shouting as he reminded me that my mistake could have cost someone's life. Needless to say, I was much more careful after that.

Was the guard justified in reprimanding me severely? Of course he was. My negligence could have had serious repercussions. But let's change the scenario. Suppose this same guard would have stopped at my house, walked into my garage, and chewed me out for leaving a screwdriver on my workbench. Would he be justified?

These two examples are completely different. A screwdriver left lying in a jail can be deadly, while one left on a garage workbench may only reveal my lack of organization. One calls for firm and serious rebuke; the other doesn't.

Perhaps the primary reason we fail to rebuke today is because we're unaware of danger. In the middle of pleasant prosperity, we tend to forget that we are involved in warfare. And once we forget the battle, there is no real reason to get excited. What does it matter if a brother gets a little caught up in materialism or chooses to waste his time and resources on a hobby? It's not that big a deal. Besides, if I rebuke him for something in his life, he might start analyzing mine! But when we really comprehend that we are engaged in active warfare and under attack, we desire warnings. Rebuke in the midst of warfare is welcome!

Several months ago I attended a meeting, and at the beginning of the presentation the speaker asked each of us to jot down four people in our lives who had influenced us most, excluding family. After I had written four names, I reviewed my list. I suddenly realized that all four of these men had rebuked me. I hadn't always liked it, and sometimes it had taken me a while to appreciate it. But these men cared enough to confront me. They had been fathers in my life.

Conclusion

Do you really care about those who are coming behind? Do you love them enough to speak the truth to them? Can you share with them, not in a condescending or judgmental way, but in true Christian love?

Relationship must precede rebuke. Most of us have heard the little quip, "People don't care how much you know until they know how much you care." Don't let familiarity with that quote diminish its truth. The church does not need more people who analyze and find fault. It needs older men and women who invest in the lives of others and care enough to rebuke when necessary.

As you contemplate living out the last half of your life, I encourage you to be a father. Take the time to build relationships with younger believers in your congregation. Be willing to humbly share your failures and allow them to learn from your mistakes. And, when necessary, give a loving rebuke.

Twenty-Four
Bankrupt Churches

In the early 1900s a man named George made a risky decision. After ten years of financial struggle on the farm, he knew something had to change. Each year he had planted in hope, and each year his dreams had been dashed. Crop failure and poor prices, combined with the loss of most of his cattle, had made George weigh his options. With his home and land mortgaged and loans on his livestock, the only way he could plant in the coming spring was to borrow yet again. But in the midst of his distress, a persistent doubt kept surfacing. *Should I really be involved in farming?*

The locals were complaining that it was several miles to the closest hardware store. The more George heard them talk, the more he wondered. Could he run a store? He was apprehensive about asking his lender, but finally, in desperation, he broached the topic. George's banker also saw the need for a hardware store and felt the bank had little to lose at this point. So after much discussion and even more debt, George found himself the owner of a small store he named Helpful Hardware.

Businesses rarely work out as planned, and looking back, it is a wonder George survived those next few years. With the challenges of learning a new industry, trying to keep up with the demands of a growing business, and dealing with the staggering debt, the old life of farming sometimes looked good. But George persevered and worked hard to please his customers. In fact, Helpful Hardware became well known for providing exceptional service. Stories were told of George getting out of bed at night to deliver something to a desperate farmer or homeowner in an emergency. Slowly Helpful Hardware grew, and after ten years it became one of the largest hardware stores in the area. Amazed by his accomplishment, George opened another store in the adjoining town.

George's diligence and hard work continued to pay off, and he watched with pride as the small chain continued to grow. His son, George Jr., worked in the business part-time while finishing his schooling, and when he finally entered the business full-time, Helpful Hardware had fifteen stores and was adding a couple more stores each year.

As a result, George Jr. began his business life much differently than his father had. He never stood behind the counter, never felt compelled to deliver a product in the middle of the night, and never needed to nervously stand before a banker explaining a request for additional funds. George Jr. never really knew what financial struggle felt like. He heard about it often from his father, but that had been years ago. He found himself working in a nice office, attending various meetings, and generally focusing on keeping his father's business on track.

George Jr. did have some ideas about business and ways he felt the company could be more productive. Sometimes he offered his ideas, but almost every time he tried to implement some change, his father explained why his ideas would probably fail. George Jr. became frustrated. But he reminded himself that his job wasn't all that bad and increasingly found activities outside of the company that interested him. Gradually, George Jr. began to pour more of his energy into these pursuits.

George Sr. had always been too busy to take vacations with the family, and as George Jr. saw his own son, George III, growing up, he decided not to make the same mistake. So George Jr. took some of his stock dividends from Helpful Hardware and purchased a second home by a nearby lake. This acquisition required a good bit of his time and energy, and consequently George Jr. spent less and less time in the office.

George Sr. could never understand this. Didn't his son understand the diligence required to run a business? Couldn't he grasp how quickly a business could lose out to competition? But George Jr. could see no reason to worry. Helpful Hardware continued to expand, and what good was a business if it tied you down? After all, a man had to have a life, and it was certainly more fun to skim across the lake than to be cooped up in an air-conditioned office.

By the time George Sr. passed away, Helpful Hardware had become quite large, and management of the company had been gradually passed on to George Jr. But his style of management was much different than his father's. His focus was primarily on maintaining what his father had created. When business decisions needed to be made, George Jr. generally chose risk-free options. He viewed Helpful Hardware as a valuable asset he didn't want to lose. As a result, business choices were made with an eye toward maintaining the wealth he had been given and avoiding any possibility of loss. Consequently, Helpful Hardware stopped building new stores or trying new product lines. After all, the business continued to bring in more than George Jr. needed. Why take unneeded risk?

George III grew up completely disconnected from the struggle his grandfather had experienced. He had very little interest in the company and really never knew much about it. The business his grandfather had started brought him a good income, but he had no interest in sitting in an office shuffling papers. He occasionally went to meetings to make his father happy, but everyone knew his heart wasn't really there. His father's second home by the lake was fun for a while, but George III soon moved on, spending most of his time traveling abroad, golfing, and living the good life. In fact, he paid so little attention to Helpful Hardware that only five years after his father's death, the business had to be sold, and George III declared bankruptcy.

This scenario has played out repeatedly in history. The first generation starts with nothing, takes great risks, works hard, and eventually hands a profitable business over to the second generation. The second generation has generally watched the first generation fight to survive, and they understand, at least partly, the effort required to start and expand a business. A steady income has now been created, and they usually comprehend what a wonderful thing they have. But instead of expanding into new areas and products, the second generation often tries to protect what has been handed to them. They become very adverse to risk and are fearful of losing what they have been given.

By the time a business is handed down to the third generation, the disconnect is usually complete. These descendants receive the results

173

of all the labor and risk that preceded their entrance onto the stage. Operating a business looks easy, and little effort is expended until, eventually, the business fails. It has been said that the first generation starts a business, the second runs it, and the third ruins it.

The Family Business Institute in Raleigh, North Carolina, has studied this subject in detail and has assembled some amazing statistics. They have found that almost 90 percent of family business owners believe their families will still control their businesses five years from when they hand them to the next generation. But the reality is much different. In fact, only about 30 percent of family businesses survive into the second generation; 12 percent are still viable into the third; and only about 3 percent of all family businesses operate into the fourth generation or beyond.[39]

Businesses can go bankrupt. The wise man said long ago, "For riches are not forever: and doth the crown endure to every generation?"[a] It isn't easy to pass on businesses, regardless of how successful, to the next generation.

But sadly, this truth applies to more than just businesses. Churches go bankrupt too. And there are some parallels in how businesses and churches lose their effectiveness. Most churches are started with great zeal and enthusiasm, often by men who have had life-changing experiences that motivated them to seek God. These men have spent much time in prayer and have earnestly sought God's will in His Word. They are willing to risk their reputations, their possessions, and even their lives in their search for truth. And out of these hazardous ventures have emerged vibrant New Testament churches.

The next generation reaps the benefits of this fervent pursuit of truth. They enjoy the blessing of parents who fought for doctrinal purity and focused on the Word of God. But their parents' original passion for truth evolves into a pattern of life and slowly becomes a culture of Christian living. The initial fight for truth is forgotten, and those who follow tend to float in the wake of those who have gone before.

While the people in the second generation know they have received something of value, their focus becomes one of preservation. Not wanting to lose the wonderful asset that has been handed down to them, they pour all their energy into maintaining the status quo,

[a]Proverbs 27:24

avoiding risk at all costs. The reference point tends to be history rather than Scriptural truth. Many of us have watched as churches lose their fervency and drift away from their original vision. Even if we haven't experienced this firsthand, history documents the downward path many churches follow over time.

Fighting, Floating, Failing

That path usually leads from a zealous fight for truth, to comfortable floating and resting on past successes, to failure and washout. At the end of the path, a passionless, apathetic group of people mechanically go through the motions but lack the vibrancy of their ancestors. Youth in these settings usually do one of two things. They either unthinkingly plod along in step with their parents, not knowing what else to do, or, disillusioned, they leave to find fulfillment in some other pursuit or church fellowship.

I am not interested in analyzing who is at fault in these situations. There is plenty of blame to go around, and people from each generation are usually partly responsible. I am interested in how this downward spiral can be avoided.

Circumstances differ, and there is great risk in making generalizations or assuming that all problems can be diagnosed the same way. Yet there is a great need for dialogue regarding the lukewarm condition in our churches today. I believe some of the responsibility for this apathy lies on the shoulders of those of us who are older.

How can we bless the younger generation? How can we encourage them to make good choices? How can we, in our older years, promote churches that are not just floating, but are fervent in their service to the King? I would encourage you to consider a few questions as you gain a vision for this time of life. These questions are not intended to condemn, but if a church is going to be effective in these last days, then it is critical that its older members do some basic self-examination.

1. What is your primary point of reference? When your church is faced with a decision, where do you turn first? First-generation churches tend to approach each decision by diligently praying and searching the Word of God. They realize this is the only trustworthy source of direction. But the next generation tends to look back at the success and decisions of the generation before. This can be good. Much can be learned from history. But what is the primary reference point? I am convinced that relying more on the past than on the Word of God is one of the first steps toward apathy.

First-generation believers tend to search the Scriptures with great humility. They know they have nothing to offer God, and they are looking for truth and direction. They understand how desperately they need God's guidance. But subsequent generations tend to stop seeking direction and begin mounting defense. Admitting that we might not have all the answers is risky and makes us feel vulnerable, so Bible reading can become primarily a search for verses to defend what we have inherited.

An older minister complained to me once that his children had little interest in reading and discussing the Word. But I wonder. Is it possible that his children saw little need for searching? Had they subconsciously been convinced that their denomination had things pretty much right and there was little left to improve? Why search for truth if there is nothing left to learn? Why spend hours seeking the face of God for direction when you sense that your leaders already believe they have all the answers?

I like to imagine churches where older ones are the first to suggest prayer when facing a time of crisis. In such churches, when older leaders are unsure which way to turn, they call their congregations to collective fasting, freely acknowledging that they don't have all the solutions. If the ones who are following can see that the older generation is leaning on the power of God rather than just precedent, they will be much better equipped to face coming storms.

What if each time there was sickness, mental or physical, one of the older members would suggest united prayer or anointing with oil? When families have wayward children or marriage struggles, what if times of fasting and corporate prayer were called? Making our primary reference point the Word of God could be risky. We might need to admit that some of our practices need to change. But as we demonstrate this level of dependence on God, we equip the younger generation for future warfare.

2. Are you focused on the Kingdom of God? This is not always easy to discern. Both people and churches tend to become self-promoting and self-serving. While we should be intent on blessing those within the church and living in peace among ourselves, our end goal should not be to just have a good time together. It is important that we periodically ask ourselves, "Are we really focused on building the Kingdom of God? Are we sure?" Our lives and churches will have a primary focus. But what is it?

When we are young, we enjoy reading accounts of the early church, and we read the book of Acts with enthusiasm. Something within us is called to action as we examine the early believers' willingness, and even eagerness, to suffer for the name of Jesus Christ. They viewed the call to follow Jesus as an appeal to surrender every part of their lives.

> *They viewed the church as a place to die, not just a place to live.*

They viewed the church as a place to die, not just a place to live. When we are young, their enthusiasm is contagious, and we long to fight the battles as bravely as they did.

But often as we grow older, something within us subtly shifts. Life has not been easy, and we long for a little comfort. The battle seems long, fatigue settles in, and we long for a quiet place to rest. Gradually our focus changes. While at one time our primary motivation was a love for the Lord, we now become increasingly concerned about how each decision will affect our lives and personal comfort. We become more and more interested in enjoying and preserving what we have, and the focal point becomes our culture rather than His Kingdom.

This change is not difficult to discern as we observe "Christianity" around us. The predominant message in many American churches seems to be how *you* can get more enjoyment from *your* Christian experience. While my flesh may enjoy this emphasis, is this really the message of the Gospel? Is it really about me?

Recently I heard a younger brother discussing his vision for expanding the Kingdom. He spoke of his desire to help start congregations in new areas. As he talked about this vision, he mentioned that it seemed the older members were the ones who opposed starting new congregations. While younger members were willing to take risks and move out into new areas, the older ones were often more fearful. Like George Jr. in the story above, they were focused on preserving what they had been given and had consequently become fearful of risk. Self-centeredness also plays a part. Sadly the brother noted, "It seems like their main objection is that their children might not all be home for Christmas."

Contrast the focus of those older church members with the focus of the Apostle Paul as he spoke to the Ephesian elders. He knew life wasn't going to be easy for him or for them in the future. He spoke of all the coming problems and then said, "But none of these things move me, neither count I my life dear unto myself, so that I might finish my course with joy."[b]

Are our lives dear to us? Our answers can be revealing. If our family, social circle, or personal enjoyment have become so important to us that they take precedence over building the Kingdom, it will be difficult for us to encourage the next generation. But if the younger generation can see older believers showing that they are unmoved by the surrounding culture and that their primary focus is on the Kingdom of Jesus Christ, they will be encouraged. They are looking for that kind of leadership.

3. Are you still willing to learn? In the corporate office of Wal-Mart in Bentonville, Arkansas, hangs a large plaque. This plaque contains the ten principles by which Sam Walton, the founder of this mammoth company, conducted his business. Sam Walton was a driven man, and he believed these business concepts were mandatory for success. He hung these principles in plain sight so that everyone who entered the office could be reminded of them.

These rules address various things businesses tend to forget over time, such as proper treatment of customers and the importance of encouragement in the workplace. But rule number seven addresses something that older businesses especially tend to struggle with. It says, "Listen to others and learn from their ideas."[40] To the end of his

[b]Acts 20:24

life, Sam Walton was searching for better ways to operate his business. He regularly walked through other stores on the prowl for new ideas, and he encouraged his employees to expose any current practice that needed improvement.

This is difficult for older business owners, because it takes humility to admit there might be a better way. Sometimes older believers have trouble with this as well. I remember hearing an older brother address this concern. He said he had seen many people become convicted of a Scriptural truth and make radical changes. But those people were usually young. In contrast, he said it was extremely rare to see anyone over forty make a major change.

Those words sent a chill down my spine. Could I possibly arrive at a point where I would be unwilling to take a fresh look at some part of my life? Is it inevitable that we become resistant to change as we age? Are we destined to subconsciously become convinced that whatever we are doing is correct? This thought troubles me, and as I look into my life, I find evidence of this tendency.

Unfortunately, this tendency can also be found in churches. Older churches, like older businesses, can become convinced they have a superior understanding of truth. When this occurs, any new thought or approach, regardless of how Biblical, is seen as a threat. In such churches younger people tend to take one of two courses. Either they become frustrated and leave the church, or they slowly lose their enthusiasm and passion for the Kingdom. Outwardly they conform to all that is required, but spiritual vitality is missing, and their vision for conquering new territory is destroyed.

All of us, both individually and collectively, have blind spots. Every believer's goal should be to become more like Jesus. But sometimes, instead of becoming more like Jesus, we redefine who Jesus is. Instead of becoming conformed to His image, we try to mold Him into ours, and our version of Christianity centers around us instead of Him. Church life can be just another way of attempting to create God in our image.

Conclusion

When a business goes bankrupt, it is immediately obvious. There is a flurry of activity. Newspapers report it, creditors are up in arms, and it becomes the talk of the town. You can't hide bankruptcy in business. But alarmingly, bankruptcy in churches can occur quite silently. Things may

continue on mechanically with the members unaware. The doors may still open at ten o'clock, and good messages may still be preached. Committees can be formed, programs put in motion, and the

> *You can't hide bankruptcy in business. But alarmingly, bankruptcy in churches can occur quite silently.*

treasury still be full. But regardless of how outwardly active it is, when love for truth has departed, a church is bankrupt.

It isn't easy to pass on a church to the next generation. But there are some ways we can aid this process in our older years.

- Be sure that the Word of God is your primary point of reference and that your church is searching the Scripture and praying fervently.

- Make sure you are focused on the King and on building His Kingdom. Be a supportive builder in your fellowship, but beware of the tendency to drift into denominational pride and a self-focused vision.

- Seek truth. Don't just defend how things are done, but be willing to re-examine your life in the light of Scriptural truth. Focus so completely on truth that you are willing to confess past failures and make changes, even in your older years.

Twenty-Five
Death and the Kingdom of God

Many of us learned about Juan Ponce de León in school. Ponce de León was a Spanish explorer who, as the story goes, grew dissatisfied with his life and material wealth and set out to search for the Fountain of Youth. In 1513 Ponce de León discovered what we now call Florida, but he was unsuccessful in his search for the fabled fountain, which reputedly restored the youth of anyone who drank from it.

The legend of the Fountain of Youth didn't start with Ponce de León. The possibility of such a spring has captured men's minds for thousands of years. What if you could find some spring of water, drink from it, and miraculously find yourself twenty years younger? What price could you put on a drink like that? Or what if the fountain would instantly cure any ailment? How long would the line be to that water? How large would the parking lot need to be? How soon would war break out nearby? We can only imagine the sudden rush to gain possession of such a fountain.

Since God first proclaimed that man would ultimately return to the ground, men have been trying to avoid death. Few things capture people's attention like living longer or better. Today, people may not be searching for a legendary fountain, but that doesn't mean the desire to avoid death is past. Men still try to pretend death isn't certain and proceed with life as though the curse proclaimed by God in the Garden of Eden can be avoided.

Recently I was walking down the greeting card aisle in a local drugstore. It was a typical Hallmark display, and I stopped for a moment in the birthday section. Looking at the large selection of cards, I realized how uncomfortable our society is with aging. Most people don't know what to do with it; they obviously would like to avoid it.

Some of the cards tried to pretend it wasn't happening. "You aren't really old if you still feel young" was their theme.

But by far the majority of the cards were humorous, with various attempts to laugh off the reality of aging.

"Aging is inevitable," one comical card read. "Maturing isn't."

If shelf space is an indicator, these humorous cards are the best sellers. "Eat, drink, and be merry" seems to be the theme jokingly promoted. "For tomorrow you die" is glaringly absent.

Some countries have tried to embrace this denial of death nationally. Several years ago I visited Tiananmen Square in Beijing, China. In the middle of this huge public square is an enormous building where Mao Zedong, the famous leader of the People's Republic of China, resides. Thousands of people come to see Mao

> "Eat, drink, and be merry" seems to be the theme jokingly promoted. "For tomorrow you die" is glaringly absent.

in his home each day. They stand in long lines to catch a glimpse, bow in reverence as they approach, and bring gifts to show their appreciation for what he has done. Every morning Mao, like so many in Beijing, rides an elevator up to work, and at night he descends to his home under the square. But there is one small problem. Mao has been dead since 1976.

Mao's body lies in an elaborate glass coffin and is transferred each morning by elevator from a safe vault underground up to his mausoleum, where a steady flow of visitors and worshipers can still see him. Many Chinese believe some supernatural force is preserving his body and maintaining its natural appearance.

However, in recent years the cost of maintaining this museum has caused concern, and Chinese scholars are asking some good questions. Why should a nation that openly proclaims that that there is nothing beyond death, pay so much money each year pretending Mao's spirit still lives? Some of the locals quietly complain. While many still worship Mao, others talk in undertones and rumor that his body is decaying rapidly. Recently, the gossip goes, his left ear fell off and had to be glued back on. Others say the cadaver has decayed so completely that the government has replaced it with a wax mummy. But others do believe that Chairman Mao lives on.

We're Smarter Than That!

None of us could be convinced that Chairman Mao has avoided death. We pride ourselves in being more intelligent than the millions of Chinese peasants who file past his remains each day. But are we really? I find the American view of dying intriguing. We accept death intellectually, yet ignore it emotionally. Most people avoid the subject. In fact, if you want to make many people extremely uncomfortable, just start talking about the reality of their death.

Recently I was discussing this topic with a physician who commented that he is continually astounded at the ability of men and women to ignore the reality of death. There is, of course, an element of surprise for anyone who first hears they have some incurable disease. But he has been amazed by the utter disbelief on some people's faces when they are told they are going to die. "I have had patients seventy-five or eighty years old," he commented, "who just can't believe this could happen to them. Sometimes I sit there and wonder, what did they think was going to happen? Did they really believe they were going to keep on living?"

Men go to great lengths to ignore the reality of death. Recently I drove past a cemetery in our area. A funeral service had just taken place, and the grieving family was making their way back to their vehicles. At the gravesite was a small tent, and the undertaker solemnly stood beside the casket. Standing off at a polite distance were a couple of men with shovels who were getting ready to bury the casket and get on with their daily routine. I marveled at the great effort men put forth to hide the reality of death. There were beautifully landscaped surroundings, flowers covering the casket, and even fake grass covering the dirt that would be used to cover the casket once it was in the grave. Now, when it was time to actually put the body in the ground, everyone was leaving so they wouldn't have to observe.

This is understandable when individuals have no belief in an afterlife. If I didn't believe that anything would happen after my funeral, I wouldn't want to think about death either. After all, it is only logical for an unbeliever to try to make this life last as long as possible and to wring as much as he can out of it.

But for a believer it is different. We understand that we are going to die, and we have accepted this truth. This reality has probably even prodded us to seek the Lord and follow Him. But there is a difference between believing death is inevitable and looking forward to death as a portal into the presence of God.

How honest are you about death and dying? Do you avoid the thought of your life ending? Does the fact that time is short and death is near affect your daily choices? Are you actually looking forward to meeting death and entering the presence of God? And if you are, do your choices reflect this desire?

Recently a well-respected bishop in his upper seventies was suddenly told he needed a major surgery. Without the operation, his life wouldn't last much longer. The bishop considered this, and after prayerfully discussing it with his family and congregation, he decided it would be wrong for him to spend such a large sum of money for an operation that would only prolong his life a few more years. "Our world is full of spiritual and physical needs where resources are needed," he said. "And these funds will do more for the Kingdom if they are used to meet some of these needs." This bishop died within a year, but his decision had a profound impact on his congregation.

I am not suggesting that medical procedures or expensive operations are wrong. Each situation is different, and we do not always know how we would or should respond. But I wonder how much society's infatuation with health and longevity has affected us. Our society knows no boundaries in its pursuit of wellness and quality of life.

People love their lives more than anything else, and death doesn't seem to be an option. But should there be a limit for the believer? Should preoccupation with physical health be a characteristic of Jesus' followers?

Holding Off on Heaven

As we grow older, most of us will experience increasing physical problems. The God who made our bodies understands this, and I think He expects us to give thought and care to our physical needs. But shouldn't there be a limit to our preoccupation? I am concerned when I see professing followers of Jesus breathlessly chase from one medical breakthrough to the next. Somehow, as I read the words of Jesus, I don't think His followers would be known for frantically pursuing the latest pill, potion, or powder. When I read the book of Acts, I see people on a passionate search, but not for some new innovation or medical breakthrough that will enable them to feel better or live longer. Notice for a moment some familiar words of Jesus that have perhaps become so familiar that we've missed their meaning. "Take no thought for your life, what ye shall eat, or what ye shall drink; nor yet for your body, what ye shall put on. Is not the life more than meat, and the body than raiment?"[a]

> *When I read the book of Acts, I see people on a passionate search, but not for some new innovation or medical breakthrough that will enable them to feel better or live longer.*

Now visualize the followers of a man who spoke such words. Would they chase every health gizmo and gimmick? Let's look at another passage that describes Jesus' followers. Notice their focus and the lack of attention they placed on their physical bodies. "And they overcame him by the blood of the Lamb, and by the word of their testimony; and they loved not their lives unto the death."[b]

[a]Matthew 6:25
[b]Revelation 12:11

If anything, Christ's followers were known not for preserving their physical lives, but for failing to give their bodies much consideration. They could say, with the Apostle Paul, that they hadn't let their bodies rule their lives.[c]

A misplaced focus on health and physical wellbeing has led many into medical scams, suspicious practices, and a continual swirl of questionable quackery. God intends that we take care of our bodies. They have been given to us by God, and as stewards we are responsible for their care. But there should be a difference between how a believer and an unbeliever approach the sustaining of life. The one is eagerly looking forward to the life to come, while the other dreads the thought that death is near.

When professing believers chase the latest medical breakthroughs, unbelievers have a perfect right to question the focus of their faith. How many seekers have become discouraged due to our obsession with physical health? How many unbelievers struggle to believe we really long for the next life when they see the great lengths we go to in order to prolong this one? Take a moment to analyze your life. Does your focus on physical health encourage or discourage the seeker?

Ready to Go!

About ten years ago a brother named Doug came to visit. Doug had been diagnosed with cancer, and he knew he might not live long. He was a physician. No one had a better understanding of what was before him than he did. But he was cheerful and gave lots of good advice that day.

The two of us took a drive, and the trip lasted all day. We lived in the state of Washington, and he wanted to see Mount Rainier, so we drove completely around the mountain. But as I told him later, we really could have just sat in a parking lot. Throughout our nonstop discussion, we hardly looked out the window. We spent the entire day discussing various topics dear to our hearts. Doug was knowledgeable, and I used this opportunity to ask him questions about death and dying. Not only was he on the threshold of death himself, he had worked with many dying patients during his career, and he had witnessed the different ways individuals faced death.

[c]1 Corinthians 9:27

Doug shared about the tremendous fear that people attach to cancer. People fear that word like nothing else. But he went on to say, "Until a man has embraced and accepted death, he cannot really live." The man who spends his days fearfully dreading the inevitable day of death can never really enjoy this life.

This message is clear in the Gospels as well. Jesus told His disciples, "Fear not them which kill the body, but are not able to kill the soul: but rather fear him which is able to destroy both soul and body in hell."[d]

> *A man's not really free to live until he's not afraid to die.*

These are astounding words! Don't fear death? How is that possible? Jesus was teaching a profound lesson. A man's not really free to live until he's not afraid to die.

Worms or Cannibals?

John Paton was pastor of a Scottish church in the mid 1800s. After he had served there for around ten years, his heart became burdened for people living in the New Hebrides. At that time the residents of these Pacific islands were known to be cannibals. Just twenty years earlier two missionaries had gone to this island to share the Gospel and had been killed and cannibalized. This was well known, and there wasn't a long line of missionaries begging to go to the New Hebrides. But John had a burning desire to reach these people, and he eventually moved there.

In his journal John tells of people who tried to convince him to give up his absurd idea. "Amongst many who sought to deter me, was one dear old Christian gentleman, whose crowning argument always was, 'The cannibals! You will be eaten by cannibals!' " But in response to this older gentleman's concern, John said, "Mr. Dickson, you are advanced in years now, and your own prospect is soon to be laid in the grave, there to be eaten by worms; I confess to you, that if I can but live and die serving and honoring the Lord Jesus, it will make little difference to me whether I am eaten by cannibals or worms."[41]

---

[d]Matthew 10:28

John Paton lived among the people of the New Hebrides for many years. Soon after arriving there, his wife and child died and he found himself alone. But as the years passed and John labored on, many of these heathen people came to know the love of the Lord Jesus. Churches were formed, and light began to shine where darkness had formerly reigned. This was only possible because John Paton had lost his fear of death.

Conclusion

Today we smirk smugly at the story of Ponce de León and his search for the Fountain of Youth. But the popular pursuits of the surrounding populace today seem no less absurd. Something about aging alarms our society, and they go to great lengths to avoid it. From anti-wrinkle creams to dyed hair to plastic surgery, the chase is on to find some product to reverse the curse. But the added wrinkles, lack of energy, and arthritic pains are just God's way of warning us. As we put on our bifocals and comb our graying hair each morning—assuming it's still there—we are reminded that the end of this life is approaching. These are God's gracious warnings. We won't be here forever.

What an opportunity to display the hope of the Gospel! We love to sing "This World Is Not My Home," but maybe our message would be more believable if our life choices demonstrated this. What would happen if every believer placed as much emphasis on the Kingdom of God as on sustaining his health and life? What if we were as eager to spread the Gospel as we are to find innovative healthcare options? What would happen if the unbelieving world could see by our choices that our lives are not dear to us? What would happen if they knew we were not afraid to die?

We love to read accounts of the early church. Their great zeal and passion for the Kingdom continues to inspire us today. But it was when they lost their fear of death that they gained the attention of the world. Their overriding goal was, as Paul said, that Christ would be magnified in their bodies, "whether it be by life or by death."[e] May the church once again be known for this kind of zeal.

___

[e]Philippians 1:20

Twenty-Six

Retirement, Savings, and Medical Insurance

J ust mention the word "retirement," and the average American thinks "savings." The two words have almost become synonymous. We are inundated by a virtual parade of information regarding the importance of saving for retirement. Advertisements from financial institutions, news articles warning of the demise of Social Security, and advice columns from economic experts keep this topic in front of us. "If you want to be happy during retirement," they tell us, "you'd better plan for it now."

One of the reasons for the recent emphasis on saving for retirement is the turmoil in our financial world. Investments that have always been regarded as reliable and impregnable, such as real estate and many blue chip stocks,[a] have revealed their vulnerability. As a result, analysts churn out more ideas, trying to find a location where retirement savings will be secure and available when needed. Ironically, their conclusions sound remarkably like the message of Jesus. Although they haven't left a stone unturned in their search, there doesn't seem to be any earthly location where money is safe. Nothing is secure.

So should a Christian save for retirement or for a time when he is unable to work? Does setting aside a certain amount each month for the coming years indicate a lack of trust? Does this violate Jesus' teaching on laying up treasures?[b] These are legitimate and important questions that each of us needs to wrestle with. They can also be

---

[a]Stocks in a corporation that has a reputation for quality and reliability. The corporation is usually known for steady profitability regardless of the current economic situation.
[b]Matthew 6:19

controversial. Some of us have strong opinions on this topic.

I am reluctant to make blanket statements on this issue. God's people find themselves in many different situations, and it is difficult to address each one. However, I would like to share some basic Biblical principles that should be considered as we approach the last half of our lives. Addressing a few of these points may help spur thought and discussion.

1. Getting older is a reality. It is easy to go through life day by day and ignore the reality of aging. If time continues, a day is coming when your body will not be able to do everything it has in the past. To ignore aging is to ignore reality. If you are the wage earner in your home, someday you will no longer be capable of earning wages. Assuming those who are depending on you for income live longer than you do, their income will then need to come from another source.

2. Some thought should be given to the financial consequences of aging. Paul told Timothy that the church should help those who are not able to provide for themselves if they do not have family.[c] In this passage we see the role of the family and the church in supporting those members who are incapable of providing for themselves. But there is also an underlying truth here. The church is not to be responsible for everyone in old age. As much as possible, each family should provide for itself. This doesn't mean that every person should have a retirement account. But it is teaching that each family should give some thought to the financial ramifications of aging, just as we would to any other known future expense. If you know, for example, that your property taxes are due several months from now, saving money to pay for them is not a lack of trust. It is the proper way to prepare for a known expense.

But saving money is not the only way to prepare for the older years, and it may not be the best way. Some people plan to sell their home when they are too old to take care of themselves and use the assets from the sale to sustain them. Others have chosen to join a church fellowship that is committed to taking care of their aged. This allows

---

[c]1 Timothy 5:3-16

families to use their resources for Kingdom building rather than feeling pressured to store up assets for the future. For this to work, however, a congregation must communicate well and be committed to their vision for the Kingdom.

It is important that we give some thought to financial arrangements for our final years. Paul told Timothy that "if any provide not for his own, and specially for those of his own house, he hath denied the faith, and is worse than an infidel."[d] These are strong words. It is evident that God intends for us to give some thought to taking care of ourselves, our families, and our dependents.

3. Recognize the limitations of any plan. Jesus asked, "Which of you by taking thought can add one cubit unto his stature?"[e] As humans, we are limited. Regardless how hard we try, there are some things we cannot do, and one of those is saving against the unknown. Have you ever tried to imagine how much money you would need to have in the bank to cover all the bad things that could occur? This fear of the unknown is one of the primary tools used by insurance companies, financial planners, and investment firms—because it works!

Fear causes us to do all kinds of things we wouldn't ordinarily consider. Jesus understood this, and He had much to say regarding how much thought to give to the unknown. In the sixth chapter of Matthew He reminds us not to be anxious about the future. We can't save enough to handle everything that might possibly come our way. And even if you did collect enough to handle every emergency, there is no promise your wealth will still be there when you need it. Earthly wealth rusts, rots, and molds. Moths can destroy it, thieves can steal it, and inflation can devalue it. Invest your money where it is safe—in the Kingdom of God.

4. Purpose is more important than the plan. Maybe your community has agreed not to have retirement accounts but expects each family to take care of their aging parents and family members. Or maybe you have some type of ongoing income from property or land and are counting on this when you are unable to work. Or perhaps you have

[d]1 Timothy 5:8
[e]Matthew 6:27

chosen to save for retirement. There are various ways to plan for your final years. It could be argued that some of these plans are better than others, but I believe the more important question is, "What is the purpose behind your plan?"

I believe any of the plans listed above could be used for the glory of God. But each can also be used to gratify your flesh as you grow older. So what is the real purpose behind your plan? Don't pass this question off lightly. It is possible to focus on the nuts and bolts and not realize we are working on the wrong machine. I have observed a tendency, far too often, among God's people to view these "golden years" as a time to enjoy life. It is tempting to think of these years as a time of reward for diligence and labor with a focus on hobbies, recreation, family time, and

> *It is possible to focus on the nuts and bolts and not realize we are working on the wrong machine.*

frivolous travel. As the Apostle Paul prepared to die, he reminded Timothy of his purpose.[f] Paul's ultimate goal in his teaching and preaching was to glorify God and build His Kingdom. That purpose drove his planning. As you look forward, what is the purpose behind your plan?

Church communities need to discuss this. Is your community united enough on its vision and purpose that members can collectively address it? Are you capable of considering financial issues as a fellowship, or has this area been relegated to each individual to decide? Our world's focus on personal independence has had an impact on the church and on brotherhood. We have drifted far from the picture we see in Acts where finances were very much a part of the church's discussion. Each locality may have a different set of issues to consider, but this is one area where honest discussion and collective agreements could bless us. If our church communities could come together and unite on vision, an amazing amount of resources could be freed for Kingdom use.

I believe you should have some plan in mind for your older years.

[f] 2 Timothy 3:10

But remember, regardless of the plan, motives must be examined closely. You can make radical choices, statements, and even collective agreements on this issue and still not focus on the Kingdom in your older years.

Medical Insurance

If saving for retirement is the most controversial financial subject among our families, the topic of medical insurance must surely be second. Some see insurance as a necessity in a world where medical operations can cost hundreds of thousands of dollars. Others see it as a lack of trust, a denial of God's faithfulness and promise to provide for His children. So which is correct? Does God intend that we purchase some type of medical coverage? Since medical costs are so overwhelming, does choosing not to purchase insurance indicate poor planning or even poor stewardship? Or is medical insurance part of Satan's sneaky plan? Is it a clever substitution designed to shift our trust from God's provision to a temporal alternative?

I understand the risk in addressing this topic. I have received letters from well-meaning individuals who view the insurance issue as the litmus test in determining where we place our trust. One reader wrote recently saying that the amount of medical insurance we carry, more than anything else, reveals which kingdom we identify with.

To some extent we are all prone to trust in something other than God. It seems we are always trying to find something to lean on in case God lets us down. Is medical insurance one of those things?

This chapter may not answer this question for you, but I would like to offer a few things to consider as you prayerfully seek direction in the area of healthcare and medical insurance.

1. God's children are subject to physical problems. God hasn't promised believers an exemption from health concerns. And while He certainly can, and does at times, step in and heal miraculously, He has not promised that this will always be the case. The Apostle Paul spoke of fellow believers, like Epaphroditus, who were extremely ill. Why did God allow this? Why did Paul leave Trophimus at Miletum, sick?[g] Why didn't he rather heal him? Why did the early church have to

[g] 2 Timothy 4:20

deal with physical problems in addition to all the other pressures and persecutions they faced? We don't have answers to all these questions, but maybe God wanted them, and us, to deal with the same physical maladies that everyone else is struggling with. Perhaps He wants the unbelieving world to observe how His children respond in times of illness and trial. God may at times provide miraculous relief—but not always.

2. You must decide if you are going to use modern medicine. How are you going to deal with physical ailments? Our world is much different than the world the Apostle Paul lived in. We have medical options never dreamed of then. Are we to use them?

In our area, some believers have chosen not to use modern medicine. When physical problems develop, whether diseases or broken bones, they rely only on prayer. To them, resorting to pills and modern procedures is a denial of God's promises and provision. It is not uncommon for someone to die from an illness that modern science would deem easily preventable.

Most of us have chosen to use modern medicine. But even if we decide to make use of the latest scientific advances, we need to address how far we will go in using modern medicine. Are there any limits? If your community shares medical costs, are there guidelines as to how much should be spent? Should individuals in their eighties ask their community to pay for a procedure that costs hundreds of thousands of dollars when it may only extend their lives a couple of years? Or what about treatments that are derived from aborted fetuses? Should we consider their source before agreeing to their use? These ethical questions should be addressed, and maybe older believers should take the lead in bringing these discussions to the table.

3. If you are going to use modern medicine, some consideration should be given to how it will be paid for. Modern medicine is extremely expensive. If we are going to make use of the medicine and technology available, it seems reasonable to discuss how we are going to pay for the services. Communities take several approaches, and there are pros and cons with each. Let's look briefly at some ways churches have addressed this issue.

- **Brotherhood medical plans.** Some churches have their own organized plans, which are similar to commercial insurance. Sometimes these are even controlled by a board of elected officials within the church. Some plans require each family to contribute a set monthly payment, and others are funded by freewill offerings. These programs are not necessarily without their stresses. Recently I was giving a financial talk at a church whose medical fund is supported by freewill offerings. Just before I went up to speak, one of the church leaders privately suggested that I mention the need for the congregation to give more in these offerings. The medical fund had been inadequately funded for some time, and this leader thought this might be a good opportunity to encourage the slackers. Lack of funding can be a concern, but blessings also accompany brotherhood medical plans. The church should be known as a place where members share their burdens and difficulties, and these plans can help foster this Biblical principle. By using a brotherhood approach, members can also be assured that their money isn't just profiting a few individuals or building more offices for an institution. The funds are actually addressing legitimate needs.

- **Parachurch insurance plans.** Many individuals use medical insurance plans that are not confined to one church or denomination. These plans usually include large groups of believers who agree to cover each other's medical needs within set parameters. Some find this to be an economical alternative to commercial insurance when their local congregation is not large enough to cover an emergency. To participate in these plans, members must usually meet lifestyle requirements such as not smoking or drinking. This excludes those whose life choices make them a higher health risk.

- **Self-insured as a brotherhood without an organized plan.** Some congregations have agreed to share medical costs as they come up. When an emergency occurs, they meet and try to address the need within their fellowship. If the need is too great, they call upon other like-minded congregations for assistance. This method of dealing with medical expense requires a congregation with a united purpose and vision, and it also requires a large enough base of participants to cover larger expenses.

- **Using a combination of commercial and self-insurance.** Some insurance companies allow a high deductible. One option is for local congregations to agree among themselves to take care of medical costs up to a certain amount and then have commercial coverage for the rare major expenses that exceed this deductible. In this way they reduce their monthly costs while still having a plan for more expensive emergencies.

- **Ignore the issue.** In some churches most of the members have commercial insurance and a few do not. When one of those who doesn't have insurance needs help, others try to assist, but often these situations create bad feelings between members. Those without coverage speak of the need for brotherhood, and those who have coverage feel they are being asked to pay for their own healthcare and assist others as well. If you are in this type of setting and plan to ask your congregation to help in times of emergency, then at the very least communicate with your leadership. You may be in a situation where, due to economic constraints, purchasing a policy isn't feasible. Or perhaps you feel commercial insurance violates a Scriptural principle. But if you will need help from your local congregation in an emergency, discuss this with your leadership before an event occurs.

These are just a few of the options being used by congregations today. My goal in outlining these approaches is to encourage thought and discussion within our congregations. There are no easy answers, but this topic needs to be addressed. For some, the issue seems straightforward and the answers simple. For others it isn't as clear, and we need charity between ourselves as we wrestle with the subject. If you belong to a large fellowship that has agreed to cover the medical needs of each member, it can be easy to accuse those who use commercial insurance of not trusting the Lord.

But in that setting, do you really trust the Lord or the deep pockets of your church group? We are not always good at honestly identifying the object of our trust, and all of us tend to lean on things other than God. God wants us to trust Him. He desires that we put our confidence in Him and His ability to deliver us. And we need to understand that insurance, savings accounts, possessions, our personal abilities, and even church fellowships can hinder our trust in God.

> *We are not always good at honestly identifying the object of our trust, and all of us tend to lean on things other than God.*

Several years ago I was talking to an American friend of mine who lives in China. He told me how he was in a train station one day and watched one man beating another. This thrashing took place in public, in view of everyone around, and no one did anything about it. But the most shocking thing to my friend was the fact that a policeman was standing nearby doing nothing. In fact, the policeman calmly turned his back and looked the other way.

This incident had a profound effect on my friend. He suddenly realized he couldn't trust in the local police force for protection. If someone wanted to rob and beat him, no one would do anything about it. He felt a sudden panic. And then the issue of trust came forcibly to his mind. For many years he had lived in the United States and firmly believed he was trusting in God. But suddenly he came face to face with the reality that he really had been trusting in more (or less) than God. It is very easy for us to conclude that we are trusting in God because of certain things we do or don't do. But sometimes the truth is more subtle.

Questions about saving for our older years and medical insurance can be difficult to address for two reasons. The first is because the Scriptures contain several concepts that must be reconciled. Paul emphasized the importance of providing for our own.[h] If you camp on that verse or one of the many others that stress the importance of diligence and hard work, you could assume that providing for self and family should be the believer's primary focus. But if you examine some of Jesus' teachings,[i] you could conclude that giving much thought at all to personal survival is a denial of God's ability to provide. Reconciling these two trains of thought can be difficult, and I suspect God wants each of us to prayerfully wrestle with this Scriptural tension in our own lives.

The second reason it is difficult to address these issues is due to our differences in personality. Making sweeping statements is dangerous due to the diverse temperaments among us. Some individuals love to plan. They tend to become anxious about the future and are never quite sure they have enough insurance or savings. Those in this category should probably read the sixth chapter of Matthew every morning and contemplate the twelfth chapter of Luke before going to bed. These people need to learn more about putting their trust in God.

Others should probably focus on some of the Proverbs. "There is treasure to be desired and oil in the dwelling of the wise; but a foolish man spendeth it up."[j] I have sat with young couples who seem to have no concern about providing for themselves. If you ask them how they would handle a medical emergency, they are pretty sure their church would take care of it. Money tends to go quickly, and they give the future little thought. Their natural tendency is to forget that God has called them to a life of financial diligence and conscientiousness.

Both of these mindsets have repercussions in our churches, and we will probably always struggle to find a balance. Mild, passive, complacent people who tend to live for today need to be encouraged to think ahead, plan, and discipline themselves. There's nothing spiritual about laziness, neglect, and chaotic living. On the other hand, goal-oriented, disciplined, self-motivated people can get off balance as well. They need to remember that all their efforts without God's blessing are in vain. King David was well aware of the need to trust the Lord. In the Psalms he describes the fallacy of depending on horses and

[h]1 Timothy 5:8
[i]Matthew 6:19-34
[j]Proverbs 21:20

chariots to save. He knew God alone was able to deliver—yet David still owned and used horses and chariots. Somehow he was able to use them while understanding that his trust must be in God.

Conclusion

At the conclusion of a recent financial seminar, I opened it for questions and discussion. A man in the back raised his hand and asked, "Could you tell us how many square feet our houses should be?" He meant well, but I still chuckle as I consider how anyone could ever answer that question. Just imagine, for example, that I had said, "Twelve hundred square feet—that should be enough." Someone there that night may well have been living a self-centered life in a one-thousand-square-foot home. He would have gone home justified, secretly condemning others who have larger homes. On the other hand, a family with a three-thousand-square-foot home might have been using every square foot to bless their community and the Kingdom of God.

> *Maybe how he will provide for those years isn't as important as how he is planning to live during those years.*

Sometimes we have all the right answers, but we're asking the wrong questions. We are quick to judge a person, for example, by what he believes about insurance or saving for his older years. But maybe how he will provide for those years isn't as important as how he is planning to live during those years. What will be his purpose and passion during the last half of his life? What does he hope to achieve, and for whom will he be living? Savings and insurance are important issues, and they need to be prayerfully discussed. But of even more importance is your overriding vision.

Some of the issues we looked at in this chapter are controversial, and I have purposely asked more questions than I have answered. These questions need to be considered on our knees and discussed in our homes and local congregations. I am often troubled as I look at how different Jesus' radical teachings were from His surrounding culture, and yet how similar many parts of my own life are to my culture. It is possible for us to rationalize every decision and then suddenly wake up (or not wake up) to the reality that our lives are nothing more than a spiritual spin on the American dream. As we prayerfully ponder living out the rest of our lives to the glory of God, let's be honest regarding our tendency to drift toward our flesh and our culture and away from the teachings of Jesus.

Twenty-Seven
Should You Be a Bank?

I was working in my office several years ago when the door opened and Frank walked in. Frank was a man of few words, and when he stopped in, it wasn't to discuss the insignificant. So when he sat down and began chatting about the weather, I knew something was bothering him. But the weather, as many of us have discovered, is a topic soon exhausted. It wasn't long until we were sitting in silence. Finally, just when the needle on the comfort dial began moving toward "uncomfortable," Frank shared his problem.

Frank and his wife had a large family. All of the children had left home. Some had good jobs and seemed to be managing well, while others had some financial difficulty. All desired to serve the Lord and seemed willing to work. But in spite of their good intentions and hard work, a couple of them habitually had difficulty keeping their bills paid. One of these sons had recently asked Frank for a loan. His son was aware that Frank had recently sold a piece of investment property and had extra money available.

Frank wanted to do what he could to bless his family. But what should he do? His children had all started out with the same opportunities. Was it right to give more help to the son who habitually made poor choices? What would happen to their relationship if the son was unable to repay the loan? And if Frank just forgave the loan, how would that affect his relationship with the rest of his children?

Many of us will face similar issues as we grow older. Experts in the lending world estimate that the default rate on interpersonal loans is fourteen times higher than the 1 to 2 percent default rate on bank loans.[42] These situations can leave damaged relationships in their wake.

It isn't always children in need of help. Others in our church communities may be in need. Should we help them? If we do, is a loan the best way? And if we lend, should we charge interest? What happens if the borrower is habitually late in making his payments or fails to repay the loan? What impact might these situations have on relationships in the church or family?

Before addressing some of these questions, let's look at what God has said on the topic. The fact that some people have more than others is readily acknowledged in the Old Testament, and God used various methods to relieve this imbalance. One of these ways was lending. God told His people, "If there be among you a poor man of one of thy brethren . . . thou shalt open thy hand wide unto him, and shalt surely lend him sufficient for his need, in that which he wanteth."[a] Notice that God doesn't say anything regarding why this man was poor. It may have been due to something outside of the man's control or a result of poor management. But when the people of Israel saw one of their own in financial difficulty, they were commanded to help, and lending was one way to assist.

When we move into the New Testament and read Jesus' teachings, this truth becomes even clearer. "And if ye lend to them of whom ye hope to receive, what thank have ye? For sinners also lend to sinners, to receive as much again. But love ye your enemies, and do good, and lend, hoping for nothing again; and your reward shall be great, and ye shall be the children of the Highest: for he is kind unto the unthankful and to the evil."[b]

The Poor Heard Him Gladly

The passage above is clear. If you have extra and someone is in need, you have an obligation to lend, even if you suspect he won't pay it back. And that isn't all. Jesus says we shouldn't even hope to receive it back. No wonder the poor heard Jesus gladly! I would like to have seen the expressions on the faces in the crowd when Jesus said this. I wonder if there weren't some rich men with perplexed faces and furrowed brows, even as some of the poor nodded enthusiastically.

[a]Deuteronomy 15:7-8
202   [b]Luke 6:34-35

So how are we to apply this today? What do we do with Jesus' words,·
"Give to every man that asketh of thee"?[c] How are we to live this out?
Does it mean we should always lend to children when they ask? Are
we obligated to issue a loan to the brother in our congregation who
habitually makes poor life choices? And when we lend to others, are
we to charge them interest?

The Old Testament has much to say regarding charging interest, or
usury. In some places God told the children of Israel it was acceptable
to charge interest of other people, but not from their brethren.[d] Other
places He told them not to charge interest of anyone, regardless of
whether they were an Israelite or a stranger.[e] But all through the law
it is clear that God frowned on lending money or food to others and
then charging for the use of it.

How does this apply to us? Interest is an integral part of our
economy. When we take money to the bank, we expect to receive
interest, and when we borrow, we expect to pay. This is how banks
operate and remain in business. But what about believers? Does God
expect us to charge each other interest?

I am asking two basic questions here. First, does Jesus expect us to
always lend to every person that asks? That is what He said, isn't it?
So what if your five-year-old son asks you for a motorcycle? Does this
instruction of Jesus demand that you comply with your son's request?
And second, when we lend to others, is it wrong to charge interest?

Fair Banking

I would like for you to back out of your culture for just a moment.
Most of us have grown up in a remarkably just economic structure.
Despite our whining, we have never experienced the daily dilemmas
faced by most of the world. We have grown used to fair banking laws
and protection for the poor. But in most Third World countries this
is not the case.

I like to ask poor individuals who reside in these poverty-stricken
countries, "If you needed to borrow money right now, what kind of

---

[c]Luke 6:30
[d]Deuteronomy 23:20
[e]Leviticus 25:35-36

interest would you have to pay to get it?" The consistency of the answer always amazes me. The reply is almost always 5 to 10 percent—per month! You may find higher rates, but rarely will you find lower.

This means that the least expensive loans are costing these poor people 60 percent each year. We would say that is ridiculous. Even our credit cards, which we think have exorbitant rates, charge far less than this. But this is reality for many people. If they have a sudden medical emergency, funeral expenses, or crop failure, they can expect to pay these kinds of rates, assuming they can even find someone willing to lend to them. This is common in countries where the people are either very rich or very poor.

As strange as this is to us who live in America, this was also reality in Bible times. The presence of a large middle class, which we have become accustomed to, is relatively new. While historians debate when the change occurred, during the time these Scriptures were written, society was divided between rich and poor. If a person was born into a poor family, rising out of that impoverished condition was difficult.

Imagine being born into a poor family today. You labor day after day as a servant, but one day you have an idea. A business model develops in your mind that has the potential to change your life, eventually providing enough income to allow you to own your own home and feed and educate your family. But when you try to find someone to lend you the money to put your plan into action, the best rate you can find is 60 percent interest on the loan. What would you do?

What generally happens is that people only borrow when they absolutely have to. Borrowing is not typically for improvements or investments. When a family becomes desperate, they visit the rich moneylender, borrowing to purchase necessities like food and medical care. Two things occur when this happens. First, if you are already poor and then are required to pay high interest for necessities, you get poorer. Second, if you are rich and lend money at 60 percent, you get richer. This is where the familiar Third World saying comes from, "The rich get richer and the poor get poorer." God hates this arrangement. And I believe this is primarily what God is referring to in Scripture.

Although our setting is not the same, the Scriptural principles apply today. I want to look at three basic principles I believe are interwoven through both the Old Testament and the teachings of Jesus. This list is not intended to be inclusive, but I believe that close adherence to these principles will keep us close to the heart of God.

1. We are not to profit at the expense of the poor. This principle is clear in Scripture and should be our guide as we consider lending and charging interest. I have seen situations in which I believe it was good for young couples to pay interest. I think this can even help people of certain temperaments be more diligent. But it is important that we not violate the principle by profiting from brothers and sisters who are sincerely in need. What are our motives in lending? Are we exploiting others in their time of weakness? One way some have dealt with this is to charge a low rate of interest and then give the interest received to a charity. In this way they can help a young couple without profiting from their situation.

2. There are times to refuse requests. James says, "Ye ask, and receive not, because ye ask amiss, that ye may consume it upon your lusts."[f] Even though God wants to give us whatever we ask for,[g] there are times He chooses to withhold even though it is within His power to give. Sometimes we find ourselves in similar situations. Someone may ask for financial help, but giving it is clearly not the right thing to do. A young man known for his lack of diligence may ask to borrow for an expensive sports car. Or someone who is already heavily in debt may ask for a loan to take a vacation. In such situations handing out a loan could harm rather than help. Other situations take more prayer and discernment. It isn't always easy to know what is best. Jesus, before going to the cross, asked His Father that the experience would pass from Him. This may be the most famous request ever made, yet it was refused. Some requests should be refused for the good of the individual and the Kingdom.

3. Their good is to be our primary objective. Although at times it is right to refuse requests, we must be sure we are not refusing for selfish motives. When Jesus said, "Give to him that asketh of thee, and from

---

[f]James 4:3
[g]Matthew 21:22; Mark 11:24; Luke 11:9

him that would borrow of thee turn not thou away,"[h] I believe He was saying we should not ignore honest requests just because of our selfishness. I have found myself turning away requests from the poor simply because I didn't feel like dealing with them. Such requests can be wearying in many countries. But even in our American setting, we might find ourselves ignoring requests because we feel like complying will just bring more difficult dilemmas. We like to help people who really deserve assistance, who normally work hard and plan well, but experienced something out of their control. But many individuals who come to you needing assistance will probably have made some poor choices, and dealing with them will require sacrifice. Before you turn them away, be sure you are doing it for their good—not yours.

There are several other things to consider when lending money. It is important to understand these principles before entering a lender/borrower relationship.

- **Loans should not be used as leverage to control.** Parents sometimes assume that by lending money they can influence their children to adopt their own lifestyle and values. They tend to feel they are doing their children a great service by providing this loan, so in response the children should show their appreciation by living as the parents wish. The result is destroyed relationships. If you are going to lend to your children or others, remember that the loan gives them no obligation to you other than to repay.

- **Loans can create, but seldom alleviate, family tensions.** Many have assumed that by doing their child this great "favor" in providing a loan, strained relationships will be restored. Again, this is a result of the parent assuming that the child views a loan as a wonderful gift. While it may be a blessing, few children will see it that way. In fact, if you loan

> *More relationships have been destroyed than restored by lending money.*

[h]Matthew 5:42

SHOULD YOU BE A BANK?

money with the subconscious desire to someday be thanked, you are probably headed for disappointment. More relationships have been destroyed than restored by lending money. There is a time to lend, but don't do it to build a relationship.

- **Be very clear with the terms.** If you decide to provide a loan to someone, be sure the terms are clear. Many of us are reluctant to talk frankly when issuing a loan. But often this is what causes damaged relationships. When do you expect the loan to be repaid? Will a payment be made monthly? Will interest be charged? After working out the details, put the agreement in writing, not because you're going to force repayment or because you don't trust the borrower, but so that there is no misunderstanding about the terms. Human memories are very fallible. If it is going to be paid back in small payments over time, then I would encourage you to also set up an amortization schedule. This will specify the amount of the payments, the amount of principle and interest in each payment, and exactly when the loan will be paid off. Taking a little time to communicate clearly in the beginning can help both of you avoid potential misunderstandings in the future.

- **People are more valuable than dollars**. Assuming you do decide to lend money, it is extremely important, from the beginning, to remember that people are more valuable than dollars. You need to begin with the mindset Jesus taught when he said to "lend, hoping for nothing again."[i] There may come a time when you need to let the loan go to preserve the relationship, and it will be much easier to do this if you began by "hoping for nothing again." I talked with a brother years ago who explained how he dealt with a loan when a borrower had difficulty repaying. When the borrower began to make late payments or miss them altogether, it began to affect their relationship. The borrower became uncomfortable around the lender and avoided him at public gatherings. The lender was determined not to

---

[i]Luke 6:35

lose the relationship. So he met privately with the borrower and told him he didn't want this loan to destroy their relationship. To avoid this, he asked the borrower to begin making his payments to a certain charity. The lender didn't want any more money to come back to him, but he did want the borrower, before the Lord, to commit to paying the loan back. If the borrower missed payments or didn't finish paying the loan back to the charity, that was between the borrower and the Lord. There are different ways of dealing with these types of situations, and I am not saying this will work for everyone. But a guiding principle must be that people and our relationships with them are much more important than money. If we enter these agreements led by this principle, I think the Lord can use personal loans as a blessing in the Kingdom.

> *A guiding principle must be that people and our relationships with them are much more important than money.*

- **Money isn't always the problem.** Often the underlying problem is not money, but management. Throwing more money at a management problem doesn't usually improve the situation and may encourage the problem. But don't let this stop you from attempting to help. Consider coming alongside and helping with more than just money. Financial counseling can be a time-consuming and thankless job, but it can accomplish much more than money alone. Many of our conservative churches are very giving and charitable. As a result, a poor manager can get an incredible amount of "help" from many well-meaning people. But this may not actually be blessing the individual. Before you write that check, make sure that you are actually helping. Contact someone familiar with the situation and inquire. If you send money without requiring accountability, you may be hurting rather than helping.

Conclusion

When my wife and I were first married, life seemed challenging. Surviving financially was difficult, and I wondered why my parents couldn't just help me out. Of course, I didn't mention this to them. But it seemed like they had more than they needed, and they knew we were starting out with nothing. Why couldn't they just help out a little?

But before too many years had passed, I was thankful they hadn't given me money to ease my situation. We learned some basic lessons in frugality during those years that we would have missed had my parents tried to make it easier.

When we purchased our first home, though, my parents did loan us money. It was understood that we were to pay it back with interest, and looking back, that was a blessing. It enabled us to buy a home before we would have otherwise been able.

If you are able to help your children financially, it will take prayerful discernment. Children have differing management skills, and it is possible to begin subsidizing poor managers. This in turn has the potential of creating friction with those who have better business skills.

You will have fewer struggles in these areas, though, if it is evident to your children and community that you are living for the Kingdom. It will be easier for a potential borrower to accept being told no, and there will be fewer interpersonal conflicts, if your lifestyle and personal financial choices declare plainly that you are focused on the Kingdom of God.

PART FIVE
A Time
to Prepare

Twenty-Eight
Closing Up Shop

D aniel grew up during the Great Depression. Times were tough for everyone, but Daniel's family was poorer than most. During his early formative years, other families in his church community took occasional trips. But Daniel's father wasn't known to be a good manager, and there never seemed to be enough extra money for outings. Daniel's father farmed, and as Daniel watched his family scrape by year after year, hardly able to pay the bills and just barely staying ahead of the creditors, he made some firm resolves.

Daniel resolved to never get himself into a position where he couldn't pay his bills. He felt ashamed as a child that his father had financial difficulties, and he didn't want his own children to ever experience that shame. So when the time finally came for Daniel to marry and begin a home of his own, he had a simple, focused prayer. "Lord, either decrease my expenses or increase my income, but please don't let me ever get to the place where I can't pay my bills."

Daniel began his married life with very little and was forced to focus on financial survival. "Looking back," Daniel said, "I believe I started with an improper focus. I was so fearful of going broke that I'm afraid I drove some pretty hard bargains. Though we were poor, it was actually a materialistic way to live, and my witness for the Lord Jesus wasn't as clear as it could have been."

In spite of his hard work and good management, Daniel was never able to accumulate much. He kept the bills paid, but there was never much left over. As Daniel raised his family, he wanted to give to others who had financial needs. He heard of people in other countries who had little, and he longed to share. But there was rarely extra to give.

Time moved on, and eventually his children all married and started homes of their own. Daniel continued farming, and as the children moved away and expenses decreased, his financial life became a little easier. And then something happened that Daniel couldn't have dreamed of when he first married.

Sudden Change

Daniel's farm was located just outside a fair-sized Midwestern metropolis, and suddenly the city began to move in his direction. Developers bought up land all around Daniel's farm, and men began to knock on Daniel's farmhouse door. Was he interested in selling the farm? How much did he want for his property? How soon could he move if he decided to sell?

At first Daniel had no interest in selling. He enjoyed farming, and the thought of turning his farmland into a subdivision had no appeal. And what would he do with all that money? He had heard the astronomical prices being paid for land, and he was concerned about the impact this might have on his children.

Finally Daniel was forced to sell his property. With housing all around him, it was difficult to farm, and with the high government assessment, his property taxes became too expensive for his farming income to cover. So Daniel sold his farm.

News of the sale quickly spread, and it wasn't long until his neighbors, those in his congregation, and his own children began to speculate. What would Daniel do with all that money? How would millions of dollars affect his life? Would he give it to his children? The Daniel they knew was a frugal man who lived a simple, godly life. Would this sudden windfall change him?

But over the years Daniel had noticed something that many others had not. Daniel was a leader in his church, and this had given him the opportunity to work with families who were dealing with interpersonal and financial difficulties. He had witnessed firsthand the effect large inheritances had on families and children, and he wanted to avoid this at all costs.

Soon after Daniel had sold his farm and moved to a smaller house, he asked all of his children to meet with him. They were well aware of the large amount of money their parents now had in their bank account, and they couldn't help being a little curious as they assembled. Daniel began by reviewing all that had happened in his life. He talked of the financial struggles he had gone through and of the sudden change that had occurred. He told them how much the farm had sold for, and he brought them up to date on his financial condition. He was getting to be an older man now, and Daniel acknowledged that he and his wife likely did not have long to live. He shared a little about what he had observed in other families where wealth had been given to children and how it had not been a spiritual blessing to them. And then, finally, Daniel shared with them his concept of stewardship.

What Does the Owner Want Me to Do?

Daniel knew he would soon stand before the Lord, the actual owner of the millions of dollars residing in Daniel's bank account. He described the difference between an owner and a steward, and he shared with his family his great desire that this money be used to bless and build the Kingdom of God. Daniel had wrestled with how God would want this money to be used.

> *Daniel knew he would soon stand before the Lord, the actual owner of the millions of dollars residing in Daniel's bank account.*

Finally, after prayerful consideration, Daniel had decided to give each of his children a small amount. It wasn't much, but since a couple of his children were in positions where a small sum could help them, he had decided to share equally with all.

After telling his children how he was planning to help them, Daniel said, "I want each of you to know that the rest of my money will be given to charity. There are so many needs in the Kingdom, and I want to use what God has entrusted to me for His glory." Daniel told his children of his plan to have nothing left to disperse at his death. He wanted to invest his money in the Kingdom as soon as possible and get it working for the Lord. Daniel also wanted to be open with his children and avoid the possibility of interpersonal conflicts after he was gone. He felt it would be best if they did not expect to receive anything at his death.

It has been several years now since Daniel and his wife discussed this with their family. Daniel's congregation has had an opportunity to observe their lifestyle since that time. Recently I had an opportunity to talk with some of the younger families in Daniel's congregation, and I asked them to share their observations. They spoke of things that had impressed them. People commented on Daniel's willingness to drive an older car. They noticed that his time was not spent on travel and hobbies, but on volunteering and visiting those in rest homes and hospitals. Some commented on how blessed they were as they observed Daniel's willingness to give up present pleasure to bless the next generation.

Daniel is in his late eighties now, yet he continues to pour himself into the study of God's Word and preaching. Daniel desires to meet God with the assurance that he was a faithful steward right to the end. He wants to be sure that when he leaves this life, he has left everything in his charge just as the Owner would want it.

Closing Up Shop

Visualize for a moment the owner of a small department store looking for someone to oversee his business. He hires a young man on trial. This young man knows that the owner has a great interest in the success of his store, and he also knows that how he manages the store will be carefully observed. The young man knows he is on trial, he needs the job, and he really wants to please the owner.

Now just imagine that one day the owner comes to the young man and says, "I need to leave this afternoon and will not return until tomorrow morning. I would like for you to close up the store tonight."

The owner leaves, and the responsibility for running the store now rests on this young man. With the owner no longer present, he must make business decisions. He feels the weight of this responsibility, and each time a decision needs to be made, he tries to make it with the good of the business and the desires of the owner in mind.

The day finally comes to an end, and it is time to close up the store. Imagine how careful this young man is. He knows the owner will return in the morning, and he wants to be sure he does everything to the owner's satisfaction. Before leaving, he makes sure the cash register is taken care of, the merchandise on the shelves looks nice, and the floors have been swept. He wants to be sure he leaves the store just as the owner would want it.

This is the desire I see in Daniel. He knows his life is almost over, and he wants to be sure that everything God has placed in his care and every task given him has been handled properly.

In the next few chapters we want to look at what it means to close up shop. How does God want us to leave this life? How can we, as good stewards, finish the business God has given us? We will look at issues like wills, inheritances, trusts, guardianship, and letters of instruction for our families. Some of these topics are easy to ignore or postpone. But as good stewards of Jesus Christ, we want to finish well and close out our earthly businesses in a way that will please our heavenly Father.

Conclusion

Recently I received a call from Daniel, and he updated me on some of the latest events in his life. Grandchildren are getting married, children are making occupational changes, he has some health concerns, and there is plenty for Daniel and his wife to pray about. But two things about his phone call impressed me. One was his concern about his congregation's materialistic focus. Members seem preoccupied with getting ahead, having nicer homes, and purchasing better vehicles. He thought it might be good for them to travel to some other parts of the world and see how people who don't have everything can still be happy.

The other thing that impressed me and the reason for his call was that he had just sold another piece of property, and he was asking where the money could be best used in the Kingdom. We discussed this for a while and shared some ideas. Before hanging up, Daniel said, "It just seems unbelievable! I am so thankful that God has allowed this poor old farm boy to bless His Kingdom in this way!"

After I hung up, I couldn't help commenting to my wife. This man hadn't even received the check yet from the sale of his property, but he had calculated what day the check would clear the bank, and he couldn't wait to invest that money in the Kingdom.

Daniel reminds me of John Wesley, who once said, "[When I die] if I leave behind me ten pounds . . . you and all mankind [may] bear witness against me, that I have lived and died a thief and a robber."[43] History records that when he died in 1791, the only money left was miscellaneous coins in his pockets and dresser drawers. Like John Wesley, Daniel desires to go to the Father with his business closed down properly. These men inspire us to keep serving, blessing, and building the Kingdom—till we are gone.

Twenty-Nine
Wills, Trusts, and Estate Planning

He was known as the Governor by his friends and fans due to the dignified manner in which he carried himself, and honors came quickly throughout his career. Rarely are offensive linemen recognized for their achievements in professional football, but Gene Upshaw was not an ordinary lineman. For fifteen years he was well known for blasting holes through opposing teams, allowing the Oakland Raider running backs to move quickly upfield. Other NFL teams learned to fear the 260-pound projectile. He was the man who prepared the way. Gene also became an active bargainer for the National Football League Players Association during the 1970s and early 1980s, helping his fellow athletes bargain for better wages. He became known as a forward-thinking planner for the association and eventually became its director.

Although he knew the importance of preparation in football, when his time of death came, Gene was unprepared. One Sunday evening, on vacation at Lake Tahoe, Gene was not feeling well and was admitted to the local hospital. The doctors diagnosed him with pancreatic cancer, and by Wednesday he was dead. His sudden death stunned the sports world.

As the media explored his story, another interesting fact emerged. At the time Gene Upshaw had been diagnosed with cancer, on August 17, 2008, he had no will. But when he died just three days later, a will was in place. While lying in the hospital, the former NFL great had hastily drafted a will and left everything to his wife.[44]

A flood of questions and accusations followed this revelation. Gene had a son from a previous marriage who was totally excluded from the will. This son had visited his father during those final days. He declared that on the day his father had supposedly made out this will, Gene was sedated and unconscious, in no condition to sign anything or dictate a will. The controversy headed to the courts, and years later strong emotions and damaged relationships trail this tragedy.

This story raises perplexing questions. Gene Upshaw was a sophisticated businessman. He was the head of the prestigious NFLPA, and the worth of his estate was estimated at millions of dollars. Why didn't he have even a basic will? How could a man known for planning the future of others fail to plan his own?

While statistics vary, it is estimated that well over half of Americans have never made out a basic will. Many wills are outdated and will not accomplish the desires of the individuals who wrote them.

In the last chapter we looked at the importance of continuing, even in our sunset years, to be good stewards of what God has entrusted to our care. One important aspect of closing up shop is giving some thought and action to developing an estate plan. An estate plan is a set of legal documents that describe our intentions for our assets after our death.

I suspect that Gene gave some thought to the importance of an estate plan during his life. It's possible that he even went to estate planning seminars, and perhaps at the end of the presentation decided to take action. But deciding to act is not the same as acting. Actually, Gene was probably not much different than many of us. We tend to procrastinate when it comes to estate planning. Time speeds along, and the topic never seems urgent enough to get our full attention. We plan to do it sometime, but so many other issues seem more important.

> *Deciding to act is not the same as acting.*

Something that deals with an uncomfortable subject like our own departure is easy to neglect.

But we want to examine this issue briefly from a Kingdom perspective. How should we finish our business here on earth? How much time and thought should be given to the time after we are gone? If God owns all and we are just stewards of His assets, how does He expect us to dispose of the resources He has entrusted into our care? And finally, what can we do to ensure that our children will still have good relationships after we are gone? Obviously, one of the most important precautions we can take is to show them, while we are living, that "a man's life consisteth not in the abundance of the things he possesseth."[a] But beyond that, how can we through proper planning avoid conflict between our children?

To help answer these questions, let's look briefly at some of the basic tools available to develop an estate plan and some ways these tools can be used.

The Will

A will is a legal document drafted during your lifetime that provides those who survive you with some final instructions.

- A will names an executor or personal representative. This person will be responsible for entering the will into probate[b] and distributing your property as you instructed. Usually the best person to do this is your spouse. But if the spouse has already died or is not willing or able to handle the responsibility, most people name one of their older children or a child who lives close by. But before naming an executor in your will, why not discuss it with your family? Everyone in the family needs to understand that being an executor is primarily a responsibility, not a privilege. If you sense there is already tension in the family, it might be better to appoint someone not in the immediate family to oversee this process.

- For young parents the most important reason to make a will is to name guardians for minor children. This

---

[a]Luke 12:15
[b]The review or testing of a will to ensure it is authentic. This process occurs in court. Probate also refers to the process by which an executor manages and distributes the property of the deceased. Depending on the size and complexity of the estate, the costs can range from 3 to 7 percent of the estate and can take from several months to several years to complete.

decision needs to be made prayerfully, with spiritual values, lifestyle, age, and availability the primary considerations. Often the first tendency is to name grandparents, but they are rarely a good choice. While they are experienced in parenting, they are also losing stamina and flexibility at the very time a teenager needs a capable authority figure. And naming grandparents robs both them and the children of a special relationship. Most grandparents confess that they love caring for their grandchildren, but they also love it when they go home again. Hopefully you belong to a church community where brothers and sisters who share your spiritual values could fill this role, sometimes better than family members. When you name guardians, be sure to discuss it with them first. And be willing to reciprocate, as they may need a guardian for their children as well. While these situations can be awkward, you will find a blessing in openly working together within your community.

- A will gives directions to your personal representative for how you wish for your assets to be disposed of. This will be discussed more later.

- A letter of instruction should be placed with your will. This gives final instructions about household goods and personal effects. The letter of instruction will be discussed more in the next chapter.

- Your will is also an excellent place to leave your children a written copy of your personal testimony. Don't pay an attorney to write this out. On a separate sheet of paper, take this opportunity to give them final encouragement to follow Jesus Christ as you have done. Reiterate some of your life experiences and share with them the blessing you have found in being faithful to God. This isn't a time to reprimand, but to give godly counsel for the last time.

Durable Power of Attorney

In our final days we may not be able to properly manage our property. A Durable Power of Attorney is a legal document that gives someone else the power to make financial decisions for us should we become unable. Again, there is a tendency to immediately turn to family, but many times this is unwise. Placing this responsibility on one of your children can result in conflict and stress. It may be better to place this duty in the hands of a respected brother in your congregation.[c] The person chosen, at what point they begin their duties, what the duties will be, and when their role will cease is decided by you and clearly stated in the document.

Durable Power of Attorney for Healthcare

A separate document can be drawn up, granting power of attorney privileges to someone who will make healthcare decisions for you if you are unable. Normally a husband and wife would do this for each other. However, in case both of you would become disabled at the same time, you should name someone else whom you trust to make decisions with your wellbeing in mind. One of your children may be the best. This document does not give the person named the right to decide at what point you are unable to act for yourself. But it does give the individual the right to make some medical decisions when you are no longer able, and it provides access to your medical records if needed.

Advance Directive to Physicians

This is a statement that gives your healthcare provider instructions regarding your wishes when you are approaching the end of life. Sometimes called a living will, it allows you, while in physical and mental health, to state that you do not wish to be kept alive by heroic means when there is no hope for survival. If you have clearly stated that you do not want to be resuscitated under certain conditions, it relieves the family from making those difficult decisions.

---

[c] In some situations, a bank trust department may be named as power of attorney. They do not have vested interests, and have experience in managing estate assets.

A Trust

A trust is a form of property ownership. It is a legal agreement that involves three parties, the person who puts assets into the trust (the grantor), the person who manages the assets in the trust (the trustee), and the person who receives the benefits of the property in the trust (the beneficiary). In this kind of legal arrangement, the grantor transfers ownership of certain assets to the trustee, who manages the assets for the benefit of the beneficiary.

A trust has a different life span than the grantor who makes it, so it can continue business as usual after his death. When a grantor sets up a trust, he decides what property goes into it, describes the powers and duties of the trustee who manages it, and defines the rights of the beneficiaries. A grantor may name himself as trustee and continue managing his property as usual, so he does not lose control of his assets. If so, he would also name someone else as the successor trustee to continue managing the trust after his death, or when he is no longer able to do it himself.

At the death of the grantor, the trust does not go through probate, but continues business as usual, with ownership passing to beneficiaries as the grantor instructed. Some trusts continue long after the grantor's death, and others are liquidated and the assets distributed to heirs. But the trustee is legally bound to carry out the instructions of the grantor and not his own wishes. Trusts are typically formed by lawyers and can be a useful tool in an estate plan.

People sometimes think trusts are only useful for wealthy families with large holdings. But trusts can be helpful in planning for estates of all sizes. Choosing to use a trust may depend on the type of property you hold, the size and nature of your estate, or whether you have dependents who will need to be provided for later in their lives after you are no longer here. A few features of trusts and ways they can be helpful in estate design are listed below.

- In some situations trusts can help avoid estate taxes. The size of your estate will determine whether or not a trust is needed for this reason.

- If your children are young and lack financial

experience, it would be unwise to give them all their inheritance at once. After your death, a trust can be used to distribute funds in smaller amounts at specific times in their lives.

- If you own property in different states, a trust can eliminate the need for probate in each state at the time of your death. This can greatly reduce the time and cost of settling your estate.

- A trust can be used to provide for management of your property in the event of your disability. Property can be placed into a trust and managed properly through a Durable Power of Attorney.

- Trusts are not required to go through probate. While creating a trust is more expensive than writing a will, even moderate-sized estates will recover these costs since they later avoid probate expenses.

- Trusts can be designed to fit your individual needs. Because there are so many options, you should seek counsel to decide if a trust is suitable and what kind of trust you need. Find someone to help you design one that best fits your estate plans.

We have mentioned some of the basic tools for estate planning, but there are many more. Your property can be placed in a charitable gift annuity. This is an agreement between you and the charity that offers the annuity. In exchange for your nonrefundable transfer of cash or other property, the charity promises to pay you a specified amount for the rest of your life, based on an interest rate determined by your age. The annual amount paid to you is fixed and does not fluctuate with the economy. After your death, the remaining balance of your original transfer goes to the charity. Because a portion of the gift annuity is actually a gift to charity, part of the annuity income you receive is nontaxable.

Payable-on-death accounts allow you to name a beneficiary while 225 you continue to control your property during life. At your death, ownership is immediately transferred, avoiding the time and costs of probate. Some of these options have significant tax advantages and allow you to direct dollars to charity that would otherwise go to pay taxes. It is helpful to have someone who is knowledgeable of tax laws and charitable options to analyze your estate.

When a person dies, his assets go to one of three places:

- His beneficiaries. This may be your spouse, children, other dependents, or individuals you simply want to bless at your time of death.

- His church and charitable organizations. These can be any charities you feel God is calling you to assist.

- The government. Many individuals end up giving more than they planned or wished to the government in taxes.

The goal of an estate design is to direct the resources God has placed into your care to the places you believe He wants them to go. But if you do not plan appropriately, the government can ultimately receive funds that could have been given to a charity or your children. Sometimes this is simply due to procrastination, and other times it is due to a lack of understanding. The following scenario explores various possibilities for the dispersal of one's resources.

> *The goal of an estate design is to direct the resources God has placed into your care to the places you believe He wants them to go.*

Sam's Situation

Let's suppose Sam was a local carpenter, but back in 1960 his neighbor offered to sell him some farmland that joined Sam's property. Sam had always wanted to farm a little land, but he really wasn't in a position to buy right then. But Sam's neighbor had always liked him, so he offered to sell the land at a very low price. He even offered to let Sam pay it off over time with no interest. To start with, Sam could rent the land to another farmer, and the income from the land would almost make the payments.

This was too good an opportunity to pass up, so Sam gave the neighbor a small down payment, leased the land to another farmer, and made yearly payments to the former owner. Let's imagine that Sam bought this property for $30,000 and had it paid off within fifteen years. His construction company continued to expand, his sons helped him in the business, and the income from the farm was put into the bank with his other income.

As time went on, Sam became more aware of Kingdom stewardship and had a growing desire to use his resources to build the Kingdom. So after talking it over with his wife, they decided to use the farm income to bless others who were in need. So each year when the rent check came in, they invested it in the Kingdom. This became a high point of the year for Sam and his wife. They felt like they were using their resources in a way that glorified God.

The time finally came when, due to Sam's health, his sons took over the construction business, and Sam began to work less. Sam needed some of the income from the property, and it bothered him that he could no longer give as much to the Kingdom. But Sam resolved that when he died, he wanted to give the entire property to charity. So he considered how he could make this happen. His sons now owned the construction business and would not need additional income from the land. Sam had originally purchased the property for $30,000, but now it would sell for around $200,000. This meant that Sam would be subject to taxes on the $170,000 increase in the value of the property, and the money he paid in taxes wouldn't be able to go to the Kingdom.

So what should Sam do? He still needs some income, he wants to eventually bless the Kingdom, and he wants charity to receive as much as possible when he passes away. Let's look at a few options.

- If Sam sells the property now and gives the money to charity, he may still have to pay some income tax, and he would lose some of the income necessary to sustain him until he dies.

- If he waits to sell the property until after his death, it will go through probate. Then it is too late to offset taxes by donating to charity.

- Sam could donate the property to charity while he is still living and receive a tax deduction. The charity could then find a buyer and sell the property. Sam could direct the charity to use the proceeds of the sale in a number of ways.

For example, a portion of the funds could be placed in a charitable gift fund. In succeeding years, as Sam becomes aware of ministry opportunities and needs, he could advise the charity to distribute money from his charitable gift fund until it is depleted.

Another portion of the proceeds of the sale might be invested in a charitable gift annuity. The annuity would provide income for Sam and his wife as long as either is living. When both have died, the balance of the funds in the annuity would be used by the charity. This way, instead of paying taxes, Sam would receive a tax deduction, have income from the annuity for the rest of his life, and have the blessing of knowing that, upon his death, the funds he did not need will be used in ministry.

Many similar options are available. Before you sell appreciated property and pay unnecessary taxes, or before you decide that all of this is too complicated, seek counsel. Find someone who can help you design an estate plan that will accomplish what you believe God desires for you. An estimated 85 percent of Christians have some type of estate plan in place. But often these plans have become outdated or are not designed correctly.

For example, I heard of an older lady who read that it was a good idea to put your property in your children's names. That way, as a person ages, the children can manage the property, and at death it won't go to probate. Well, this woman wanted her estate to be passed to her three children, and she wanted to avoid probate, so she deeded the property to one of her daughters in order to take it out of her own name. At the time of her death, her will was read, stating that part of her estate should go to her church, and the rest was to be divided among her children. But it didn't work out that way. Her church didn't receive anything, and two of her children didn't either. Why was that? Wasn't her will clear enough? Did the attorney take advantage of an old woman? Was her will invalid?

No, there was nothing wrong with her will. But her home was her major asset, and since she had deeded it to her daughter, the woman no longer owned it. At her death, ownership transferred to the daughter also named on the deed. Of course, if the daughter had been upright, she would have found a way to honor her mother's wishes. The point to remember, however, is this. Since only those possessions that are in your name will flow through your will, the title on your property is extremely important if you want your will to achieve your desires. It's a good idea to have someone familiar with estate design examine your estate plan.

Conclusion

Understanding that we are stewards and God expects something from us will help us avoid procrastination. We will soon stand before God. In light of the resources I have at my disposal here in America and the great needs that exist around the globe, what does God expect from me as I close up shop here? How can I design an estate plan that will continue to build His Kingdom even after I am gone?

When writing to the church at Corinth, the Apostle Paul encouraged them to send a financial blessing to struggling saints in another country. The Corinthian church was wealthy. They had much more than they needed, and Paul reminded them that God desires equality among his people. "I mean not that other men be eased, and ye burdened: But by an equality, that now at this time your abundance may be a supply for their want."[d]

Death is a certainty, and we want to meet the Owner knowing we have been faithful.

There is a great imbalance in our world today, and God still

---

[d]2 Corinthians 8:13-14

desires equality. I believe our estate plans should be used to build the Kingdom. With all of the tax laws and different investment vehicles available, this can become confusing. If you have questions or would like advice in this area, help is available.[45] Death is a certainty, and we want to meet the Owner knowing we have been faithful.

Thirty

Avoiding Family Conflict

My father passed away in March 2003, and soon after this my mother began thinking of how she wanted to deal with her possessions and the possibility of moving to a smaller home. Different times she expressed a desire to simplify her life. She wanted to give away as much as she could and dispose of as much as possible while she was alive. One of the things I remember hearing her say was that she didn't want her children to disagree about possessions after she was gone.

So she gathered her children and grandchildren and had them go through all of her household items. When all the family had taken what they wanted, my mother called in the young couples in her congregation and gave them an opportunity to take whatever they could use. Some of her children hauled the rest of her unneeded belongings to a local mission thrift store. A few years later when my mother passed away, there was little left to dispose of. As a family, we have good memories of getting together and dispersing these belongings. But you don't have to live very long to find that this has not been everyone's experience.

Experienced estate planners will tell you that most family feuds are not over millions of dollars. Most are either about who was chosen to be the personal representative for the estate or over personal effects and household items. Generally, plans for larger property have been identified in the estate design, and instructions have been given as to where it should go. But sometimes the small items, the antique hutch or the family shotgun, were deemed too insignificant to leave instructions about, and they create hard feelings and stress. "Money brings out the best and the worst in families," said Doug Flynn, a certified financial planner in Garden City, New York. "I've seen people nearly fight to the death over an ashtray. And the nicest people often end up getting the short end of the stick."[46]

"Never say you know a man," said Swiss poet and pastor Johann Lavater, "until you have divided an inheritance with him."[47] It would be nice if we could report that conflict occurs only in unbelieving families. But unfortunately, feuds over personal effects and household items have been known to happen in professing Christian homes as well.

As parents design their estate plan, they should always consider what steps they can take today to ensure that their children will still love each other tomorrow. Imagine the shame and disgrace that comes upon the Kingdom of God when it becomes known that a "Christian family" is fighting over an end table or a grandfather clock. I can think of few rumors that have more potential to impact evangelism negatively than those that circulate about professing Christians arguing over material goods. So how can this be avoided? What steps can be taken to keep this from occurring in our families?

> *I can think of few rumors that have more potential to impact evangelism negatively than those that circulate about professing Christians arguing over material goods.*

You cannot control what happens to your children after you are gone. Most of us have discovered we aren't always especially wise in guiding our children while we are alive. We have to assume that controlling them from the grave is even more difficult. But I want to look at simple steps that can help your family maintain good relationships after you are gone. Even more important, these steps will bless the Kingdom of God and help to ensure that your estate is not a hindrance to the Gospel.

1. Distribute as much as possible while you are alive. The book of Proverbs tells us "Where no wood is, there the fire goeth out: so where there is no talebearer, the strife ceaseth."[a] We all understand the lesson. If you remove the wood from the fireplace, the fire won't last long. Conversely, if you add more wood to the stove, the fire will grow. The same is true in our estates. The more wealth, collectibles, and antiques you have, the more potential for unrest after your death. Distributing as much as possible now can help reduce the potential for conflicts. As stated earlier, disagreements often arise over who receives insignificant items. It doesn't take a large estate to create a fuss. But large estates do raise expectations, and when those expectations are not met, feelings can be strong. Another proverb says, "Hope deferred maketh the heart sick."[b] By distributing as many assets as possible before you die, you greatly reduce the possibility of disappointment.

2. Be transparent with family members. For nearly thirty years Evelyn and Diana Sakow believed that their father had died penniless and without a will in 1956. The girls worked their way through college and became public school teachers. The two women lived happy, uneventful lives until 1983 when Diana uncovered a secret while taking a night course in real estate. Not only had her father owned as many as one hundred properties in the Bronx, Brooklyn, and Manhattan, but he had also left a handwritten will leaving Evelyn, Diana, and their older brother Walter each a portion of the estate. Walter, who had been named the executor, had used all their father's assets to build a real estate empire without telling his sisters.

When this discovery was made, lawyers were hired and lawsuits filed, and for the next twenty-five years the three children fought over those properties. To this day, even though most of the properties have been divided, the feelings are bitter in the family. The "conspiracy to deny us our inheritance destroyed my family, broke my heart, and left me with scars that I have painfully struggled with and have not fully overcome even now, after all these years," Diana, 68, said in a recent affidavit.[48]

All of this could have been avoided if the father had given more thought to his will and been more transparent with his children. By

---

[a]Proverbs 26:20
[b]Proverbs 13:12

not telling some of his children about assets he owned, he set up his family for conflict. In the end this man's possessions became a curse to his family.

3. The letter of instruction. Next to a letter designating guardianship of minor children, perhaps the most important document in your estate design is your letter of instruction. As mentioned earlier, this letter designates who will receive household items and family treasures. View this as your last opportunity to share with your children. It should be kept with the will, but don't pay an attorney to do this; write it in your own handwriting. Tell your children who is to have the dining room table and the old pitcher that was handed down to you from Aunt Betsy. Specify who is to receive any item that you suspect might create conflict in your family. Creating a letter of instruction for your children can save them a tremendous amount of confusion and conflict.

Grandma's Clever Plan

While researching estate planning, I listened to many stories. Some were sad, some inspiring, and others just plain humorous. One man told about his grandma who had always been a hoarder. She was raised during the Great Depression, so her cupboards were filled with things like empty cottage cheese containers, and her attic and garage were crammed with clutter that, according to the rest of the family, belonged in the landfill. Everyone dreaded the thought of going through Grandma's stuff after she was gone.

When Grandma was about to leave this life, all of the family gathered around the bed. Just before she died, Grandma told the family she had hidden a large amount of money somewhere in the house. Shortly after revealing this astonishing fact, Grandma passed away. Grandma was well aware of the family's distaste for her miserly ways, and she also had a good sense of humor. Though the family pleaded to the end for her to reveal where the money was hidden, she just smiled and remained silent. As you can imagine, immediately after the funeral the house was cleaned out in record time. All the clutter the children had predicted would take months to dispose of was gone in a few days.

But they didn't find the money.

Finally, after the house was completely cleaned out, one of Grandma's brothers came over, loosened up a few floorboards, and uncovered the secret stash. It turned out that the "huge fortune" was only $2,000. Grandma had told her brother what she was up to and where the money was hidden but had made him promise not to say anything until the house was cleaned out. This may not have been the best way to finish things up, but the family laughingly had to admit that Grandma still knew how to inspire her children to get the work done.

Thirty-One
How Much Do My Children Need?

B illie sat in his easy chair one evening comparing his lottery Quick Pick numbers to the Sunday newspaper. He studied the sequence of numbers again and began to realize that his wildest dream was becoming reality. He and his wife Barbara Jean held the only winning ticket to the Lotto Texas jackpot of $31 million.[49] Billie Harrell was known as a religious man who attended a Pentecostal church, and he just *knew* this money was a godsend. He had been laid off from a couple of jobs in the last few years, and recently he had been stocking shelves at a local Home Depot. Life for forty-seven-year-old Billie, his wife Barbara Jean, and their three teenage children had been a string of financial difficulties.

But recently Billie had been purchasing lottery tickets. He knew they were a poor investment, and he should have known that covetousness and a desire to be rich are strongly condemned in the Bible,[a] but he had purchased the tickets anyway. And now, staring at the winning ticket on that warm night in June, his only thought was that his problems were over at last.

One month later Billie, his family, their minister, and Billie's attorney traveled down to Houston to collect his first check for $1.24 million. They had a little ceremony there, and Billie gave a speech. "Life has been tough," he told the media and those who had come to listen, "but I've persevered. I wasn't going to give up. Everyone kept telling me it would get better. I didn't realize it would get this much better!"

Life suddenly looked great to Billie. But unknown to him, his

---

[a]1 Timothy 6:6-10

problems had just begun. Upon returning home, he purchased a ranch, bought six homes for himself, and bought a new vehicle for each member of his family. He also made a large contribution to the church, and if anyone needed help, Billie was known as the man with the cash.

But then Billie discovered that his life was coming apart almost as fast as it had come together. He liked to help, but it seemed that people—family, friends, fellow worshipers, and strangers—showed up continually at his door, all wanting a fraction of his fortune. Choices about how to spend the money had to be made, and all the spending and lending put a terrific strain on his marriage and his relationships with his children. One day in early 1999, less than a year and a half after receiving the first of twenty-five payments of $1.24 million, Billie confided to a financial adviser, "Winning the lottery is the worst thing that ever happened to me."

The pressure continued to build, and finally Billie snapped. On May 22, 1999, just twenty months after winning the lottery, Billie locked himself into an upstairs bedroom where, according to investigators, he took his life. The very thing that had seemed like a blessing from heaven had actually been a curse to Billie and his family. The same family members who had initially rejoiced with Billie now turned on each other. The grandparents and grandchildren were at odds. A family war ensued over the remains of the fortune, and accountants couldn't be sure there would even be enough left to pay the estate taxes after all the legal fees were paid.

Sudden Cash, Sudden Conflict

Many of us have read accounts like this of individuals who received large sums of money and are thrust into sudden turmoil. But this doesn't only happen with lotteries. Sometimes well-meaning parents leave wealth to their children when they die, and those results can be devastating as well. The writer of Proverbs said a long time ago, "An inheritance may be gotten hastily at the beginning; but the end thereof shall not be blessed."[b]

There was a time when most families survived in a land-based

[b]Proverbs 20:21

economy. "A good man leaveth an inheritance to his children's children"[c] was a familiar verse regarding the importance of handing land down to the family. Loss of farmland was devastating. Land was the primary provider of income, so it was essential for it to stay in the family. The coming generations were depending on that land for survival.

In that economy a certain mindset developed that assumed the parents' wealth should always be passed on to the children. But in recent years many have challenged this assumption. Most of us are not living in a land-based economy. In our income-based economy there are many ways to provide for a family without land. So is it still best to pass the family's accumulated wealth to the children? Are you actually blessing your children when you leave large sums of money for them at your death?

Years ago an older farmer lived in an area where irrigation was necessary, and he had always wanted to upgrade the irrigation system on his farm. He had struggled with the old system for years, and he decided it would be a nice gift to his children if he installed a new system before he died. This change was an expensive undertaking, but the father really wanted his children to know how much he loved them, so he spent the final days of his life and over half a million dollars getting the new irrigation system installed. But even though the expense was great and the energy required took a great toll on him during his final days, this older farmer consoled himself with the knowledge that his children would be blessed for years to come. His children wouldn't have all the difficulties he had experienced with the old irrigation system.

The new system was finally completed, and the old farmer died. But when the children received the farmland, they discovered something. This new irrigation system had radically raised the value of the land. Suddenly some of the children realized how much money the land could be sold for and all the things they could buy with that money. Why keep farming land when you can get that much cash from it? Some children were in favor of selling the property and others wanted to keep it, and the contention became so intense that the issue finally made it into court. The end result was years of litigation, an estranged family, and legal fees that consumed much of what they had received.

The saddest part of this story is that none of these children even needed the money to begin with. They all had their own careers and good incomes, but this inheritance became the wedge that drove the family apart.

So what are we to do with the resources in our care at the time of death? Sometimes we know that additional money probably won't bless our children, but what if they expect to receive our assets? How will they respond if we don't give our wealth to them? What is the right thing to do?

These are very real questions that many of us will need to deal with, and there is not a standard answer that addresses every situation. But let's go back and establish in our minds some basic Biblical principles.

God Is the Owner of All

As believers, we all say we believe this. The Bible is clear that God owns everything we see. He says, "If I were hungry I would not tell thee: for the world is mine and the fullness thereof."[d] Paul told Timothy, "We brought nothing into this world, and it is certain we can carry nothing out."[e] We come empty-handed and we leave the same way. The question is not whether or not you are a steward, but whether you choose to work within a stewardship paradigm. If you choose to accept your role as a steward, then there are two important questions you must consider.

First, what does the Owner want you to do with the goods He has entrusted to

> *The question is not whether or not you are a steward, but whether you choose to work within a stewardship paradigm.*

you? Secondly, how many of these resources are for you and your family? These questions should guide us as we think about estate design and decide how to distribute assets owned by God.

[d]Psalm 50:12
[e]1 Timothy 6:7

How Much Do My Children Need?

When designing an estate plan, how much do your children actually need? This question will require prayerful consideration. Each child's situation is different and must be considered. But more important, consider why you are giving the money to them. Are you doing it from a stewardship perspective? Or do you feel compelled to follow tradition and custom? We mentioned that each child's needs are different, so let's consider some potential scenarios.

Paul told Timothy that we have a responsibility to provide for those under our care.[f] This verse addresses dependency. We have an obligation to provide for those who are dependent upon us for support. So let's assume you have a family of six children and the oldest is fifteen years old. You have one hundred thousand dollars of equity in your home, and you wonder where God would want that money to go if something should happen to you and your spouse. You are excited about different missions and places where money is desperately needed, and you wonder if maybe that is where it should go. But remember: your first responsibility is to provide for your dependents. Stewardship does not mean ignoring dependents. If something happens to you and your spouse, who will take care of your children? How will those expenses be met?

Suppose, on the other hand, that your children are older, have occupations, and are providing for themselves. They no longer depend on you, and the situation is entirely different. Now the assets in your care could be allocated to a Kingdom-building project you feel the Lord has put on your heart. Always be sure that you first address the needs of those who depend on you. As time progresses and your children become more financially independent, a will or trust can be adjusted to reflect this change in dependency.

Another concern many parents secretly wrestle with is how *not* receiving a large inheritance will affect their children. If children are aware that their parents have assets, what impact will it have on them if they don't receive the assets when the parents pass away?

Recently a mother who was working on her estate plan shared

this concern. She has a daughter who left home as a teenager, and her relationship with this daughter has been rocky ever since. The mother was concerned how the daughter would use the money if she did receive it, and what kind of effect it might have on her spiritually if she didn't. Her concern is legitimate, and there are two points to consider when dealing with it.

- **Make your decision from a spiritual rather than a traditional mindset.** In other words, decide how much to give your children with their spiritual good in mind. While money itself is amoral, an abundance of it can be detrimental. Wealth itself does not make a person holy or unholy. But wealth does provide opportunity, and some of us are not ready for the temptations that accompany wealth. In fact, most of us are probably less prepared than we suppose we are.

- **Don't try to project too far into the future.** If your spouse is still living, sit down and discuss how much should be given to each of your children if you were to distribute your assets now. Don't try to calculate how much they might be able to handle in the future. Analyze their need, decide how much would be good for them spiritually today, and let that drive your decision. As time goes on and conditions change, that decision can be altered.

As I interviewed older parents who have been godly role models in their latter years, I asked how they dealt with this issue of passing wealth on to their children. Almost all of them made similar comments. They first tried to live in a way that their children knew they were focusing on the Kingdom while they were alive. They were not waiting until death to bless those in need.

"My goal is to die with absolutely nothing," one told me with a smile. "But it would be a lot easier if the Lord would just tell me when I am going to die!" This older believer wanted all his assets to go to the Kingdom, and his children have the same desire. They have been blessed by their father's example of Kingdom living and are trying to walk in his footsteps.

Conclusion

Recently I heard a financial counselor say that of the situations he works with, most of the couples who are having financial difficulty either had received an inheritance or were hoping to. I do not believe many of us understand how crippling a future inheritance is for a child. It is difficult for some families to get serious about financial stewardship to begin with. But when a child knows there is a high probability of receiving a large sum of money in the future, there tends to be even less inclination. Many families in this situation go heavily into debt, assuming a future inheritance will bail them out. "People are leading lifestyles they can't sustain," one news article reported. "Kids run up bills they think they'll be able to pay off with their inheritance. When the money is bequeathed in a way they did not expect . . . the heir has a terrible problem."[50] We do our children a great disservice when we let them presume upon a future inheritance.

Go back to the foundational principle that God is the owner of all. If you actually believe and embrace this, then deciding where your resources should go after death will not be difficult. You will want them to go where you believe the Owner wants them to go. Every situation is different, and there is more than one correct way to distribute assets. But we have a wonderful opportunity to demonstrate a Kingdom focus—even after we are gone!

PART SIX

A Time to
Finish Faithfully

Thirty-Two

What Am I Supposed to Do?

We have spent considerable time addressing our responsibility as stewards. We have discussed the importance of focusing the last half of our lives and our accumulated resources on the Kingdom of Jesus Christ. But what exactly does that mean? We understand what it means to waste time and money. We know it is wrong to focus on ourselves during our latter years, but what is the alternative? And even more specifically, in your situation, what kind of changes would need to be made? What does a Kingdom-focused "retirement" look like? And what are you supposed to do with your abilities, time, and money?

Each of us will need to bring these questions before the Lord in prayer. But I believe one of the reasons we struggle with them is that we tend to divide the spiritual and the physical worlds. We think of prayer, Bible reading, and Bible study as spiritual activities, while our occupations and the labor required for survival are thought of as physical activities. The spiritual activities are seen as good and holy, but the others are a necessary evil. With this kind of mindset, being spiritual means spending less time at work and more time in prayer. But is that correct?

I am convinced that God never intended that we divorce our work from our worship. Rather than asking whether or not I am working too much, I need to examine why I am working at all. Sometimes I hear older people say, "I don't

> *God never intended that we divorce our work from our worship.*

believe in retirement, and I am going to keep working until I die."
While this may sound wonderful, it really doesn't tell us much. Maybe
they just like working better than sitting on the couch. The real question we need to ask ourselves is why we are working. Is the focus of my
life really to glorify God and build His Kingdom? If I am continuing
to work only for my own personal pleasure, then from a Kingdom
perspective, it may not matter whether I am at work or on the couch.

Sometimes we assume that choosing to focus on the Kingdom means
a radical change in our occupation and lifestyle. It can seem that our
occupation is carnal and that it must be discarded to really work for
the Lord. We picture service as living in a mud hut somewhere in
Africa, subsisting on grasshoppers and drawing our water from an
open well. We assume that anything short of subsistence living is
compromise. But does God really call everyone to that lifestyle? Does
every committed follower of Jesus need to live in a mud hut?

I don't know what your focus has been. Maybe you do need a radical
change in your standard of living. Perhaps you have drifted into a
materialistic, self-centered lifestyle that needs to change drastically.
Maybe God is even calling you to a mud hut. We live in the midst of
a self-seeking society, and its values can easily and quite subtly become
ours as well.

But when we conclude that the only way to really serve the Lord is
to live in a shack, and when we assume that anything short of living
in abject poverty is second best, we are tempted to subconsciously
give up on Kingdom-focused living. Many of us have responsibilities,
spouses, and local obligations that prohibit us from moving off to some
distant land. Perhaps we have health issues, aging parents, or church
responsibilities to consider. Moving away might be unfaithfulness to
what God has already given us to do. I can think of individuals here in
America whose flesh would love to move to some remote location just
to avoid the local obligations that have been laid upon them.

There are many different needs in the body of Christ and in society
around us, and we can't individually fill them all. But you can do
something. Even though you may feel insignificant, God has work
prepared for you.

Edward Hale said many years ago, "I am only one, but still I am one.

> *I am only one, but still I am one. I cannot do everything, but still I can do something; and because I cannot do everything, I will not refuse to do the something that I can do.*
> —Edward Hale

I cannot do everything, but still I can do something; and because I cannot do everything, I will not refuse to do the something that I can do."[51] The fact that she was blind and deaf makes this quote even more powerful.

Begin Where You Are

As you try to discern God's will for your final years, I want to encourage you to begin where you are. Don't just sit idly while waiting for revelation. Jesus said, "If any man will do his will, he shall know of the doctrine, whether it be of God, or whether I speak of myself."[a] This truth is powerful. Too often we pray for direction and plead that God would give us more information. But Jesus says to go ahead and do what you already know to do, and as you do this, He will give you more light. He may want you to use your current occupation.

I have been blessed as I have watched men and women use their livelihood, experience, and God-given talents to bless the Kingdom of God. I have watched those with medical skills help after a natural disaster. Individuals who raise fruit and vegetables provide the local Gospel mission with fresh produce. Cabinetmakers ship new kitchen cabinets across the country to help after a house fire. If an individual has a strong desire to bless the Kingdom, almost any occupation can be pressed into service.

Merchandise Ministry

I remember hearing of a merchant who saw a need. Many church groups were gathering occasionally to put relief packages together to be sent to other countries, and he noticed that they were paying higher prices than they needed to. As a merchant, he knew of better ways to purchase things, so he put together a catalog and distributed it

<hr>

[a]John 7:17

to interested churches. By purchasing in large quantities and donating his services, he was able to provide these supplies cheaper than these groups could have bought them anywhere else. This merchant was using the resources he had been given, his abilities and finances, to make the donations of others go much further. Rather than abandoning his occupation, he was using it.

Recently I received a phone call from a brother who works in plastics. He was working on an idea to take plastic trash that lies along roadsides and clogs streams in some Third World countries and transform it into building blocks for use in that country. He was combining his knowledge of plastics with his desire to help these people, and the potential result may bless many.

I also heard of an Amish man who designs horse-drawn equipment for his people, but has a desire to bless the larger Kingdom too. He has been working on a piece of farming equipment that has great promise in Third World countries. Even though he will receive no financial benefit from this project, he is excited about the ways this could help impoverished people. He will not even travel to these countries, but that hasn't dampened his eagerness. He is simply using his occupational skills and abilities and partnering with those who can travel to bless others.

Sometimes we assume that we will do more when we reach a certain income level or station in life. But go ahead and start in your present situation. Regardless of the many mistakes you may have made in the past or how unimportant you may feel, don't waste another day. Begin where you are!

God Loves to Work With Nothing

One of Satan's primary tactics as he attempts to make us ineffective in the Kingdom is to remind us of our insignificance. He loves to haunt us with memories of past failures, criticism we have received, and glaring daily inadequacies. We all have them. And it is easy to let these things hinder our Kingdom activity. When we were young, we felt like we had a lot to offer the Lord. But as time progressed, we began to understand our weakness. This knowledge can either cause us to lean more heavily on the Lord or retreat in fear of failure. But I want to

> *Our Lord loves to work with nothing.*

remind you that our Lord loves to work with nothing.

As I think back over the individuals who have challenged my spiritual walk and inspired me to do better, the faces that come to mind are not always well-known and respected leaders. While good speakers and writers have made an impact on my life, I have found myself at times challenged more by common people who live uncommon lives—individuals who have few resources but are determined to use them for the Kingdom.

Mina's Ministry

One of those is a lady known as Sister Mina, who lives alone in a little house in central Honduras. I have visited her several times and always come away awed by the experience. Sister Mina is blind, bedridden, and diabetic. She has lost both of her legs. Someone has to bring food and medicine to her, and she has little ability to do anything. She has very few earthly possessions, partly because other villagers have repeatedly robbed her, taking advantage of her blindness. So what is so inspiring about a blind, crippled diabetic? She is surrounded by extreme poverty, and she can't get out and help others. She can't take tortillas to the neighbor whose drunken husband just beat her up or help care for the children of the overburdened mother across the street. So what good is Sister Mina to her community and the Kingdom of God?

Sister Mina is a woman of prayer. When she hears the beating, she prays for the abused woman who lives next door. She prays for the discouraged mother across the street. She prays for the believers who regularly bring her food, water, and medicine. She wakes herself up in the middle of the night to pray. Sitting up in bed, she commits long periods of time to intercessory prayer. Sometimes she gets so sleepy she raises her arms just to stay awake. But she prays.

The other activity Sister Mina is involved in is counseling. No, she has never attended a counseling seminar, graduated with a degree in psychology, or even read books telling how it should be done. But many discouraged individuals have found their way to Sister Mina's bedside over the years. They shuffle in off the dirt path that goes by her house, share their struggles and discouragement, and then head back out with renewed purpose and vision. They sense in her an unconditional love and a desire to help. But something else generally occurs as they sit on that old folding chair beside her bed. It would be difficult to find a situation worse than Sister Mina's, yet she is rarely without a smile. She loves to share how the Lord is continually blessing her life. Her positive and thankful attitude is contagious. Listening to Sister Mina praise the Lord for His goodness in spite of her difficulties has a way of causing you to reevaluate your woes. If she can sing, pray, and continually trust in the Lord despite all her ailments, why can't I?

One pastor told me Sister Mina has never failed him yet. He pointed to that old beat-up folding chair and said, "Just a couple of hours sitting in that chair listening to her share the goodness of the Lord is enough to change the outlook of the most discouraged person." By earthly standards, Sister Mina doesn't have much. If there was ever a person who had the right to fear the future, you would think it would be her. Yet she is taking the few resources she has been given and using them to bless the Kingdom, right where she lives.

Stay Centered and Connected

Something about a merry-go-round attracts young children. Usually one child tries to make it go faster while another secretly wishes it would slow down. Though it makes them frightfully dizzy, children find the merry-go-round just scary enough to be attractive. But you will notice two things about frightened children on a merry-go-round. First, they hold on tightly, and second, they migrate toward the center.

There is a simple explanation for this. If you don't hang on tightly, you will be thrown off, and the closer to the center you stay, the less centrifugal force you experience. In fact, if you sit right in the center of that merry-go-round, you will feel little pull at all. The center is the safest place to be.

In midlife many of us become like children on a merry-go-round. Often life has sped up. We have tried to make serving God the center of our life, but there are many pulls. We know that prayer and spending time alone with God are essential, but these other pulls tend to draw us away from that which is most important. Often these are good things—family needs, community involvement, church activities, and requests from others who need our attention. But all of these draw on our time.

The merry-go-round of life spins faster and faster as all of these needs cry out for attention around the perimeter of our lives. Sometimes it seems there aren't enough hours in a day to meet the requests, and in the breathless pace and demands of the day, our dependence on the power of God relaxes. There just isn't enough time to deal with all these urgent situations and also spend quiet time with God. Something has to go. So, slowly we edge toward the pressing demands on the perimeter and slip away from our vital connection with God. The urgent becomes more pressing than the essential.

This phenomenon has been referred to as the tyranny of the urgent. We are constantly bombarded with requests and immediate needs, and in the midst of responding, we forget to stay centered and connected. We forget the vital importance of our life source. Jesus spoke of the importance of this connection. He said, "I am the vine, ye are the branches: he that abideth in me, and I in him, the same bringeth forth much fruit: for without me ye can do nothing."[b]

Recently I asked a grape farmer how long it takes for a branch to wilt after it is disconnected from the vine. He replied that you will see the effect in just a few minutes, especially in hot weather. It is obvious why Jesus chose the vine for His lesson. We are totally dependent on our connection to Him. If you desire wisdom to know where God wants you to serve, it is absolutely necessary that you stay centered and connected. Don't let the urgent pull you away from the essential.

---

[b]John 15:5

Conclusion

On July 21, 1969, Neil Armstrong stepped off the lunar module and onto the surface of the moon for the first time. An estimated 450 million people listened as Neil uttered the famous quote, "That's one small step for man, one giant leap for mankind." It was just one small step, much like a house painter stepping off his extension ladder after completing a project. And yet much of Neil's past had been spent preparing him for this moment. His education, career as a test pilot, and even mistakes along the way had been preparation for this assignment.

I don't know what God has for your latter years, and maybe you don't either. But I want to suggest that you do have a mission. God has been preparing you for something. He has been using your occupation, your life experiences, and even your mistakes to educate and prepare you for the task ahead. Your job may be one that others will observe and appreciate. Or it may be a calling similar to Sister Mina's that brings little praise and is unnoticed by others. Your work may even be misunderstood. But whatever it is, pursue it.

Finding our mission begins by taking one small step. Too often we wait for God to speak through a loud voice or a bolt of lightning. But is it possible that God has already opened a door that you are not recognizing? Is there some menial task that comes to your mind occasionally—something that would bless the Kingdom of God, yet seems insignificant? Go ahead and walk through that door. As you faithfully follow in the little tasks that God places before you, He will lead you on. Just begin where you are. Remember, God doesn't need much to work with; He only requires willing believers who stay centered and connected.

> *Finding our mission begins by taking one small step.*

Thirty-Three

For Such a Time as This

On May 2, 2008, the cyclone Nargis struck the country of Myanmar (Burma) with incredible ferocity. It was the deadliest storm in Myanmar's history, and the government estimated that at least 138,000 people were killed. Unfortunately, we will never know the total extent of the destruction or loss of life. Myanmar is governed by an extremely secretive and oppressive regime, and this sudden devastation presented them with a great dilemma. Their country was extremely impoverished before the disaster, and in the wake of this cyclone, the needs were overwhelming. But since the government had always tried to portray to the rest of the world that their country had no problems, it was reluctant to let any foreigners inside to assist.

Immediately following the storm, many countries offered assistance, only to be rejected and told that the government had the situation well in hand. But truth, in a country of fifty-five million people, is difficult to hide. Finally, bowing to international pressure, the country allowed certain organizations to enter. Just as the government had feared, once foreigners and their cameras entered the country, the devastation was no longer a secret. Various organizations tried to help, but the government did everything it could to make the relief effort difficult. Myanmar has a history of persecuting Christians, so it was difficult for people connected to Christian organizations to even get visas to enter the country. And yet, despite all the rigorous restrictions, much aid and literature did find its way into the country.

One year after the devastating cyclone, I was asked to go to Myanmar to investigate the results of aid that had been sent. Funds had been provided to help individuals get back on their feet following the storm, and some of this money had been given in the form of small business loans. In October of 2009 I landed in Yangon, the capital, to visit some of the recipients of this program and inspect some of the small businesses that had been created. I met with some leaders who had been in charge of administering the program and was assured that these loans had been a great blessing to the people who had received them. But I wanted to get out into the countryside and visit the recipients. The leaders explained that they would try to take me, but it was difficult for foreigners to leave the city. The government closely monitored all outsiders, and although I had received permission to visit Yangon, getting permission to travel farther out was more difficult.

Day after day passed, and I still hadn't been able to visit the place where the funds had supposedly gone. The time for my departure drew closer, and I became more suspicious. Had all the money really been used correctly? I was running out of time and feeling a little frantic. Would I have to go back without ever seeing any proof that the money had been spent as intended?

Finally I was told we would travel out to investigate the day before I was to fly home. I was ready bright and early. I had been told it was about a four-hour drive, so it didn't take much calculation to understand that if we wanted to get back in good time, we needed to get going. But that morning had delay after delay. No one was in much of a hurry, and I began to wonder if they were just stalling for time.

It was after noon before a rickety old van appeared with a driver, and we were finally off. I must confess that even though we were moving, I was extremely frustrated. My list of personal grievances was long. They had waited until the last part of the last day, the driving was going slower than they had predicted, and this old vehicle looked like it could conk out at any moment. Even if the trip went as planned, I wouldn't have more than an hour of daylight to see anything. Besides, the weather was oppressively hot and humid, and it seemed they could at least have provided a vehicle with air conditioning. So as we bumped along, I nursed my complaints and grumbled inwardly.

Then it got worse. We were stopped at many military checkpoints, and the government obviously was taking travel into this particular area seriously. I had understood that the locals I was traveling with had received clearance to bring a foreigner in, but as we stopped at one checkpoint, the driver handed a large stack of brand new shirts to the guard. Obviously, we weren't supposed to be here and were just bribing our way through. There is something a little disconcerting about traveling through a country like Myanmar without approval. The government is known to be ruthless toward offenders, and they have no qualms about eliminating those they don't appreciate.

Needless to say, when we arrived at our destination in the dark to "see" the results of this lending program, I was not in a good frame of mind. The heat was still oppressive, and as we left the vehicle and began hiking through high weeds in a swamp, my guide turned and in broken English informed me to watch carefully for poisonous snakes. I am not sure when I have felt as sorry for myself. As I tried to keep up with the guide, in the dark, without a flashlight, alert for snakes, and swatting at bugs in the sweltering heat, life just didn't seem fair.

After a nerve-wracking walk and a dark boat ride, my frustration mounting all the while, we came to a clearing where a shelter had been erected. Through the darkness I could see hundreds of people sitting cross-legged on the ground under one lonely light bulb.

We entered the area, and there I experienced one of the most humiliating events in my life. I listened as an interpreter explained that all of these people had come, some from a great distance, to say thank you for the help they had received. They stood in line that night, each wanting to shake my hand and tell how the aid they had received had impacted their lives. I stood there listening to their thankfulness, comparing it to my own ungratefulness that day.

Everything these individuals had owned had been swept away by the storm, yet they came with tears of thankfulness in their eyes. And what were they thankful for? They had each been given a fifteen-dollar loan to help them start a small business. Over the past six months they had faithfully paid back their loans in payments of sixty cents a week, and now they wanted to say thank you for the opportunity that these fifteen dollars had given them. Mothers surrounded by small children told how the fifteen-dollar loan had changed their lives. Some had used it to buy a few ducks and then sold eggs to repay the loan. Others bought and sold vegetables and earned enough to feed their children in the process.

I had tears in my eyes that night as well, but mine were tears of shame. I had spent my day wishing for air conditioning, a better van, more efficient travel, and daylight. But these Burmese were extremely thankful for just a fifteen-dollar loan.

Before we left, they wanted to pray. I cherish the memory of seeing rows of these poor people sitting in the semidarkness, open hands outstretched, singing "Praise God From Whom All Blessings Flow" in their own language. I think of them often when I start to complain because something isn't just right, and I thought of them as I returned home and stopped to get sandwiches in an American airport. The cost of that meal for my wife and me was fifteen dollars!

I wonder if any of us can really comprehend the disparity in our world. The inequality is mindboggling, yet it provides us with wonderful opportunity. As you consider how you want to use the final years of your life, think about some blessings and opportunities that are yours.

1. The truth of the Gospel. Millions of people travel through this life unsure why they are here. If you have received and responded to the message of the Gospel, you possess an incomprehensibly valuable gift. But while you rejoice in this gift, remember that many know nothing of it.

A few years ago a friend from China visited in our home. She is a first-generation Christian, and her face shines with a perpetual glow. She is used to worshiping in secret and rarely sees more than twenty believers in one room. After she attended our church, I asked for her impression, and her immediate response was, "So much light in one little room." She then asked why we needed so many believers in one place. "Why not spread out more?" We forget the great blessing we enjoy in knowing Jesus. But she remembers. She was in high school before she even heard there was a man named Jesus. And she is aware that many still haven't heard.

2. Ability to travel. If you have an American passport, you can enter almost any country on the globe. It is truly an unparalleled time, and we have been given an amazing opportunity. That doesn't mean that everyone should travel, but it does open doors for proclaiming Christ in places where Christian witness is scarce. I have been especially blessed as I have seen older believers use this opportunity to travel into isolated parts of the world and provide teaching for church leaders there. Many churches are pleading for good, sound doctrinal teaching. Many ministers, especially in places like Asia, have had very little experience, and many have been believers for only a few years themselves. They will sit for hours and days, if only someone will come and teach. In some of these settings, cults have moved in and filled this void. Many of us could help provide sound teaching to these first-generation believers who are crying out for Biblical instruction. Prayerfully consider using a week or two a year to serve the Lord in this way.

3. Financial resources. Living in a developed country, it is easy to feel sorry for ourselves. Others seem to have more and get along better financially. We know we should not compare ourselves among ourselves, and yet we do. And for some reason we tend to look up the ladder instead of down. We are sure the wealthy in the world should share with the poor, but we seldom stop to realize how wealthy we are. Leaving our safe and sheltered setting can be an eye-opening experience. As you prayerfully consider how to live out the remainder of your life, remember to give financially. Don't wait until your house, your bank account, and your life are just the way you want them. All of us need to share. You may not believe you have much to contribute, but people in places like Myanmar would disagree. Even if all you have is fifteen dollars, you can use it to bless someone!

> *For some reason we tend to look up the ladder instead of down.*

Conclusion

Sometimes I think we forget the uncommonness of our time. We have grown up in the midst of prosperity, and this is all most of us have ever known. All around us is plenty. We forget it hasn't always been like this, and in many parts of the world it still isn't. But there is something else we tend to forget.

It may not always be like this. Wealth and opportunity have changed hands throughout history, and the opportunity and prosperity we now enjoy may not always be with us.

Immediately after the Civil War, the Southern currency became worthless. People who had saved their Confederate States of America (CSA) dollars suddenly found themselves holding paper money that meant nothing. I wonder how many of them wished they could back time up and exchange their CSA dollars for something that would retain its value. But now it was too late. The war was over, and the time of opportunity gone.

We will face a similar scenario. A time is coming when everything around us, things that now captivate men and hold great value, will be worthless. Even in the short term, our economy is shaky at best. We have no promise of continued prosperity. How disappointing to suddenly find that money or possessions we have been hoarding are suddenly worthless. While we have the opportunity, let's use "our" resources to bless the Kingdom. As Mordecai told Esther many years ago, "Who knoweth whether thou art come to the kingdom for such a time as this?"[a]

> *A time is coming when everything around us, things that now captivate men and hold great value, will be worthless.*

[a]Esther 4:14

Thirty-Four
The Spirit of Caleb

On April 13, 1888, Alfred Nobel sat down to read his French newspaper and received an unpleasant shock. There across the front page in bold print the headlines screamed, *"Le marchand de la mort est mort* (The merchant of death is dead)." Alfred sat in stunned amazement and read his own obituary. He and his brother Ludvig were both famous inventors, and the newspaper had mistakenly thought Alfred had died instead of Ludvig. As the morning progressed, that headline wouldn't leave Alfred's mind.

Merchant of Death

Was that really what the world thought of him? When he died, was that how he would be remembered? Alfred had invented dynamite. His objective had been the common good by providing a better way to construct tunnels, canals, and bridges.

Though Alfred's goal had been to help humanity, this article went on to portray him as responsible for the arms race of the day. It described him as a killer, a "bellicose monster" whose inventions had served to "boost the bloody art of war from bullets and bayonets to long-range explosives."[52] A peaceful man at heart and an inventor by nature, this strong indictment was unsettling. Was this the legacy he was leaving? Had all of his work in explosives just furthered the cause of warfare and fueled the continual conflict that consumed humanity?

Alfred was a wealthy man, as the article noted, and that morning he resolved to make some changes. Not wanting to go down in history with such an awful epitaph, Alfred Nobel created a will that shocked his family and established the now-famous Nobel Peace Prize, designed to reward individuals who encourage peace between nations. Today Alfred Nobel is better known for his contribution to world peace than for his invention of dynamite.

Alfred had an opportunity that most of us do not have—a chance to reevaluate his legacy late in life and make some adjustments. How would your obituary read? What would you be best known for if you died today? If someone wrote an article about your life, your pursuits, and your accomplishments, what would it say?

The Orange Revolution

The morning of November 25, 2004, Natalia Dmytruk, forty-eight, soberly walked into the studio of the state-run television station in Ukraine.[53] Natalia couldn't help but tremble as she considered the task before her and the potential cost to herself and her family. Yet as she said later when interviewed, "I was sure I would tell people the truth that day. I just felt this was the moment to do it."

The national presidential elections in Ukraine that year had been a messy affair. Ukrainian reformer Viktor Yushchenko was running against the Russian-backed incumbent prime minister, and in the middle of the race, Yushchenko had suddenly been poisoned. The mysterious dioxin poisoning had almost killed him and permanently disfigured his face, and Viktor's family and friends had pled with him to withdraw from the race. But Viktor Yushchenko refused to give up so easily, and by election day, polls showed him with a comfortable 10 percent lead. The people of Ukraine were obviously ready for change.

But the existing regime had only begun to fight. Throughout the election process there were widespread reports of corruption. Election monitors reported extensive vote-rigging, and despite Viktor Yushchenko's popularity, the government prepared to announce that the incumbent president of Ukraine had been reelected.

As Natalia Dmytruk entered the television studio that morning, she had a choice. She could tell the public what the government was saying, or she could tell them the truth. Natalia was not a primary anchor for the television station; her job was to communicate with the hearing impaired. As Ukrainians watched the news, Natalia appeared in a small box in the lower corner of their televisions as she translated the newscaster's message into sign language.

So on that Thursday morning, as the newscasters broadcasted the government-scripted message to the general public, Natalia signed. But when the newscasters relayed the false message that the government-backed candidate had won, Natalia, in a daring protest, signed to the deaf who were watching, "I am addressing everybody who is deaf in the Ukraine. Our president is Victor Yushchenko. Do not trust the results of the central election committee. They are all lies . . . And I am very ashamed to translate such lies to you. Maybe you will see me again—" she concluded, hinting at what might happen to her when the authorities found out. She then continued signing the rest of the officially scripted news as it was given.

Natalia's defiance of the regime started what has become known as the Orange Revolution. Deaf citizens used their cell phones to send text messages carrying the real story to others, and within a matter of hours, masses of Ukrainian citizens spilled into the streets protesting the fraudulent election results. Natalia's act of defiance emboldened public protests that grew until the government finally buckled. A new election was held, and the opposition candidate, Viktor Yushchenko, was eventually declared the winner.

A Christ-Centered Counter-Culture Demonstration

Natalia Dmytruk was given only a small window on the big screen, but she used it in a powerful way to expose truth. As I consider the events surrounding the Orange Revolution and the impact of her message in the little window at the lower right-hand corner of the screen, I am reminded of the opportunity we have been given.

The prevalent message going out is that wealth, fame, and natural beauty matter. I am amazed by our society's infatuation with celebrities. I see older people on airplanes poring over glossy magazines, admiring and discussing the rich and famous. Never mind that many of these famous folks do not retain a relationship more than a few years, or that they seem to be constantly entering or leaving a rehab facility for drug abuse. Even though they represent the segment of society least capable of coping with life, the public admires and emulates them.

Our culture has developed a kind of point system. Good looks, physical ability, wealth, and fame each bring with them a certain number of points. Our value as individuals depends on how many points we have. When a movie star is good looking, wealthy, and famous, the world beats a path to his mansion. Natural ability, fame, and fortune obviously control the big screen.

But this entire message of the age is false. Everything around us, all the earthly power, possessions, and prestige, will soon be worthless. That is the truth. And each of us has been given just a little corner of the screen to proclaim this reality. Our responsibility is to use our corner to faithfully deliver the Christ-centered, counter-culture truth. Regardless of the fact that the big screen is continually screaming a self-centered, self-indulgent, materialistic message, we know better.

So how are you using the small corner of the screen you have been given? What kind of message is coming from your life? What message do you envision coming out of your final years?

A Cloud of Witnesses

Immediately following the catalog of the faithful in the eleventh chapter of Hebrews, the writer says, "Wherefore seeing we also are compassed about with so great a cloud of witnesses, let us lay aside every weight, and the sin which doth so easily beset us, and let us run with patience the race that is set before us."[a] The writer had just enumerated many faithful men who had served the Lord, and he refers to them as a "cloud of witnesses." He encourages us to imitate their faithful lives.

> *How are you using the small corner of the screen you have been given?*

After interviewing many faithful examples and reading stories of others, I think I know a little of what the writer of Hebrews must have felt. I could tell about John, who, though not wealthy enough to give of his own resources, gleaned produce in orchards and fields after harvest and took his grandchildren with him while he distributed

---

[a]Hebrews 12:1

what he'd gleaned to the poor. Or Timothy, who, fighting cancer and grieving the death of his wife of forty-seven years, committed the remainder of his life to evangelizing and counseling dysfunctional families in the inner city. I think of Luke, whose wife left him four years after their marriage. His testimony of fidelity, even though it meant living alone for over sixty-five years, encouraged many who came after to remain faithful and take their vows seriously. And Mike and Edna, who, though they could afford to travel anywhere in the world, chose to use their vacation time and money to aid in disaster relief work. I remember Robert, who, despite having lost both his legs, traveled with a work team to help earthquake victims in Haiti. I could list dozens of other older believers who have used their little corner of the screen to proclaim truth in their day and who have left behind a legacy of Kingdom building.

Biblical stewardship is not a way of giving, but a way of living. What really inspires us in the lives of others? What causes us to sit up and take notice? Some of the examples I mentioned were raised in wonderful godly homes. Others were not. Some had wealth and ability, while others had little of either. So what did all of these people have in common? What qualities in the lives of older mentors motivate us to change our own lives? What are the ingredients for a dynamic, Spirit-filled, Kingdom-focused life that inspires others?

An Old Testament character had those ingredients. The Bible doesn't give a lot of detail about his life, but it gives enough for us to understand that this man had something different. His name was Caleb.

> *Biblical stewardship is not a way of giving, but a way of living.*

The Spirit of Caleb

When the twelve Israelite spies returned from spying out the land of Canaan, the Bible says only two of the spies brought back a report that was pleasing to God. God mentions Caleb specifically by name when He makes this wonderful declaration: "But my servant Caleb, because he had another spirit with him, and hath followed me fully, him will I bring into the land whereinto he went; and his seed shall possess it."[b]

Something in Caleb was different. Caleb saw the same giants in the land of Canaan the other spies had seen. He knew those mighty Canaanite armies were more powerful than the Israelites. He had seen the walled cities and the mighty fortresses. He was even well aware that the children of Anak lived there—men rumored to be nine feet tall and extremely fierce. Caleb knew all this. He knew the Israelites were like grasshoppers beside this kind of enemy. So why did Caleb indignantly face the people and say, "Let us go up at once, and possess it; for we are well able to overcome it"?[c]

God answers that question for us. He says, "Because he had another spirit with him."[d]

Another Spirit!

Something different was driving Caleb. He saw something the others did not and arrived at conclusions that seemed strange and wrong to the majority. Caleb didn't win the argument at Kadesh Barnea, and for almost forty years he found himself plodding along in the dusty desert, listening to the murmuring of the faithless masses.

But at the end of Caleb's life, we get one more glimpse into this spirit. If there was ever a qualified candidate for retirement, it was Caleb. If anybody deserved rest from the battle, wasn't it him? Moses was gone now, and with a large family, a long history of faithful service, and the normal aches and pains that eighty-five years brings to a body, surely it was time for the La-Z-Boy. But instead we find Caleb begging Joshua to let him take on those same giant Anakims his peers had been so fearful of and who still resided in the hill country. "Now therefore give me this mountain,"[e] Caleb pled with Joshua.

Picture this in your mind. An eighty-five-year-old man begs his commander to be allowed to take one more mountain! Imagine the effect this had on younger soldiers! How many young men went out to battle with renewed vigor because of the inspiration of Caleb's

---

[b]Numbers 14:24
[c]Numbers 13:30
[d]Numbers 14:24
[e]Joshua 14:12

example? The Lord said Caleb had another spirit, but what kind of spirit was it? What would inspire a man like Caleb to keep asking for more battles and more opportunities to fight? Let's look at some characteristics and attitudes that define the spirit of Caleb.

> *We like to assume that peer pressure is a problem only for youth, but most of us are very susceptible to it even in old age.*

1. Caleb stood for truth. We like to assume that peer pressure is a problem only for youth, but most of us are very susceptible to it even in old age. Can you imagine standing up against ten other spies and all the tribes and stating an opinion so wildly unpopular that they were ready to stone you? The visible facts were not in Caleb's favor. There really were giants, walled cities, and much bigger armies in that land. We can only imagine the murmuring. *What kind of a man would try to take us and our children into that kind of slaughter?* But Caleb trusted God and was willing to stand for truth in the face of the opposition. That was part of the spirit of Caleb. And I am thankful to see that same spirit in many older believers I know.

2. Caleb was a man of persistent pursuit. Caleb never lost his vision for following God. All through those years of wandering in the wilderness, his pursuit of the will of God was clear. It would have been tempting to succumb to discouragement out there. Caleb couldn't understand from the beginning why the rest of the people wouldn't just believe what God said. And after many years of putting up with their unbelief, it would have only been normal to feel like surrendering. But Caleb didn't give up.

Years later the Apostle Paul described that same passionate desire to follow God when he said, "I press toward the mark for the prize of the high calling of God in Christ Jesus."[f] Those are the words of a man who, with purpose of heart, is pursuing God with all he has. Caleb and the Apostle Paul both exhibited a single purpose in their lives that was contagious.

3. Caleb compared the problem to the promise. It seems like Caleb couldn't even imagine a promise from God not being performed. Too often I find myself considering the obstacles, and there are always plenty of them to examine. Sometimes I think I even have a "gift" for this! There is nothing wrong with examining problems. I think God wants us to be realistic about our obstacles, and I believe Caleb was. He saw the giants just as clearly as any of the other spies did. But while the ten spies compared their ability to the problem, Caleb compared the problem to the promise.

4. Caleb didn't live in the past. We have a tendency as we grow older to focus more on past battles than on present warfare. Caleb didn't do that. Think what wonderful history tours Caleb could have conducted! Can you imagine the stories he could have told and the talks he could have given? There is a time to look back and learn from the past. There is nothing wrong with recounting history, admiring days gone by, and reliving victories past, but it is valuable only if it equips us for the battle today. We are not living in the time of the early church or the Reformation. While there is much we can learn from those eras, we need to keep our primary focus on the mountains that haven't been conquered.

Caleb lived out this truth. He didn't allow the victories of the past to so envelop his mind that he became useless in fighting the battle in his day. He didn't try to take all the mountains, and neither did he let the fact that there were many mountains keep him from his. Where is your focus? What is the battle in your day? What

> *While the ten spies compared their ability to the problem, Caleb compared the problem to the promise.*

[f]Philippians 3:14

is the mountain on which God is calling you to fight? You will need to prayerfully address this question in your own life, but rest assured, God has a mountain for you.

Conclusion

Alfred Nobel made a midcourse correction in his life. Many never have that opportunity. Take time to analyze your life. Examine it carefully and then answer this question: Would the way you envision living the last half of your life make sense if the Gospel didn't exist?

Many of us find it easy to believe we are living lives of self-denial and dedication to Jesus, when in reality we may simply be conforming to the expectations of our particular church or culture. Some of the things we like to think are a sign of selfless living may actually make our lives much more enjoyable and stress-free. There are enough natural benefits in belonging to conservative churches that, even if the Gospel were a myth, there would be plenty of reasons to continue living as we are.

But what I have consistently noticed in believers who are sold out for Christ is that their lives would be pure foolishness were it not for the Gospel. Their dedication to Jesus Christ causes them to make choices that don't make earthly sense.

I am blessed as I see a growing number of middle-aged and elderly believers taking another look at what it means to live the Christian life. They have the spirit of Caleb, a desire to conquer more mountains for the Lord.

May the spirit of Caleb describe your life as well. My prayer is that your generation be recognized not for casually coasting but for continuing to conquer. May you be known for intentionally pursuing the enemy, encouraging your fellow soldiers, and fighting for the Kingdom. And may you keep on going in His strength—till you're gone!

Now also when I am old and grayheaded, O God, forsake me not; until I have shewed thy strength unto this generation, and thy power to every one that is to come.[g]

---

[g]Psalm 71:18

Endnotes

[1] Alan Farnham, "Baby Boomers to Inherit Trillions," <http://abcnews.go.com/Business/baby-boomers-inherit-116-trillion-historic-transfer-wealth/story?id=12427504>, accessed on December 8, 2011.

[2] Robert Frank and Amir Efrati, " 'Evil' Madoff gets 150 Years in Epic Fraud," *The Wall Street Journal,* June 30, 2009, <http://online.wsj.com/article/SB124604151653862301.html>, accessed on August 4, 2011.

[3] Steve Fishman, "Bernie Madoff, Free at Last," *New York Magazine,* June 6, 2010, <http://nymag.com/news/crimelaw/66468/>, accessed on August 4, 2011.

[4] <http://www.timesonline.co.uk/tol/news/world/us_and_americas/article5904340.ece>, accessed on August 4, 2011.

[5] Foster Farms, <www.fosterfarmsfoodservice.com>, accessed on October 18, 2010.

[6] Tom Brokaw, *The Greatest Generation*, Random House Publishers, New York, 1998, p. 12.

[7] Christopher Chabris and Daniel Simons, *The Invisible Gorilla and Other Ways Our Intuitions Deceive Us,* Crown Publishing, New York, 2010.

[8] <http://www.siasat.pk/forum/showthread.php?39184-The-Monkey-Business-Illusion>, accessed on October 25, 2010.

[9] Thieleman J. van Braght, *Martyrs Mirror,* Herald Press, Harrisonburg, VA, 2007, p. 453.

[10] Eric de Jong, *Nature and Art: Dutch Garden and Art: Dutch Garden and Landscape Architecture, 1650-1740,* University of Pennsylvania Press, Philadelphia, 2000, Ch. 5.

[11] James Urry, "Wealth and Poverty in the Mennonite Experience: Dilemmas and Challenges," *Journal of Mennonite Studies,* Vol. 27, 2009, p. 31.

[12] *Martyrs Mirror,* p. 8.

[13] Jean M. Twenge, Ph.D., *Generation Me,* Simon and Schuster, New York, 2006, <http://www.generationme.org/aboutbook.html>, accessed on March 28, 2011.

[14] David Platt, *Radical,* Multnomah Books, Colorado Springs, 2010, p. 70.

[15] "Hunger and World Poverty," <http://www.poverty.com/>, accessed on March 31, 2011.

[16] Anah Shah, <http://www.globalissues.org/issue/587/health-issues>, accessed on March 31, 2011.

[17] Jeffrey Sachs, *The End of Poverty: Economic Possibilities for Our Time,* Penguin Press, New York, 2005, p. 28.

[18] Data from the World Bank, Figures are in 1993 purchasing parity dollars, World Development Indicators, 2008.

[19] United Nations Development Program, Human Development Report 2007, (Palgrave Macmillan, New York, 2007), p. 25. Also see: Steve Corbett and Brian Fikkert, *When Helping Hurts,* Moody Publishers, Chicago, 2009, p. 42.

[20] Dom Helder Camara, *Revolution Through Peace,* Harper & Row, New York, 1971, pp. 142-143.

[21] Molly Edmunds, *Nature's Most Amazing Events,* HowStuffWorks.com, 2011, <http://dsc.discovery.com/tv/natures-most-amazing-events/how-stuff-works/salmon-run.html>, accessed on April 6, 2011

[22] American Pets Products Association, <http://www.americanpetproducts.org/press_industrytrends.asp>, accessed on March 12, 2011.

[23] Anah Shah, "Today, around 22,000 children died around the world," <http://www.globalissues.org/article/715/today-over-22000-children-died-around-the-world>, accessed on March 12, 2011.

[24] David Bercot, *Will the Theologians Please Sit Down,* Scroll Publishing, Amberson, PA, 2009, p. 8.

[25] Dr. Jordan Grafman, Chief of Cognitive Neuroscience Section of the National Institute of Neurological Disorders and Stroke (NINDS), October 17, 2006, quoted in "Joy of Giving," ScienCentral Archive, <http://www.sciencentral.com/articles/view.php3?article_id=218392880>, accessed on July 27, 2012.

[26] Randy Alcorn, *Money, Possessions, and Eternity,* Tyndale House Publishers, Wheaton, IL, 1989, p. 207.

[27] Irenaeus Against Heresies, *The Ante-Nicene Fathers,* Eerdmans Publishing Company, Grand Rapids, MI, 1989, (c. 180, E/W), Vol.1, pp. 484-485.

[28] <http://ssjothiratnam.com/?p=747>, accessed on August 1, 2011.

[29] Nathan Overholt, "How Can We Inspire Our Men to Fight?" April 15, 2008. Used by permission. Condensed and adapted.

[30] Social Security Online, <http://www.ssa.gov/policy/docs/quickfacts/stat_snapshot/>, accessed on June 5, 2011.

[31] Larry Burkett, *Preparing for Retirement,* Moody Press, Chicago, 1992, p. 27.

[32] Larry Swedroe, <www.moneywatch.bnet.com/investing/blog/wise-investing/how-to-create-and-live-a-fulfilling-retirement/2285>, accessed on April 25, 2011.

[33] Harold Kushner, *When All You've Ever Wanted Isn't Enough,* Simon and Schuster, New York, 2002, p. 20.

[34] Quiet Hour Ministries, "The Face of Jesus," February 18, 2007, <http://www.qhministries.org/Document.Doc?id=56>, accessed on April 3, 2011.

[35] J. M. Darley and C. D. Batson, "From Jerusalem to Jericho: A study of Situational and Dispositional Variables in Helping Behavior," 1973, <http://faculty.babson.edu/krollag/org_site/soc_psych/darley_samarit.html>, accessed on April 4, 2011.

[36] <http://www.brainyquote.com/quotes/authors/m/mother_teresa.html#ixzz1IgS523ob>, accessed on March 10, 2011.

[37] James Gilchrist Lawson, *Deeper Experiences of Famous Christians*, Warner Press, Anderson, IN, 1911, copied by Stephen Ross, <http://www.wholesomewords.org/biography/biomoody4.html>, accessed on May 8, 2011.

[38] Don Stephens, *Ships of Mercy*, Thomas Nelson, Inc., Nashville, TN, 2005, p. 15.

[39] Family Business Institute, <http://www.familybusinessinstitute.com/index.php/Succession-Planning/>, accessed on June 6, 2011.

[40] Michael Bergdahl, *The Ten Rules of Sam Walton*, John Wiley and Sons, Hoboken, NJ, 2006, p. 150.

[41] *John G. Paton, D.D., Missionary to the New Hebrides: An Autobiography*, Hodder and Stoughton Publishers, London, 1891, p. 56.

[42] Annelena Lobb, "Fighting Family Feuds," May 21, 2002, <http://money.cnn.com/2002/05/17/pf/q_family_feud/index.htm>, accessed on August 17, 2011.

[43] United Methodist Foundation for the Memphis and Tennessee Conferences, "Quotes on Stewardship," <http://www.umfmtc.org/quotes-on-stewardship.html>, accessed on January 25, 2012.

[44] Tom Jackman, "Gene Upshaw's dramatic death-bed scene: The rest of the story," *The Washington Post*, Post Local, May 5, 2011, <http://www.washingtonpost.com/blogs/the-state-of-nova/post/gene-upshaws-dramatic-death-bed-scene-the-rest-of-the-story/2011/05/04/AFSF86tF_blog.html>, accessed on July 6, 2011.

[45] You can contact Christian Aid Ministries Biblical Stewardship Department at 330-893-2428, or contact them at kingdomfinance@camoh.org. The staff there can help design your estate plan. There is no obligation or charge for these services.

[46] Annelena Lobb, "Fighting Family Feuds," May 21, 2002, <http://money.cnn.com/2002/05/17/pf/q_family_feud/index.htm>, accessed on August 17, 2011.

[47] Quotations Book, <http://quotationsbook.com/quote/20985/>, accessed on August 17, 2011.

[48] Charles Bagli, "Family Feud Over Estate Ends After Twenty-Five Years," *New York Times*, (New York Edition), March 29, 2009, p. 23.

[49] Steve McVicker, "Billie Bob's (Mis) Fortune," *Houston Press*, February 10, 2000.

[50] Ken Kamen, quoted by Sheryl Nance-Nash, "Plan Now to Avoid an Inheritance Feud Later," *Daily Finance*, February 27, 2011, <http://www.dailyfinance.com/2011/02/27/how-to-avoid-an-inheritance-feud/>, accessed on June 28, 2011.

[51] Quotations Book, <http://quotationsbook.com/quote/45550/>, accessed on June 30, 2011.

[52] Sevastian Winters, *The Resurrection of Alfred Nobel,* December 11, 2006, <http://www.associatedcontent.com/article/94675/the_resurrection_of_alfred_nobel.html>, accessed on August 17, 2011.

[53] Nora Boustany, "As Ukraine Watched the Party Line, She Took the Truth Into Her Hands," *The Washington Post,* April 29, 2005.

About the Author

Gary Miller was raised in an Anabaptist community in California and today lives with his wife Patty and family in the Pacific Northwest. Gary's desire has been to encourage Christians in developed countries to share their resources and focus more on the Kingdom of God. He also continues to work with the poor in Third World countries and manages the SALT Microfinance Solutions program for Christian Aid Ministries.

Gary's enthusiasm for Kingdom building has prompted him to share his vision in writing. Seeing a need for Christians in all age groups to take a fresh look at their goals and priorities in life, especially in finances, Gary began to develop the Kingdom-Focused Living series. His first book in the series, *Kingdom-Focused Finances,* was released in 2010, and his second book, *Charting a Course,* in 2011.

If you have comments about any of the Kingdom-Focused Living books, you can share your thoughts by sending an e-mail to kingdomfinance@camoh.org or writing to Christian Aid Ministries, P.O. Box 360, Berlin, Ohio, 44610.

Christian Aid Ministries

Christian Aid Ministries was founded in 1981 as a nonprofit, tax-exempt 501(c)(3) organization. Its primary purpose is to provide a trustworthy and efficient channel for Amish, Mennonite, and other conservative Anabaptist groups and individuals to minister to physical and spiritual needs around the world. This is in response to the command ". . . do good unto all men, especially unto them who are of the household of faith" (Gal. 6:10).

Each year, CAM supporters provide approximately 15 million pounds of food, clothing, medicines, seeds, Bibles, Bible story books, and other Christian literature for needy people. Most of the aid goes to orphans and Christian families. Supporters' funds also help clean up and rebuild for natural disaster victims, put up Gospel billboards in the U.S., support several church-planting efforts, operate two medical clinics, and provide resources for needy families to make their own living. CAM's main purposes for providing aid are to help and encourage God's people and bring the Gospel to a lost and dying world.

CAM has staff, warehouse, and distribution networks in Romania, Moldova, Ukraine, Haiti, Nicaragua, Liberia, and Israel. Aside from management, supervisory personnel, and bookkeeping operations, volunteers do most of the work at CAM locations. Each year, volunteers at our warehouses, field bases, DRS projects, and other locations donate over 200,000 hours of work.

CAM's ultimate purpose is to glorify God and help enlarge His kingdom. ". . . whatsoever ye do, do all to the glory of God" (I Cor. 10:31).

The Way to God and Peace

We live in a world contaminated by sin. Sin is anything that goes against God's holy standards. When we do not follow the guidelines that God our Creator gave us, we are guilty of sin. Sin separates us from God, the source of life.

Since the time when the first man and woman, Adam and Eve, sinned in the Garden of Eden, sin has been universal. The Bible says that we all have "sinned and come short of the glory of God" (Romans 3:23). It also says that the natural consequence for that sin is eternal death, or punishment in an eternal hell: "Then when lust hath conceived, it bringeth forth sin: and sin, when it is finished, bringeth forth death" (James 1:15).

But we do not have to suffer eternal death in hell. God provided forgiveness for our sins through the death of His only Son, Jesus Christ. Because Jesus was perfect and without sin, He could die in our place. "For God so loved the world that he gave his only begotten Son, that whosoever believeth in him should not perish, but have everlasting life" (John 3:16).

A sacrifice is something given to benefit someone else. It costs the giver greatly. Jesus was God's sacrifice. Jesus' death takes away the penalty of sin for everyone who accepts this sacrifice and truly repents of their sins. To repent of sins means to be truly sorry for and turn away from the things we have done that have violated God's standards. (Acts 2:38; 3:19).

Jesus died, but He did not remain dead. After three days, God's Spirit miraculously raised Him to life again. God's Spirit does something similar in us. When we receive Jesus as our sacrifice and repent

279

of our sins, our hearts are changed. We become spiritually alive! We develop new desires and attitudes (2 Corinthians 5:17). We begin to make choices that please God (1 John 3:9). If we do fail and commit sins, we can ask God for forgiveness. "If we confess our sins, he is faithful and just to forgive us our sins, and to cleanse us from all unrighteousness" (1 John 1:9).

Once our hearts have been changed, we want to continue growing spiritually. We will be happy to let Jesus be the Master of our lives and will want to become more like Him. To do this, we must meditate on God's Word and commune with God in prayer. We will testify to others of this change by being baptized and sharing the good news of God's victory over sin and death. Fellowship with a faithful group of believers will strengthen our walk with God (1 John 1:7).

Additional Resources
by Gary Miller

Kingdom-Focused Finances for the Family
This first book in the Kingdom-Focused Living series is realistic, humorous, and serious about getting us to become stewards instead of owners.

Charting a Course in Your Youth
A serious call to youth to examine their faith, focus, and finances.

The Other Side of the Wall
Gary Miller continues his Kingdom-Focused Living series with a thorough look at God-centered giving. He stresses Biblical principles that apply to all Christians who want to reflect God's heart in giving, whether by meeting financial needs in their local community or by seeking to alleviate poverty abroad.

Budgeting Made Simple
A budgeting workbook in a ring binder; complements *Kingdom-Focused Finances for the Family.*

Small Business Handbook
A manual used in microfinance programs in Third World countries. Includes devotionals and practical business teaching. Ideal for missions and churches.

AUDIO BOOKS, NARRATED BY THE AUTHOR
Kingdom-Focused Finances for the Family, Charting A Course in Your Youth, Going Till You're Gone and *The Other Side of the Wall.*

AUDIO AND POWER POINT SEMINARS

Kingdom-Focused Finances Seminar—3 audio CDs
This three-session seminar takes you beyond our culture's view of money and possessions, and challenges you to examine your heart by looking at your treasure.

Kingdom-Focused Finances Seminar Audio Power Point—3 CDs
With the visual aid included on these CDs, you can now follow along on the slides Gary uses in his seminars while you listen to the presentation. A good tool for group study or individual use. A computer is needed to view these CDs.